The Biosocial Construction of Femininity

Recent Titles in
Contributions in Women's Studies

The Biosocial Construction of Femininity

Mothers and Daughters in Nineteenth-Century America

NANCY M. THERIOT

Contributions in Women's Studies, Number 93

GREENWOOD PRESS

New York • Westport, Connecticut • London

Library of Congress Cataloging-in-Publication Data

Theriot, Nancy M.
   The biosocial construction of femininity : mothers and daughters
in nineteenth-century America / Nancy M. Theriot.

      p.   cm.—(Contributions in women's studies, ISSN 0147–104X ;
no. 93)
   Bibliography: p.
   Includes index.
   ISBN 0–313–25483–4 (lib. bdg. : alk. paper)
   1. Middle class women—United States—History—19th century.
2. Mothers and daughters—United States—History—19th century.
3. Sex Role—United States—History—19th century.   4. Femininity
(Psychology)   I. Title.   II. Series.
HQ1426.T48   1988
305.4′2′0973—dc19   87–29545

British Library Cataloguing in Publication Data is available.

Library of Congress Catalog Card Number: 87–29545
ISBN: 0–313–25483–4
ISSN: 0147–104X

First published in 1988

Greenwood Press, Inc.
88 Post Road West, Westport, Connecticut 06881

Printed in the United States of America

The paper used in this book complies with the
Permanent Paper Standard issued by the National
Information Standards Organization (Z39.48–1984).

10   9   8   7   6   5   4   3   2   1

For my mother

Patty Brown Theriot

Contents

Acknowledgments

I want to thank M. Jane Slaughter for her direction and inspiration when this work was in its early stages. I also want to thank Anne Boylan, Charles Biebel, Helen Bannan, and Susan Tiano for their helpful suggestions throughout the development of my work. At the University of Louisville, I am especially indebted to Ann Taylor Allen for her careful reading of the manuscript and her difficult but stimulating questions that helped me to formulate my ideas in a clearer way. Thanks also to my other colleagues in the History Department and to the University of Louisville for their encouragement throughout the final stages of this project.

I also want to thank my son, Devin Thantsideh Theriot-Orr, for keeping me tethered to the real world, and his father, William Orr, for his support and help.

The Biosocial Construction of Femininity

Introduction

Writing 150 years apart, Margaret Fuller and Adrienne Rich offered two perspectives on the relationship between women and sexual ideology. In *Woman in the Nineteenth Century* (1840), Fuller urged her countrywomen to begin the difficult task of developing a feminine ideal out of the wildest, freest visions of their woman-souls.[1] Inspired by German Romanticism and American transcendentalism, Fuller recognized two important points about sexual ideology that most later writers have forgotten. She clearly saw that women participate in the creation of "femininity," and she realized that the raw material of that creation is the female life-process. In *Of Woman Born* (1976), Adrienne Rich described the relationship between women and sexual ideology from a different point of view.[2] Approaching her topic from a radical feminist perspective, Rich saw the ideology surrounding motherhood as a cultural veil between a woman and the potency of her female body. While Fuller described the power of women in forming ideology, Rich was concerned with the effect of ideology in overshadowing and predicting women's experience. Although they appear contradictory, Fuller and Rich have described forces that are interrelated.

This study is an attempt to elaborate the essential dialectical relationship between physical life and sexual ideology that Margaret Fuller and Adrienne Rich partially described. My focus is feminine ideology and middle-class women's reproductive experience in nineteenth-century America. While historical sources provide my basic data, the impetus behind this study is a desire to address questions and entertain speculations that have remained outside the traditional historical frame of reference. Historians of American women have done detailed work on feminine ideology; on the history of childbirth, abortion, and contraception; and on women and family roles. They have documented changes in women's reproductive experience and have traced the shifting focus of feminine ideology; however, most historians have been reluctant to speculate on connections or to theorize about feminine "reproductive consciousness."[3]

What is needed at this point in the historiography of nineteenth-century American women is careful but imaginative speculation about the relationship between sexual ideology and women's material lives and about women's role in the creation and evolution of "femininity." Such a project necessitates an interdisciplinary approach and an eclectic methodology. Using nineteenth-century popular literature written by women, medical literature, and autobiographies, my intention is to offer a theoretical framework for viewing gender as an historical process and women as agents in gender formation. Social psychology, object-relations psychoanalytic theory, and phenomenological sociology have aided me in explaining what I see as the generational interconnection of body experience, sexual ideology, and feminine consciousness in nineteenth-century America.

My hypothesis is that feminine ideology and female body experience are related in a dialectical way, such that each is agent and product, formed and reformed in continued contradictory interaction. Within the family setting, specifically the mother/daughter relationship, sexual ideology enters feminine consciousness as a gender script; it shapes the daughter's sense of body and of female place. As the daughter grows to womanhood, her life experience, including her sex-specific physical experience, challenges or validates the maternal message (the sexual ideology) of childhood. Based on the material conditions of her life, the daughter-as-woman formulates a slightly different version of her original script. Put in terms of the dialectic, the sexual ideology a woman grows up with becomes the "thesis" of her feminine identity; it defines the expectations and limitations of her womanhood. But the woman's life experience provides an "antithesis" to her inherited script; the material conditions of one generation do not fit exactly with the ideology produced by the previous generation. The woman forms a "synthesis," a new, altered version of the feminine script, out of the contradictions and similarities between hers and her mother's life worlds.

Thus, at different points in the female life cycle feminine ideology is a different phenomenon to the woman. In childhood and adolescence it is a cultural imperative; in young womanhood, as the old script is altered according to new conditions, feminine sexual ideology is a search for meaning and validation; and in maturity, it is an interpretation of womanhood, based on life experience, passed on to the next generation. As Adrienne Rich suggested, the ideology is powerful and defining; but as Margaret Fuller hoped, women play a central role in revising the meaning of "feminine." Sexual ideology is both woman-forming and woman-formed.

By tracing the changes in sexual ideology and physical experience among nineteenth-century middle-class American women, I hope to call attention to gender as an historical process. The term "sex/gender system" was coined by an anthropologist, but it is imperative that women's historians find a way to investigate sex (body) and gender (cultural definitions of body) in their systematic interconnection over time.[4] Because historians are rarely (consciously) theoretical and because social and psychological theorists are accused (rightfully) of being ahistorical, my first task is to develop a methodological framework for describing what l see as an historical body/culture relationship. Therefore, the opening chapter of this study is devoted to explaining a theoretical way to approach the sex/gender system as a category for historical study.

Chapters two through four describe the formation of feminine ideology in the first part of the nineteenth century by focusing on what I am calling the "maternal generation"—women born in the early part of the century who popularized (or read about) a middle-class feminine script centered around an idealized notion of powerful, yet self-sacrificing and suffering, motherhood. Although home-centered mothering (the feminine sexual ideology described in chapter two) was perfectly congruent with the socioeconomic conditions of middle-class women's lives, the idealization of suffering cannot be explained by looking only at general material conditions (the socioeconomic "setting" described in chapter three). When women's reproductive experience is considered, however, the "suffering mother" is understandable. Middle-class women began using male physicians in the early nineteenth century and thus encountered a new reproductive ritual. Chapter four details the results of this change in women's experience of fertility control, pregnancy, and birth. Because of the state of medical knowledge in the early decades of male midwifery, women's physical experience was filled with new dangers, alienation, and pain. Out of their experience, women created a sense of the "feminine" that defined suffering motherhood as central to "true womanhood." These chapters are meant to demonstrate the link between the ideological celebration of suffering and women's new experience of the body.

The maternal generation passed on this synthesis to their mid-century daughters, the focus of the last five chapters. The internal dynamic of the sex/gender system—the mother/daughter relationship and the daughter's nascent sexual identity—is the subject of chapter five. Considering women who were girls in the mid-century period as the "daughters' generation," in this chapter, I describe the mother/daughter world of the time and analyze the daughters' process of gender-learning. The final four chapters take the daughters' generation into adulthood and demonstrate the impact of changes in sex-specific experience, including changes in physical experience, on the daughters' inherited script. As women, the daughters encountered new material conditions (described in chapters six and seven) that caused them to question the necessity of suffering. Chapter eight is a discussion of psychosomatic illness as a minority response to the maternal messages daughters encountered. Based on their new experience, most middle-class daughters did not respond with illness; they altered the feminine script to accommodate their new life conditions. The daughters' synthesis, the subject of the final chapter, contained traces of early-century ideals but reflected the life experiences of the new generation. Late-century "true womanhood" was still other-directed but not painful, still nurturing but not family confined. Throughout the nineteenth century, feminine sexual ideology, passed on from mother to daughter, influenced women's sense of self and possibility even while that ideology was altered by women responding to new material conditions.

Although I believe that the dialectical pattern described here is basic to the social construction of femininity, I am also aware that my historical sources are limited to middle-class white women. I used woman-authored popular non-fiction as evidence of a collective mentality that one generation passed on to the next in more private ways, and I read other forms of women's writings, such as autobiographies and monographs of more serious intent, as personal testimonies about women's perception of their experience. Because this literature was produced and read primarily by middle-class white women, conclusions can only be drawn about this group. The second area of primary documents I used, medical literature by both women and men, also limits this study to the middle class. Male-authored literature provided information about the attitudes a typical nineteenth-century physician took to his female patients. Female medical writers supplied information on the state of women's health, the experience of women as patients, and the level of knowledge and ignorance of women about their bodies. Although poor and working-class women, black and white, provided the raw material of medical education and experimentation in the nineteenth century (as hospital patients), middle- and upper-class women were the first to use professional physicians voluntarily as the health care practitioner of choice. Published medical literature described middle-class women's experience as health care consumers, and middle-class women also recorded their perceptions of that experience.

Analyzing the link between the external and internal dimensions of women's world is the major challenge for feminist theory today; illustrating that link in history requires imaginative use of sources and interdisciplinary methodology. As John Demos pointed out in his introduction to *A Little Commonwealth*,[5] the most difficult and, for many of us, the most interesting historical questions are only approachable by stretching the limits of historical empiricism to include careful but courageous theorizing. Applying phenomenological and social psychological methodology to historical materials, the work that follows is a suggested framework for understanding the relationship of female body and feminine sexual ideology and for viewing the mother/daughter dyad as central in women's personal and collective history.

NOTES

1. Margaret Fuller, *Woman in the Nineteenth Century* (New York: W.W. Norton & Co., 1971).

2. Adrienne Rich, *Of Woman Born: Motherhood as Experience and Institution* (New York: W.W. Norton & Co., 1976).

3. Gayle Rubin, "The Traffic in Women: Notes on the 'Political Economy' of Sex," in *Toward an Anthropology of Women*, ed. Rayna R. Reiter (New York: Monthly Review

Press, 1975), pp. 157–210, was the first to use the term "sex/gender system." Joan Kelly, "The Doubled Vision of Feminist Theory: A Postscript to the 'Women and Power' Conference," *Feminist Studies*, 3(1979), 216–227, urged theorists to work on describing the external and internal dimensions of women's lives in their "systematic connectedness."

4. Mary O'Brien, *The Politics of Reproduction* (Boston: Routledge & Kegan Paul, 1981), uses the term "reproductive consciousness" in her analysis of the culturally constructed yet biologically based origin of patriarchy.

5. John Demos, *A Little Commonwealth: Family Life in Plymouth Colony* (New York: Oxford University Press, 1980). Mary Daly, *Beyond God the Father: Toward a Philosophy of Women's Liberation* (Boston: Beacon, 1973), pp. 11–12, also discussed the necessity to go beyond "methodolatry," the limiting deification of empirical method.

CHAPTER 1

Gender in History: A Methodological Proposal

Since the emergence of women's studies in the early 1970s, scholarship on women has stretched and challenged the methodological assumptions of every field. Feminist scholars in the social sciences and humanities found that research on women was not simply a matter of adding to the information in their various fields, but involved a rethinking of the basis of the knowledge. The clearest manifestation of the critical attitude of women's studies was and is its inter-disciplinary approach, its blurring of traditional categories. Women's studies from its beginning represented a critique of methodology as well as method, a reappraisal of assumptive frames of reference as well as an addition to content.

Women's history has, for the most part, been an exception to this critique. Certainly feminist historians have challenged conventional notions of what con-stitutes "significant" events and individuals and what determines an historical "period." Likewise, the women's history of the past decade and a half has asserted the importance of the ordinary individual and the "private" aspects of people's lives. This in itself has challenged the traditional idea of what history is. With this challenge has come interest in the history of the family, the history of sex-specific experiences such as childbirth and abortion, and the history of sexual ideologies. In spite of these new questions and new directions, however, women's history has not presented the methodological challenge that feminist anthropology, feminist criticism in literature and philosophy, feminist psy-chology, and femininst sociology have raised in their respective fields. Most women's history is revolutionary in its subject matter and sometimes in its method, but traditional in its methodology. This is because women's historians have not examined the full implications of gender as a category of historical analysis.

Gender is the social transformation of perceived differences between the sexes into differing norms, expectations, roles, and power for women and men. For the most part, women's historians have described and analyzed the constraints of gender in women's lives. This is a necessary first step in understanding gender in history, and the work to be done still appears limitless. However, perhaps because there is so much research yet to be done to outline a "women's" history, women's historians have been less interested in the theoretical questions raised by gender as a category. I am interested in two such questions, which I believe are central to understanding gender in history.

The first was suggested in 1978 by Joan Kelley in an article in *Feminist Studies*.[1] In that article, "The Doubled Vision of Feminist Theory," Kelley outlined the basic methodological problem of women's studies, a problem still unaddressed by women's historians. Kelley argued that, in order to understand women's experience in contemporary or past societies, we need to go beyond the internal/external, psychological/socioeconomic dichotomy; we need to bridge the gap between "private" family issues and "public" questions of status and power. Traditional historical methodology has no way to answer Kelley's challenge. Except in biography, where the task is to place the personal life within the historical moment, historians tend to concentrate on the "public" questions and rarely address the public/private dichotomy.[2] If women's experience is to be taken seriously in history and if women's history is to offer a true critique of the discipline, we need to develop a theoretical frame of reference to bend the seemingly parallel lines of public/private, individual/collective, and biological/social.

The second question is contained in the first: How do we account for the physical (biological) component of gender? Body or physical being is the basis of gender. Simone de Beauvoir introduced us to the central paradox of body/gender by pointing out that biological sex (body) defines woman's place, yet a woman is not born, but made.[3] Anthropologist Gayle Rubin coined the term "sex/gender system" to refer to the universal, yet historically specific transformation of biological sexuality into a social product.[4] What is the process by which bodies are given meaning? What effect does physical change have on meaning change? How does gender predetermine our physical experience and our perception of the world, and how do we integrate new experience into our concepts of gender? These questions lead us to regions untouchable by traditional empirical methodology. We need a different set of epistemological assumptions to approach the relationship between body and gender in history.[5]

One of the most important and least appreciated points of the new women's history is that historians have been limited, shaped, determined by their methodology: their assumptions about the nature of history, what is important, and how change occurs. But methodology is more than that. It is a point of view about the relationship between individuals and society, about the relationship between historian and material, about reality itself, and about what constitutes knowledge; it is a metaphysics and an epistemology. Historical methodology, for the most part, still is rooted in a nineteenth-century empiricism, in that traditional historians limit themselves to questions approachable through "objective," sometimes quantifiable data. This method renders many questions

invisible or unanswerable and provides a false sense of objectivity. Early twentieth-century sociology, philosophy, and psychology offer a more "modern"
methodology for historical research than the empiricism of the nineteenth century, a methodology based on the world view of twentieth-century science.[6] It
is time for historians to explore these theoretical possibilities. If we see human
beings and the relationship between human beings and society in a way similar
to George Herbert Mead, William James, and the contemporary sociologist
Peter Berger,[7] we can answer Joan Kelley's challenge and have a language to
talk about body and gender.

Historians are notoriously antitheoretical, and even historians such as myself
who are interested in theory find it difficult to explain theoretical frameworks
in the abstract. Therefore, 1 want to begin by explaining my title and move on
through some concepts that are important to my work. In doing this, I am
moving backwards: from the result of research/thinking to the necessary root
ideas. In reality, the ideas and the concrete material of my study (sources) were
in constant relationship. Questions raised by my research were unanswerable
in traditional modes of thinking, and my frustration led me to explore a more
daring perspective, which was again altered by the material itself. What follows
is an account of a process, necessarily frozen for purposes of explanation and
analysis; but in reality never fixed, always blending theory into material and
material into theory.

"The Social Construction of Femininity" is a loaded phrase. The easiest
term is "femininity." I mean by that term the ideology surrounding womanhood:
the set of ideas about appropriate womanly behavior, aspirations, and feelings
that rest on assumptions about female nature. That seems fairly straightforward,
but is really very complex. Any writer who discusses femininity or sexual ideology
has more than a definition in mind; she/he also has assumptions about the
groups or social and economic forces shaping sexual ideology, about the relationship of ordinary individuals to ideology, and about how ideas come to
change over time. For example, historians interested in American women's
history at first assumed that ideas about femininity were created by men and
that women were victims of the ideology.[8] Later historians, among them Nancy
Cott and Daniel Scott Smith, demonstrated how women manipulated repressive
ideology to their advantage.[9] The assumptions behind any writer's definition
of femininity are not "provable" in any empirical way, yet they provide the very
foundation of the work and determine what will be seen and what will go
unnoticed.

My frame of reference for considering femininity is in the rest of the phrase:
"social construction." I assume that ideology (sexual or otherwise) is not the
creation of a ruling class or ruling sex, but is a collective creation of individual
human beings acting on the material conditions of their lives in an attempt to
make their experience meaningful. This does not mean that all groups have
equal input into one ideology, but that there are competing ideologies with the
hegemonic group influencing but not determining the beliefs and world views

of the various "out" groups by exerting power over the material conditions of these groups' existence. The material conditions of womanhood are determined by the socioeconomic structure and cultural values of a specific time and place, and vary according to class and race. Men influence women's concepts of femininity because men set legal, economic, and physical limits to women's lives. In addition, in a situation of sexual inequality women must learn men's expectations of them in order to survive. Women responding to the conditions in which they find themselves create ideas of femininity that resemble, but are not identical to, male views of femininity. The resemblance is due to male power in determining women's life conditions. Feminine sexual ideology is a metaphorical construction, an attempt by women to give meaning to their experience and to their world. This view of sexual ideology allows us to see women as neither victims nor all-powerful actors, but as people constantly responding to and interpreting their life situations within unchosen constraints.

If femininity is the creation of women, what is the process of that creation? Another way to ask that question is: How does femininity change over time? As the rest of my title indicates (*Mothers and Daughters in Nineteenth-Century America*), I see femininity as socially constructed within a generational dynamic. In order to clarify this way of seeing and demonstrate how it provides a satisfactory framework for understanding the relationship of public/private and body/gender, five key concepts must be analyzed: body, self (or consciousness), generation, sexual ideology, and the material conditions of gender (socioeconomic and physical restrictions that divide the life worlds of women and men).

Of these concepts, body is the most concrete and the most confusing. This is because body is two different experiences which we usually do not differentiate. As James, Mead, and Berger have pointed out, we *are* bodies and we *have* bodies at the same time, due to our being self-conscious animals.[10] These two experiences of body play different roles in psychological and cultural development. The body that I *am* involves the fusion of self and body that occurs in infancy and early childhood through human socialization. Because the human animal is social and learns about self and environment through physical and social interactions, throughout the early developmental stages the body is the self and the self is the body.

The second experience of body, that of *having* a body, is a later development in that it presupposes a former sense of self: one must first *be* before one can *have*. In this second experience the body can be considered part of the material conditions of gender (and of life) with which the self must deal. In a classic Marxist sense, the fact of body (*being* a body) requires that human beings provide food and shelter for themselves and that they reproduce; the consciousness of body (*having* a body) makes possible such human inventions as food taboos, clothing styles, and gender. When we discuss the material conditions of gender we will return to this second sense of body, but for now it is important to keep in mind that although we regard our bodies as separate (and create elaborate and diverse rituals for physical needs and events), we experience our bodies as our selves.

Peter Berger and Thomas Luckmann, in *The Social Construction of Reality*, elaborate the implications of our being bodies who are dependent on a caretaker for an extended period of time and who are unequipped with instinctual survival skills. We learn about the world, and about ourselves, only through relationship; the world we learn is the world our primary caretaker introduces us to. What is to be feared, what is to be eaten, what is appropriate shelter, what is reality itself comes to us through relationship and not through discovery of an "external" world-as-it-is. Our perception of the world is inherently active, meaning-making, and subjective because our survival as a physical entity is dependent on communication, on social interaction. Berger and Luckmann do not raise the question of sexual difference in their work, but their understanding of social interaction as the basis of self-construction and world-construction has implications for the study of gender. If the primary caretaker is female, then the world we're given is her world and the meaning we associate with our bodies' needs, wants, and being is her meaning.

Psychoanalysis, and especially object-relations theory, elaborates the biosocial construction of a gendered self within the mother/child dyad. Feminist theorists have made use of this perspective to describe the link between the sexual identity formed in infancy, the personality traits of the feminine woman, and the ideology of femininity.[11] Nancy Chodorow's *The Reproduction of Mothering* is the most ambitious attempt to use object-relations theory as an analysis of gender. Chodorow argues that the sexually dichotomous structure of the nuclear family, in which only women mother, produces certain psychological characteristics in women that are rooted in the infant body/self experience with a same-sex parent. Women's tendency towards dependency, self-sacrifice, and over-involvement in relationships is based on psychosexual development which in turn is based on a certain family structure.[12]

There are many problems with this approach for historians: the assumption of a universal, historically static family form, the strict structuralism, the circularity of the argument itself.[13] However, if we take her general approach about the process of gender formation and avoid her structurally specific conclusion, Chodorow is very useful to the task of understanding body and gender. The process that Chodorow describes is an elaboration of Berger and Luckmann's ideas about the social construction of self in relation to the primary caretaker. The gendered self is a product of infancy; by the age of eighteen months a child has both a sense of her self as female and a beginning sense of what it means in her culture to be a female.[14] The gendered self comes out of the mother/daughter relationship, and mother is both the biosocial "first cause" of gender and the cultural transmitter of gender throughout childhood. Because gender identity is formed at an early pre-verbal time in human development, it continues to be a core part of being a body throughout life; and because gender identity for the girl comes out of a mother/daughter, female to female relationship, the experience of having a female body (like mother's, like the primary caretaker's) continues to be a significant variable in the daughter's life.[15]

All of this assumes mother as the primary or only caretaker in a nuclear family setting, and if we look at the nineteenth-century middle-class family, we see a pattern very close to Chodorow's theoretical construct. Among the middle class, an increasingly private family form developed in the nineteenth century, in which the husband left home to work, childrearing became a focused and private female activity, and women were economically dependent. If Chodorow's theory is culture-bound in positing a particular family structure as universal, that structure was indeed the predominant family type among middle-class nineteenth-century Americans.

Assuming Chodorow's points about the psychosexual development of daughters in this particular family structure are relevant whenever and wherever such family configurations appear, the mother/daughter relationship is a significant area to study in order to understand the link between body and gender for nineteenth-century women. Maternal attitudes about the female body and the feminine role and the way mothers lived those attitudes were important factors in forming a daughter's core gender identity.

While psychoanalysis and object-relations theory is useful in understanding the importance of the primary caretaker to the child's sense of being a female (or male) body, this framework is problematic in providing a definition of "self" or "consciousness." A historically useful definition of self must go beyond the static "identity" definition usually associated with Freudian work; psychoanalysis assumes that identity is formed in early childhood and remains fixed.[16] A historically useful definition of self must also assume, but surpass the social learning theory idea of imitation and reinforcement. Because "self" in social learning theory is always acted upon, always a reflection of family and culture, it offers no way to explain historical change except structurally.[17] We also need a definition of self that can describe identity and change without presupposing the historical idea of "individualism," a fairly recent development.

Cognitive-developmentalists in psychological learning theory and symbolic interactionists in sociological theory offer a workable definition of self for a historical study of gender. According to these groups, self is not a static, ahistorical entity with inaccessible private layers; nor is it a simple reflection of cultural messages. Self is a variable and constant reservoir of personal identity that is established, maintained, and altered through social interaction.[18] In other words, self is the cognitive, emotional, physical process of socially-rooted human behavior. A self can be individualistic or community or tribe oriented. The important universal characteristic of self is its socially situated development over time.

This idea of self-as-process is the link between body and society, individual and culture, private and public. The core of self is the gendered body, which is a product of a particular set of childrearing patterns in a particular historical time and place. The gendered body or core self carries the maternal messages of gender throughout life. But the self interacts with people and environment, and continually re-forms itself according to experience. The self interacts constantly with new stimuli and new situations, and each interaction carries a potential for altering the self or being altered by the self.[19] This means that the gendered body of infancy, the core of self-identity, is not frozen or determined throughout life. If this were so, gender would never change; each generation would be exactly the same as the one before. But since self is a process based on social interaction, the maternal imprint of infancy is malleable, though not erasable. The gendered body is the starting point for the on-going, socially-rooted reinterpretation of self, body, and culture based on life experience.

The self-as-process and the mother/daughter relationship are most accessible to historical investigation through biography, but it is also possible to draw conclusions about self and relationship by looking at generations. Karl Mannheim has pointed out, in "The Problem of Generations," that generation is more than a biological cohort; it is a "location" in social/historical time.[20] Generation limits its members to a specific range of potential experiences and predisposes them for certain modes of thought, feeling, and action. A generation is a "tendency" towards certain cognitive and emotional patterns. Put in terms of the sex/gender system, a generation shares basically the same gendered body, the same core identity. And a new generation, a new social/historical "location," is created not by years alone but by a new experiential package: new ideology and new material conditions. For example, in this study I am discussing two generations of women. The first, the "maternal generation," reached reproductive adulthood in the early to mid-nineteenth century. They shared a specific childbirth ritual and were the first American women to occupy an increasingly non-productive "home" sphere in the early decades of industrial development. These were among the experiences which made them a "generation." Their daughters, the "daughters' generation," also shared a specific social/historical "location." The daughters reached reproductive adulthood at least by mid-century, when anesthesia, followed by other medical advances, altered the childbirth experience of middle-class women and when higher education and more job opportunities were opening to women of that class. These were among the experiences that made them a "generation." Similarly, the generation that launched the new women's movement of the 1970s shared a specific educational and reproductive experience. This sense of "generation" as social/historical position, as a group sharing a specific ideology and set of material conditions, is crucial to an understanding self-as-process, the mother/daughter relationship, and also the connection between public and private. This brings us to the final categories essential to an understanding of gender as a historical process.

Thus far our explanation of methodology has centered on the internal dimensions of the sex/gender system: how the human animal forms a primary gender identity in infancy and childhood which changes in relation to people and life events. This internal area is usually outside of historical investigation and also outside of what is called "social science." But the external dimensions of the sex/gender system—sexual ideology and the material conditions making the lives of the two sexes different—are both subjects of empirical scholarship. In spite of, or perhaps because of so much scholarly activity, "sexual ideology" and the "material conditions of gender" remain cloudy concepts.

I am defining "sexual ideology" as a set of ideas about female and male that divides the sexes according to prescribed norms of behavior, feeling, roles, and personality type, and that reflects male supremacy. But it is not enough to define sexual ideology simply as ideas; a sense of "cause" or interaction always accompanies the definition. As I said earlier, I see sexual ideology as a collective creation of women as well as men, with men influencing women's sense of femininity by exerting control over the conditions which define and confine women's lives. This means that sexual ideology is a human product, not something that "follows from" any particular structure. Socioeconomic structure does not produce ideology; it presents a situation that people make meaningful with ideology.

But if ideology is human-made, as opposed to structurally produced, it is also human-making. Because we learn about self and world through an acculturated caretaker, we never experience the conditions of our lives "directly"; instead, our caretaker's point of view is the lens through which we filter reality and come to "see" ourselves. We encounter sexual ideology as we develop gender identity, in early childhood, and that set of ideas influences our experience of self and world. To understand sexual ideology as human-made and human-making, we need to look more closely at the "material conditions of gender."

Usually social scientists mean "socioeconomic structure" when they speak of material conditions, but Marx included the physical environment (nature) as part of the material conditions of life (in fact, as the original material condition). It is only because nature has been acted on again and again by human culture that we can think of socioeconomic structure as a kind of "physical environment." Still, this definition is instructive because it points to the fact that the material conditions of one's life do indeed provide an environment, a physical limitation of possibilities. The material conditions of female life provide the external limits (legal, social, economic) to women's life actions in a particular time and place.

When speaking of the material conditions of *gender*, body must also be considered.[21] The body that I *have* (as opposed to the body that I *am*) is a material condition relevant to the sex/gender system because the constraints of female body in a given time and place, in conjunction with socioeconomic structure, define women's outermost limits of action. Just as the development of smallpox vaccination altered the material conditions of colonial people's lives, the technological possibility of fertility control, the availability of anesthesia for childbirth, and even the marketing of sanitary napkins and tampons have profoundly changed the material constraints of women's lives. Since gender is based on body, is the social transformation of body into culture, the changing conditions surrounding female body are important to an understanding of the sex/gender system.

The reader has probably noticed that each concept we have discussed thus far—body, self, sexual ideology, and material conditions of gender—requires the other concepts. This is because the four categories are not only overlapping, but are part of a dialectic. In many diverse areas of social science, the concept of a dialectic is employed to analyze social change and the development of individual consciousness. While the most familiar use of the dialectic method is the Marxist description of historical change, dialectic is also used in psychological learning theory, linguistics, and the sociology of knowledge to describe the process of human enculturation. By applying this concept to gender, we can connect the public/private, external/internal in one process.

Theorists who write about the internal dialectic stress the original Hegelian notion of separation as well as the idea of contradiction.[22] Human beings, as they become self-conscious (conscious of the difference between self and not-self), experience separation and alienation from the world. In the drive to make the world knowable and part of the self once more, the drive toward unity, the primary caretaker (mother) mediates between self and culture so that the child (female or male) receives mother's world (categories, attitudes, language patterns, values) as *the* world. In the process, the child comes to see that view of the world as objective reality, as real and as "fixed" as the earth itself. Throughout life there is a constant dialectic relationship between the maturing consciousness (self) and the external reality it encounters, with categories of consciousness defining perception and being altered by experience at the same time.[23] The "social construction" methodology is dialectic.

Traditional Marxists usually apply the dialectic in such a way as to eliminate the private, inner world of consciousness (and with it, human agency) from history.[24] However, both Hegel and Marx were interested in the development of human consciousness as well as in the impact of human consciousness on historical development. The internal and external dimensions of human life can be theoretically linked by viewing consciousness (self) as the locus of ideology and mediator between animality and culture.[25] In terms of women and sexual ideology, the dialectic can describe the categories of body, self, sexual ideology, and material conditions of female life as two dimensions of the same social-historical movement: the one internal, between the female animal and her socially produced identity (self); the other external, between the socialized woman (self) and the social world.[26] With self as a link, the two dimensions are not dichotomous spheres of activity. Using the definitions we have developed, the girl-child inherits a sexual identity based on her mother's generation's sexual ideology and life world. Her self contains the maternal ideology (the culture becomes individual). As she matures, new material conditions, including new physical conditions of being female, conflict with and alter her gendered self (ideology is changed by experience). The woman's altered self is then translated into sexual ideology and sometimes into action and material changes, and is passed on to the next generation as the new "thesis" (individual becomes culture).

Seen from this perspective, feminine ideology is both woman-creating and woman-created, and two important features of that movement are the mother/daughter relationship and the culturally shaped sex-specific experiences of female life, including but not limited to physical experience. This study concentrates on those two dimensions of the nineteenth-century sex/gender system, arguing that cultural values about womanhood, transmitted in the mother/daughter relationship, were formed and altered by women in response to changes in their sex-specific experience, especially physical experience.

Although many aspects of the material conditions of women's lives changed during the nineteenth century, not enough attention has been paid to physical change and its effect on women's collective sense of self. Similarly, historical work on women's relationships has not concentrated on the mother/daughter relationship or on the implications of the mother/daughter dynamic in terms of sexual ideology. It is not so much that these areas have been left unexamined, but that women's physical experience and the mother/daughter relationship have been seen within a limited methodological context. The questions we ask, what we think of as sources of information, and how we define "information" itself rest on the methological assumptions of the investigator. Within the theoretical framework I have outlined, what are the epistemological assumptions? From what vantage point are questions posed? If we view the sex/gender system as a personal and cultural dialectic, what historical material can be used as sources of information about the process of gender?

I begin with the phenomenological assumption that subjective experience is a trustworthy source of information about human beings, in that we share the characteristic of being "embodied consciousness" (self-conscious animals) who act purposefully in a particular environment.[27] Because we have this in common, we know certain things about past people and our contemporaries who are culturally distant. For example, we know that all societies have had to find ways to feed themselves, even if we don't know the variety of ways people have devised to provide nourishment. We also know from our late twentieth-century experience that communication media influence our perception of "reality"; therefore we know that people in the past and contemporary people with communication technology different from ours were or are affected by the way in which they tell each other about the world.[28] We know certain categories of thought and experience shared by temporally and culturally distant people, without knowing the content of the categories, because we share the status of being self-conscious animals.

All of this is to begin an explanation of how I came to see the two questions of this study—the roles of sex-specific physical experience and the mother/daughter relationship in women's changing sense of self—as important and approachable. My experience as a late-twentieth-century American woman provides evidence that female body experience is a significant variable in women's sense of self. The availability of reliable contraception and legal abortion has altered women's experience of heterosexual relationships and prompted a change in meanings and values. The possibility of elementary school sports experience for girls has altered how young women see themselves as strong or weak. In a situation of sexual inequality, whether or not a woman's body approximates the male ideal of beauty affects her sense of self and the way she interacts with others. All of these sex-specific experiences, though rooted in a particular time and place, indicate that the technological and cultural constraints on female body are important conditions of women's self-concept and sense of "reality." It is because technology has freed American women from many of the traditional constraints of female body that we can envision equality as a question of law and money. Experiencing the world through our largely unburdened female bodies affects what we see as possible and what we see as real.

In order to understand women from a different time (or place), we need to reconstruct as closely as possible their particular frame of reference, including the sex-specific physical experiences they shared. The nineteenth century was a time of great change in women's experience of their femaleness. The technology of contraception, the legality of abortion, the sex of the childbirth attendant, the technology surrounding childbirth: in all of these areas of women's experience there was change. Although there are numerous excellent studies dealing with these areas of change, I am less interested in the changes themselves and more interested in seeing these physical conditions of womanhood as powerful determinants of women's sense of self and world. This entails reconstructing the material conditions surrounding female body, about which much has already been written, with sensitivity to clues as to how those conditions were experienced. So the first step is to look with a different point of view at the information we already have.

The next step is to read women's published writing as a source of information about "collective mentality."[29] Popular fiction and advice literature written by women for women constitutes a public discourse on women's experience of their life world. Although there is a danger in reading "shoulds" as indicative of behavior, popular literature does reflect shared, sanctioned versions of reality. If we see "femininity" as a metaphor created and communicated by women to make meaning of the historical "moment" in which they find themselves, woman-authored popular literature provides abundant examples of this metaphorical thinking. It also contains information about what some women did do, as well as what some women thought women should do. Reading this popular literature, with autobiographies as a "check" as to the extent that certain ideas were shared, provides a way to see how women responded to the sex-specific conditions framing their life world.[30]

The second question I am interested in, the importance of the mother/ daughter relationship in the sex/gender system, like the first, stems from my experience as a late-twentieth-century American woman. Since the early 1970s there has been a growing awareness among feminist writers of the significance of the mother/daughter relationship for daughters and for mothers.[31] Certainly this awareness stems from an historically specific situation, but the fact that human beings in all times and places are embodied consciousness who must be introduced to culture by another human being in order to survive means that the relationship between the infant/child and the caretaker(s) is significant, regardless of temporal and cultural variation. The first step in investigating that relationship in a past society is to look at the conditions of childrearing unique to that time/place.

Throughout the nineteenth century, among the middle class an intensely private nuclear family form was most common. Not only was childrearing women's most time-consuming and culturally significant occupation, but the women's community was physically and ideologically separate from the world of men. What did this mean for mothers and daughters? Were nineteenth-century daughters closer to and less ambivalent about their mothers than late-twentieth-century daughters? How did the mother/daughter relationship in a world of women affect daughters' sense of self and world?

We can learn much about the mother/daughter atmosphere of a particular time by looking at women's published writings with generation in mind.[32] A generation of women writing a similar message about female body and femininity, especially if much of that writing is directed to "daughters" or "girls," can be interpreted as public expression of the privately enacted mother/daughter relationship. The unconscious levels remain inaccessible, but consciously transmitted maternal values can provide an outline of one dimension of the mother/ daughter dynamic. If a set of documents from one generation expresses the maternal message, which becomes the core sexual identity of the next generation, then the writings of the daughters' generation may indicate a shift. The process of self is visible when women's writings on femininity and the female life world are examined with sensitivity to generations. Once again, autobiographies can be used to validate the mother/daughter atmosphere found in women's popular fiction and non-fiction.

I do not mean to imply that women's sex-specific physical experience and the mother/daughter relationship are the only two variables, or even the most important variables, in the examination of the sex/gender system, but only that they have not been given the attention they deserve. Within the methodological assumptions I have outlined, these two variables are crucial to an understanding of women as creators and products of culture. Adopting this framework allows us to see gender as a process, and gives us a way to approach Kelley's public/

private question and de Beauvoir's body/gender riddle. This study is offered as a first step in a new direction.

NOTES

1. Joan Kelly, "The Doubled Vision of Feminist Theory: A Postscript to the 'Women and Power' Conference," *Feminist Studies*, 3(1979), 216–227. Since Kelly's article, other theorists have focused also on the public/private link. See Zillah Eisenstein, "Developing a Theory of Capitalist Patriarchy and Socialist Feminism," in *Capitalist Patriarchy and the Case for Socialist Feminism*, ed. Zillah Eisenstein (New York: Monthly Review Press, 1979), pp. 5–40; the introduction in *Women: Sex and Sexuality*, ed. Catharine R. Stimpson and Ethel Spector Person (Chicago: University of Chicago Press, 1980); Lydia Sargent, ed., *Women and Revolution* (Boston: South and Press, 1981).

2. I do not mean to imply that all historians concentrate on "public" questions, but only that conventional history is concerned with those questions. An example of an American women's historian who has been very interested in the public/private connection is Mary P. Ryan. See especially her *Cradle of the Middle Class: The Family in Oneida County, New York, 1790–1865* (New York: Oxford University Press, 1981). Another example is Barbara Leslie Epstein, *The Politics of Domesticity: Women, Evangelism, and Temperance in Nineteenth-Century America* (Middletown, CT: Wesleyan University Press, 1981).

3. Simone de Beauvoir, *The Second Sex*, trans. H. M. Parshley (New York: Vintage Books, 1974).

4. Gayle Rubin, "The Traffic in Women: Notes on the 'Political Economy' of Sex," in *Toward an Anthropology of Women*, ed. Rayna R. Reiter (New York: Monthly Review Press, 1975), pp. 157–210.

5. The boldest work done so far in this area by a women's historian is Carroll Smith-Rosenberg, *Disorderly Conduct: Visions of Gender in Victorian America* (New York: Knopf, 1985).

6. The view of "reality" that comes to us through twentieth-century science calls into question many empirical assumptions, such as the idea of an "objective" observer who does not influence the results of the experiment, the idea of absolute certainty and fixity, and the idea that discovery is collecting data. Science posits a much more interactive view of consciousness and "reality."

7. George Herbert Mead, *Mind, Self, and Society*, ed. Charles W. Morris (Chicago: University of Chicago Press, 1935); George Herbert Mead, "The Social Self," *Journal of Philosophy*, 10(1913), 374–380; William James, *Psychology* (New York: Henry Holt & Co., 1892); Peter L. Berger and Thomas Luckmann, *The Social Construction of Reality: A Treatise in the Sociology of Knowledge* (London: Allen Lane, 1966); Peter L. Berger and Stanley Pullberg, "Reification and the Sociological Critique of Consciousness," *History and Theory* IV:2(1965), 196–211. See also: William H. Desmonde, "George Herbert Mead and Freud: American Social Psychology and Psychoanalysis," *Psychoanalysis* 4–5(1957), 31–50; Herbert Blumer, "Sociological Implications of the Thought of George Herbert Mead," *American Journal of Sociology*, 71(1966), 535–544; Robert Wuthnow, James Davison Hunter, Albert Bergesen, Edith Kurzweil, *Cultural Analysis: The Work of Peter L. Berger, Mary Douglas, Michel Foucault, and Jugern Habermas* (Boston: Routledge & Kegan Paul, 1984); R. Gordon Kelly, "The Social Construction of Reality: Implications for Future Directions in American Studies," *Prospects: The Annual of Amer-*

ican Culture Studies, 8(1983), 49–58. For a discussion of the application of phenomenology to social science see: Maurice Natanson, ed., *Phenomenology and the Social Sciences*,
2 vols. (Evanston: Northwestern University Press, 1973). In the first volume, note
especially the articles by Eugene T. Gendlin, "Experiential Phenomenology," pp. 281–
319; Joseph J. Kockelman, "Theoretical Problems in Phenomenological Psychology,"
pp. 225–280; Maurice Merleau-Ponty, "Phenomenology and the Sciences of Man,"
pp. 47–108; Edward A. Tiryakian, "Sociology and Existential Phenomenology," pp.
187–222. In the second volume, note Gerhard Funke, "Phenomenology and History,"
pp. 3–101; and Donald M. Lowe, "Intentionality and the Method of History," pp. 103–
130. See also Donald M. Lowe, *History of Bourgeois Perception* (Chicago: University of
Chicago Press, 1982); Helmut R. Wagner, ed., *Alfred Schutz, On Phenomenology and
Social Relations* (Chicago: University of Chicago Press, 1975); C. A. Van Peursen, *Body,
Soul, and Spirit: A Study of the Mind/Body Problem*, trans. H. H. Hoskins (London:
Oxford University Press, 1966). See also Kenneth A. Rice, *Geertz and Culture* (Ann
Arbor: University of Michigan Press, 1980).

8. Barbara Welter, "The Cult of True Womanhood: 1820–1860," *American Quarterly*, 18(1966), 151–174, while not specifically blaming men for repressive feminine
ideology, implies that women were passive in relationship to the ideology.

9. Examples of historians who have demonstrated women's positive use of feminine
ideology include: Epstein, *The Politics of Domesticity*; Nancy F. Cott, "Passionlessness:
An Interpretation of Victorian Sexual Ideology 1790–1850," *Signs*, 4(1978), 219–236;
Daniel Scott Smith, "Family Limitation, Sexual Control, and Domestic Feminism in
Victorian America," *Feminist Studies*, 1(1973), 40–47; Anne M. Boylan, "Evangelical
Womanhood in the Nineteenth Century: The Role of Women in Sunday Schools,"
Feminist Studies, 4(1978), 62–80.

10. James, *Psychology*, pp. 189–190; Mead, *Mind, Self, and Society*, pp. 171–173;
Berger and Luckmann, *The Social Construction of Reality*.

11. Feminist theorists who make use of psychoanalysis are numerous. For example
see: Shulamith Firestone, *The Dialectic of Sex* (New York: Bantam Books, 1970); Eli
Zaretsky, *Capitalism, The Family, and Personal Life* (New York: Harper, 1973); Juliet
Mitchell, *Psychoanalysis and Feminism* (New York: Random House, 1974); Ann Foreman,
Femininity as Alienation: Women and the Family in Marxism and Psychoanalysis (London:
Pluto, 1977); Nancy Chodorow, *The Reproduction of Mothering* (Berkeley: University of
California Press, 1978); Ethel Spector Person, "Sexuality as the Mainstay of Identity:
Psychoanalytic Perspectives," in *Women: Sex and Sexuality*, pp. 36–61; Jane Flax, "Po-
litical Philosophy and the Patriarchal Unconscious: A Psychoanalytic Perspective on
Epistemology and Metaphysics," in *Discovering Reality*, ed. Sandra Harding and Merrill
B. Hintikka (Boston: D. Reidel, 1983), pp. 245–282.

12. Chodorow, *The Reproduction of Mothering*.

13. Judy Housman, in "Mothering, The Unconscious, and Feminism," *Radical America*, 16:6(1982), 47–61; and Marcia Westkott, in "Mothers and Daughters in the World
of the Father," *Frontiers*, 3(1978), 16–21 offer critiques of Chodorow.

14. Theorists and practitioners from every persuasion in learning theory agree that
children have a sense of self as one sex or the other and a sense of what that means
before two years of age.

15. Another theorist who uses the idea of being/having a body (but in a different
way) is Dorothy Dinnerstein, *The Mermaid and the Minotaur: Sexual Arrangement and
Human Malaise* (New York: Harper & Row, 1976). She argues that the meaning we

place on sexual difference (the body that I have) is directly connected to early experiences of powerlessness and dependence as the body that I *am* which occur with a female (mother).

16. One problem with the psychoanalytic definition of self is that it remains fixed over time, so that Chodorow can envision change in the psychological characteristics of women only by postulating a change in the structure of infancy. For an explanation of identity in object-relations theory, see Fred Weinstein and Gerald M. Platt, *Psychoanalytic Sociology* (Baltimore: Johns Hopkins University Press, 1973).

17. On social learning theory, see Walter Mischel, "A Social-Learning View of Sex Differences in Behavior," in *The Development of Sex Differences*, ed. Eleanor E. Maccoby (Stanford: Stanford University Press, 1966), pp. 56–81; Walter Mischel, "Sex-Typing and Socialization," in *Carmichael's Manual of Child Psychology*, vol. II, ed. Paul H. Mussen (New York: John Wiley & Sons, 1970), pp. 3–72; Albert Bandura, ed., *Psychological Modeling* (Chicago: Aldine, Atherton, 1971); Albert Bandura, *Social Learning Theory* (Englewood Cliffs: Prentice-Hall, 1977). An excellent critique of social learning theory is Dorothy Z. Ullian, "The Development of Conceptions of Masculinity and Femininity," in *Exploring Sex Differences*, ed. Barbara B. Lloyd and John Archer (London: Academic Press, 1976), pp. 25–48.

18. This particular definition is my own, but both groups define self as a process of interactions. See Ullian, "The Development of Conceptions of Masculinity and Femininity"; Regina Yando, Victoria Seitz, Edward Zigler, *Imitation: A Developmental Perspective* (Hillsdale: Lawrence Erbaum Associates, 1978); Rebecca Meda, Robert Hefner, Barbara Olenshansky, "A Model of Sex-Role Transcendence," in *Sex-Role Stereotypes: Readings Toward a Psychology of Androgyny*, eds. Alexandra G. Kaplan and Joan P. Bean (Boston: Little, Brown & Co., 1976), pp. 89–97; Lawrence Kohlberg, "A Cognitive-Developmental Analysis of Children's Sex-Role Concepts and Attitudes," in *The Development of Sex Differences*, pp. 82–173. In sociological theory, self-as-process is a popular concept among symbolic interactionists and people who write about the sociology of knowledge. For example, see Berger and Pullberg, "Reification and the Sociological Critique of Consciousness"; Peter Berger and Hansfried Kellner, "Marriage and the Construction of Reality," *Diogenes*, 46(1964), 1–24; Gregory P. Stone and Harvey A. Faberman, eds., *Social Psychology Through Symbolic Interaction* (Waltham, MA: Ginn-Blaisdell, 1970), p. 86 on "self" in symbolic interaction theory, and pp. 367–372 on the use of the term "self" as opposed to the term "personality" in sociology. See also Gardner Murphy, *Personality: A Biosocial Approach to Origins and Structure* (New York: Harper & Row, 1947). Mead, in *Mind, Self, and Society*, described self as "an eddy in the social current and so still a part of the current. It is a process in which the individual is continually adjusting himself in advance to the situation to which he belongs, and reacting back on it" (p. 182). This idea of self as a process is also central to phenomenology.

19. This back and forth motion of self and society is described in all of the sociological theorists cited above and in phenomenologists' writing. In addition, see L. S. Vygotsky, *Mind in Society* (Cambridge, MA: Harvard University Press, 1977).

20. Karl Mannheim, "The Problem of Generations," in his *Essays in the Sociology of Knowledge* (New York: Oxford University Press, 1952), pp. 276–320. See also Annie Kriegel, "Generational Differences: The History of an Idea," *Daedalus*, 107(1978), 23–38; Alan B. Spitzer, "The Historical Problem of Generations," *American Historical*

Review, 78(1973), 1353–1383; A. P. Simonds, *Karl Mannheim's Sociology of Knowledge* (Oxford: Clarendon Press, 1978).

21. Hegel and Marx both consider body important. On Hegel, see Mary O'Brien, *The Politics of Reproduction* (Boston: Routledge & Kegan Paul, 1981). On Marx, See Foreman, *Femininity as Alienation*.

22. O'Brien, *The Politics of Reproduction*.

23. All of Peter Berger's work illustrates this point, and it is also a basic idea in Mead's *Mind, Self, and Society* and in phenomenologists' writing.

24. Feminists writing from a socialist-feminist perspective have criticized traditional Marxism for this blind spot. See Eisenstein, "Developing a Theory of Capitalist Patriarchy and Socialist Feminism"; Sargent, *Women and Revolution*. Socialist scholars are beginning to take note of this problem. See: Zaretsky, *Capitalism, The Family, and Personal Life*; Joseph Interrante and Carol Lasser, "Victims of the Very Songs They Sing: A Critique of Recent Work on Patriarchal Culture and the Social Construction of Gender," *Radical History Review*, 20(1979), 25–40.

25. See Guy Swanson, "Mead and Freud: Their Relevance for Social Psychology," *Sociometry*, 24(1961), 319–339; Mary O'Brien, "Feminist Theory and Dialectical Logic," in *Feminist Theory: A Critique of Ideology*, ed. Nannerl O. Keohane, Michelle Z. Rosaldo, Barbara C. Gelpi (Chicago: University of Chicago Press, 1982), pp. 99–112; Bernhard Waldenfels, Jan M. Broekman, Anet Pazanin, eds. *Phenomenology and Marxism*, trans. J. Claude Evans, Jr. (London: Routledge & Kegan Paul, 1984).

26. This is a paraphrase of what Berger and Luckmann say about human beings in general in *The Social Construction of Reality*, p. 201.

27. Two very good explanations of this point of view are Tiryakian, "Sociology and Existential Phenomenology," and Lowe, *History of Bourgeois Perception*; but all the phenomenologists cited and Peter Berger's work also explain this idea.

28. Lowe, *History of Bourgeois Perception*, discusses the effect of communication media on people's view of reality.

29. See Murry G. Murphey, "The Place of Beliefs in Modern Culture," in *New Directions in American Intellectual History*, ed. John Higham and Paul K. Conkin (Baltimore: Johns Hopkins University Press, 1979), pp. 151–165. Examples of literary critics using popular fiction as a kind of public discourse include Elizabeth Long, *The American Dream and the Popular Novel* (Boston: Routledge & Kegal Paul, 1985); Mary Kelley, *Private Woman, Public Stage: Literary Domesticity in Nineteenth-Century America* (New York: Oxford University Press, 1984); Jane Tompkins, *Sensational Designs: The Cultural Work of American Fiction, 1790–1860* (New York: Oxford University Press, 1985). Jay E. Mechling, "Advice to Historians on Advice to Mothers," *Journal of Social History*, 9(1975), 44–63, cautions historians about using advice literature to draw conclusions about behavior. However, it is a different thing to use women's popular writing to understand the meaning women gave to experience, instead of using it to determine what women literally did. We should not write off this literature simply because it may not be a source of information about behavior.

30. I selected hundreds of monographs written by women from the microfilm collection of the Schlesinger Library. I was especially interested in titles with the words "mother," "daughter," "girls," "women's place," "children," "childbirth," "girlhood," and "womanhood."

31. One popular treatment of the mother/daughter theme is Nancy Friday, *My Mother/My Self* (New York: Delacorte Press, 1978). See also Chodorow, *The Reproduction*

of Mothering; Carol Gilligan, *In a Different Voice* (Cambridge, MA: Harvard University Press, 1982); Adrienne Rich, *Of Woman Born* (New York: Norton, 1976).

32. In this study, reading the literature before deciding on generational dates was important. After reading monographs published during a certain time frame and getting a sense of the patterns and when the patterns changed, I then could go back and look at birth dates of authors to establish a rough sense of generation. Beginning with age cohorts and then going to the literature might have caused me to miss the two generations as social/historical "locations."

CHAPTER 2

Imperial Motherhood: The Early-Nineteenth-Century Feminine Script

Early-nineteenth-century popular literature reflected a new set of common values about American womanhood based on a glorified notion of women's reproductive role. Celebrating the private, nuclear family and the moral bond between women and children, popular writers defined the home as the "empire of the mother" and praised domesticity and child-centered motherhood as the apex of womanly fulfillment.[1] As the major script of true womanhood between 1830 and 1860, imperial motherhood defined the boundaries of female propriety, created a new sense of "feminine" personality, and specified a uniquely female avenue of power. Before considering the socioeconomic and psychological roots of the early-nineteenth-century feminine script, it is helpful to examine the assumptions, behavioral prescriptions, and promises in the "moral mother" ideal.

Imperial motherhood was an early-nineteenth-century development and differed from previous feminine ideals in its focus on reproduction and its assumption of qualitative sexual differences. During the colonial period, the major role definition of the middle-class American woman did not revolve around her reproductive function, but rather centered on her household production. The colonial "helpmeet" role stressed the reciprocal nature of the marriage relationship and the quantitative, rather than qualitative differences between women and men. Although colonial women were not considered equal to men in intelligence, strength, or even virtue, the differences between the sexes were seen as a matter of degree, not of kind. The helpmeet differed from the man in her relative physical, mental, and moral weakness; she performed her economically essential labor under his guidance. Their work was separate and equally important, but he was her superior.[2]

By the time of the American Revolution, a new dimension was added to the helpmeet role: republican motherhood. Linda Kerber's and Mary Beth Norton's studies of revolutionary women indicate that republican motherhood was more an extension of the helpmeet idea than an entirely new feminine script.[3] In addition to doing her economic duty in the household, the republican mother was also expected to train her children in citizenship skills. While republican motherhood required that the woman take on another task, it did not change the nature of her work, demand a special personality type, or celebrate women's reproductive capacity *per se.*

In the early nineteenth century, however, a new feminine script emerged, which idealized and elaborated women's reproductive nature. Imperial motherhood was based on the new assumption of qualitative differences between the sexes, symbolized by their different reproductive functions. Women and men were seen as different kinds of creatures, with maleness implying aggression, competitiveness, and market-related skills, and femaleness including nurturance, emotion, and altruism.[4] Motherhood became the most important symbol of true womanhood, the major cultural metaphor for femininity; the moral mother seemed to encompass all the characteristics newly assigned to the female sex. Unlike the helpmeet ideal, imperial motherhood organized gender literally on the basis of body; an idealized notion of the maternal role was taken as the measure of female nature. Thus, body and role were blurred, so that the moral mother ideal and femininity in general seemed to spring from female biology, and "masculine" and "feminine" seemed as irreconcilably different as day and night.

The mother-role that women encountered in the pages of advice literature and domestic fiction involved a many-faceted script. It is helpful to speak of the script as having three major dimensions. First of all, the new mother-role required strict adherence to a child-centeredness that was newly valued. Second, the script defined a new realm of feminine power. Lastly, the mother-role contained a promise of fulfillment by associating womanhood with maternity, thus claiming that physical mothering was essential to feminine happiness. The combination of these three characteristics produced a compelling new role for early-nineteenth-century American women.

The clearest aspect of the new maternal script, child-centeredness, was a development intricately connected to the rise of a new concept of childhood. Although there were a variety of views about children from neo-Calvinist to extreme romantic, nineteenth-century people recognized childhood as a distinct period of life and the child as more or less malleable. The most popular middle ground was expressed by Horace Bushnell who argued that parents were responsible for the "Christian nurture" of children. According to Bushnell, the child was born with some natural propensities that parents could cultivate or weed out.[5]

This view of the child's possibilities and innate plasticity changed the expectations of parenthood. At a time when men increasingly left home to work, parenthood actually meant motherhood; according to critics, middle-class fathers were not very involved in parenting.[6] The image of "mother" as the all-important characteristic of adult womanhood developed alongside this new image of childhood. The new child required a different kind of mothering. Since the child was a "tender bud," constant, selfless care was necessary. Since the child was a "kernel of possibility," adult character defects or lack of religious feeling were attributable to faulty caretaking. The mother-role fit the needs of the malleable, delicate child by asserting that good mothering involved willing, child-centered self-sacrifice. Whatever the physical or emotional requirements, mother was to be constantly available, constantly selfless in her attention to detail. Motherhood was a commitment of body and soul to the service of offspring. In exchange, a woman was assured that she held the most powerful role in the world: the molding of the future, the care of souls.

The child-centeredness of motherhood was a point that was stressed repeatedly by popular writers. Sarah Josepha Hale, writing in *Godey's Lady's Book*, insisted that children were "woman's true mission ground," and another advisor wrote that a woman's children must be "the principal objects of her attention."[7] One male writer went so far as to say that a woman seeking to escape the constant care of her children was unnatural, and that such an escape would transform her into a "monster." He added that "she who can wish to throw off such cares must be capable of any wickedness."[8] The insistence that mothers be totally immersed in their children involved physical and attitudinal expectations that bound mothers spatially, behaviorally, and emotionally to their children's welfare. According to the script, motherhood demanded that a woman be child-identified.

The first thing expected of the child-centered mother was that she surrender her body to her child. The pregnant woman was admonished to take proper care of herself for the sake of her unborn charge. This advice included food and exercise precautions as well as sexual abstinence.[9] Lydia Maria Child went even further in her requirements for expectant mothers. She expressed the popular notion that a woman's moods could adversely affect the fetus. "If a mother indulges violent temper, or habitual gloom and discontent, before the birth of a child, it is very apt to have an unfavorable effect both on the character and health of the infant." She warned mothers that "it is a duty to make considerable effort to resist melancholy and fretfulness."[10]

The physical requirements of the child-defined woman also specified that she nurse her infant for the first nine to eighteen months of its life. During the same period when the invention of the rubber nipple made bottle feeding more feasible, lactation was spoken of as a "peculiar, inexpressible felicity" for the woman, and as the source of "the only proper nourishment" for the child.[11] William Alcott expressed the common feeling of horror over women who gave "excuses" for not nursing their children. The "good" mothers who nursed their children were then warned by Alcott to refrain "from all causes which tend to produce a feverish state of . . . fluids. Among these are every form of premature exertion, whether in sitting up, laboring, conversing, or even thinking."[12]

The body requirements of motherhood were stressed during pregnancy and lactation, but once infancy was successfully weathered, the child-defined woman was to concentrate her energies in molding her youngster's character. According to Mrs. Sigourney's *Letters to Mothers*, one of the most popular advice books of the day, a woman must "impress on her offspring that goodness, purity, and piety, which shall render them acceptable to society, to their country, and to their God."[13] Lydia Child in the *Lady's Book*, reiterated the same theme, calling on mothers to teach "truth and justice ... patriotism and duty."[14] Eliza Farnham held mothers responsible not only for their children's character, but also for their future capacity for independence and happiness. She wrote that true motherhood must "penetrate beyond the crust of external needs, touch the inner springs and harmonize them for future independent action. Not to supply happiness, alone, but to create permanent sources of self-supply."[15]

In addition to holding the woman responsible for the future happiness and character formation of her child, the maternal script specified that the mother's most important task was preparing the infant soul for eternal life. Mrs. Sigourney summarized this responsibility in the Preface of her *Letters to Mothers*. She wrote, "Every trace that we grave upon it [the infant soul], will stand forth at the judgment ... every waste-place, which we leave through neglect, will frown upon us."[16] This type of advice reflected the new belief in the malleability of the child's soul, and also left no question as to who was responsible for the child's ultimate salvation. The "soul-education" of the child was definitely considered the major concern of the child-centered mother.[17]

Not only did the early-nineteenth-century advisors describe the details of the new mother-role, they also provided practical guidance for the script's performance. The first behavioral requirement for the child-defined woman was that she remain at home. Advisors emphasized that home should be "the center of her joys, and the principal scene of her exertions" if a woman aspired to be a good mother. The reason mothers should always be home was that children demanded "the constant watch and instruction of a mother." The editorial page of *Godey's Lady's Book* cautioned mothers to study "the temperament and dispositions of her children, and the effects which her treatment and the circumstances that surround her and them produce, day by day, on their feelings and characters."[18]

Besides careful attention to children's physical and psychological needs, the mother, simply by being at home and doing her duties there, would inspire a love of domesticity in her daughters and sons. An author who called herself "An American Mother" urged mothers to make home a pleasant place for children because "a love of domestic life is, next to religious principle, the surest safeguard of our sons from crime, of our daughters from sorrow."[19] Another advisor warned mothers to make the home inviting, and so "not drive them [children] to seek comfort and amusement elsewhere." She further specified that the household should be "so regulated that the family are not made uncomfortable by any strings being ajar, or screws loose, in the domestic instrument."[20]

Being at home was the first essential step in becoming a successful mother. The second requirement was that the mother realize and be careful of her power of example. In a two-volume work entitled *Claims of the Country on American Females*, the author informed her readers that mothers have "the duty of exhibiting a lovely and consistent example" for their children.[21] Another writer warned mothers that all their actions influence their children, and went on to caution them against "every equivocation, every deviation from truth, every burst of passion, every uncharitable speech." The good mother was admonished to be very aware that every aspect of her conduct was scrutinized and mimicked by her children. Her very life was the lesson book her children daily studied and imitated.[22]

Of all the emotions mothers were told to control for the sake of a good example, the most important was anger. Lydia Child wrote in *The Mother's Book*, "The first rule, and the most important of all . . . is that a mother govern her own feelings. . . . The simple fact that your child never saw you angry, that your voice is always gentle, and the expression of your face always kind, is worth a thousand times more that all the rules you can give him."[23] This admonition against the display of anger was a popular theme, and one writer, guessing the difficulty of the task, even had practical suggestions to offer the fiery-tempered mother. Mrs. Chapone told women that when provoked they should "immediately resolve either to be silent, or to quit the room." By so conquering anger, she promised "you will, by degrees, find it grow weak and manageable."[24]

This advice against the display of angry feelings highlighted the central theme of the motherhood script's behavioral imperative. Besides seeing their lives as examples and conquering harsh emotions, mothers were expected to embrace self-renunciation as a total lifestyle. Mrs. Sigourney stated it bluntly: "No longer will you now live for self," and others elaborated this theme.[25] Even the positive virtues associated with motherhood had a ring of "other-directedness" to them. Eliza Farnham enumerated these motherly traits as "steadily hopeful, sustaining, compassionate, helpful, loving."[26]

The advisors defined motherhood as a complete self-surrender. Calm endurance of trials and pain and constant suffering without complaint were spoken of as essential characteristics of good mothering. Mary Ryan, in her study of early-nineteenth-century family ideology among the middle class, found painful images of motherhood in women's popular literature. "Moans," "fears," "wasting," "grief," "sorrow," and similar words were associated with the mother/child relationship.[27] After discussing women's maternal function, Eliza Farnham wrote, "To be a woman is to suffer, thus far in the human career." It was assumed that suffering was part of motherhood just as it was a part of physical birth, and that in keeping quiet about it women accepted this divine arrangement. Catharine Beecher wrote that a woman "needs to cultivate the habitual feeling, that all the events of her nursery . . . are brought about by the permission of our Heavenly Father, and that fretfulness or complaint, in regard to these, is, in fact, complaining and disputing at the appointments of God." Another writer described the "Character of a Wise and Amiable Woman" thus: "A peevish complaint does not escape from her lips.... Even in sickness [those around her] almost forget that she suffers any pain."[28]

The maternal experience, according to popular advisors, was one of total self-abandonment and child-centeredness. Just as the woman was to care for her pregnant body for the sake of her child, she was to fashion and conduct her life also for that child. The body was given up as receptacle and nourisher, the life was offered as caretaker and Christian example. Women were told that their maternal joy would come through suffering, just as birth itself involved happiness in pain. The mother was not to complain and was not to be congratulated for her patience because suffering was part of the divine plan of birthing/mothering.

In exchange for physical and psychological child-centeredness, women were promised an empire. The maternal ideal defined influence and soul-formation as a new realm of feminine power. It was not enough to speak of motherhood as a "mission from God," though many writers described it as such; mothers were also compared to kings and heads of state to illustrate the absoluteness of their authority and weightiness of their positions. One woman described maternal power as "greater than any monarch's who has ever reigned," and the power of mothers over children was celebrated and elaborated by other writers as well.[29]

Lydia Sigourney told her readers that upon becoming mothers, they "gained an increase in power." She went on to describe it: "The influence which is most truly valuable, is that of mind over mind. How entire and perfect is this dominion, over the unformed character of your infant." Another writer, in *Woman's Influence and Woman's Mission*, emphasized that the child's first impressions come from its mother: "She is its first book, and from her comes all which is to elevate or degrade." Mary Atkinson Maurice told mothers that their influence was supreme, and their early impressions on the minds and hearts of their children were unerasable.[30] The general message of these advisors was that mothers are powerful, simply in terms of their absolute authority over impressionable youth.

Maternal power over children was not confined to the individual child, but through the child the mother controlled future generations. Hale, writing in the Editor's Table of the *Lady's Book* of mother's influence over children, promised women that through this power over hearts and minds they "direct the movements of society ... more surely than the legislator can by his laws."[31] This idea of social power through maternal formation of future generations was a common theme of the advice literature. Mrs. A. J. Graves wrote of the indirect political power of the mother: "in every son she is entrusted with a being who ... will exercise a voice in the promotion of measures to operate either for his country's weal or woe. It is for her, then, to form good citizens as well as good men."[32] Not only could sons become political citizens, but some would be rulers. During the early nineteenth century a large number of books about mothers of famous men were popular. Lizzie R. Torrey described such a mother for her readers: "The influence of that humble matron, through the son, now become great and powerful, rules the hearts of thousands."[33]

Another aspect of maternal power was over the immortal souls of children. As one writer put it, "She [mother] holds 'the key to its infant soul,' " and another, more poetically, "Let every young mother . . . feel with the artist that she is labouring for 'immortality.' "[34] What more power could a person crave than the responsibility of damning or saving a soul? According to the advisors, such was the awesome potency of motherhood. No matter the sex of the child, its level of resistance to mother's temporal authority, or its susceptibility to maternal impressions—all children's souls were in the power of mothers. Her control and responsibility were direct and absolute.

The child-centered mother was not only promised power and influence; she was also promised complete feminine fulfillment. Although some historians have argued that women's relationship with family has been "at odds" with women's sense of self, the early-nineteenth-century moral mother ideal defined female fulfillment as rooted in the family-bound maternal experience.[35] Popular writers described motherhood as woman's most complete happiness, on the one hand, and as her only source of adult status, on the other. For the early-nineteenth-century women who lived with this script, it was not a question of family interests versus self-interest; the means of self-actualization was thought to be within the family, in the mother-role. The experience of caring for and educating the young was seen as personally satisfying and socially important. It was not that the female self was blotted out or thwarted by the mother-role, but that the mother-role was a vehicle for female self-expression and female power.

The early-nineteenth-century advisors celebrated motherhood in glowing terms, describing it as an experience that carried a woman to the limits of earthly bliss. Lydia Sigourney told her readers that in becoming a mother "you have reached the climax of your happiness and you have also taken a higher place in the scale of being." She later said that only the physical ills of maternity kept the experience from being "one of too unmingled felicity, for a mortal."[36] Another writer spoke of maternal duties as "the best pleasures of a woman's life."[37] According to many early-century writers, maternity was transforming and elevating mostly because the woman, upon becoming a mother, was initiated into the "deep and holy spell" of mother love.[38] Writers were in agreement that the love of a mother for her child was more perfect and more divine than any other earthly love. "Nobody loves you, nobody ever will love you, as she does," one woman wrote of maternal feeling. Another called mother love "the most constant, the most devoted, the most unalterable of all loves."[39]

The special ingredient making maternal love transcending to the mother and unique for the child was its selflessness. Advisors pointed out that such love was based on the helplessness of infancy and willing self-abnegation of motherhood.

Some compared mother love to a lover's feeling for his bride or a father's for his son, and found masculine emotion deficient and inferior. Father love was "pride," and sexual love was not selfless enough to compare with maternal feeling.[40] In a poem entitled "Maternal Affection" Mrs. Hemans wrote almost bitterly of sexual love (" 'tis mockery all"), and father love ("*You* ne'er made / Your breast the pillow of his infancy, / You ne'er kept watch / Beside him, till the last pale star had set"). She told the reader: "There is none, / In all this cold and hollow world, no fount / Of deep, strong, deathless love, save that within / A mother's heart.[41]

In popular nineteenth-century literature, the mother-role was the source of feminine happiness and transcendence. By becoming a mother, a woman would experience the highest form of love and the most complete sense of well-being. In addition to celebrating the inherent happiness of the maternal script, the advisors went further in claiming that motherhood was the natural state of womanhood. Being born female gave a person a special insight into children and a natural source of that unique maternal emotion. "To love children, is the dictate of our nature," wrote Mrs. Sigourney, and another writer added, "There are . . . very few women not replete with maternal love."[42] Since women (and girls) supposedly had a natural tendency to love children, it seemed obvious to the popular writers that the purpose of womanhood was maternity.

Not only was the moral mother ideal seen as natural to women, it was also seen as the mark of adult status. Sigourney wrote that motherhood "breaks the bonds to the father's home and attaches them to husband and child."[43] The clearest and most direct statement that the mother-role was the highest goal of womanhood was from Eliza Farnham's two-volume work, *Woman and Her Era*. The thesis of the book is that women are organically superior to men because they are "co-workers with Nature, in her grand design of Artistic Maternity." Farnham divided woman's life into three stages—ante-maternal, maternal, and post-maternal—and said that "motherhood is the ideal state of womanhood."[44]

The advice literature and domestic literature of the early nineteenth century provide an interesting type of evidence that maternity was seen as the natural culmination of womanhood. In all the literature dealing with mothers or the maternal role, at least at some point the writers identified "mother" with "woman." The traits described as ideal maternal behavior were seen as "womanly," and the feelings associated with an adult female were "motherly." The fact that "mother" and "woman" were used synonymously reveals the authors' basic assumption that maternity was a necessary aspect of womanhood.

If the moral mother was necessarily self-renouncing and long-suffering and if motherhood was the major characteristic of female maturity, it followed that suffering and self-sacrifice were somehow inherent in femaleness. Because the traits were associated with mothering, they were also associated with "femininity." The theme of "suffering womanhood" appeared throughout the advice literature and domestic fiction of the early and mid-nineteenth century.

The necessity of female suffering was discussed in diaries and popular writing as a matter of common knowledge. It would seem that woman was sent into the world for "trial and suffering," one woman wrote in her diary. She went on to comment: "In how many instances are the best years of her existence marked but by sorrow, and by sacrifice."[45] Other writers described womanly suffering as almost a joy in itself, and as a definite indication of woman's superiority. Farnham celebrated the feminine willingness to abandon self for others, describing woman as possessing "wonderful endurance . . . sublime self-poise, where self-poise would seem to be the last thing we could reasonably expect."[46] Sarah Josepha Hale wrote that woman's heroism consists in "the calm endurance of afflictions." She went on to say, "Female genius never appears so lovely as when like the trodden chamomile, it springs, apparently, from the very pressure that threatens to destroy it."[47]

Even more than a feminine virtue, suffering was viewed as the major avenue of womanly transcendence. Women wrote of regenerating the world through patient endurance of hardships, and of winning heaven through "the perfection of suffering."[48] In a two-volume book entitled *Claims of the Country on American Females*, its author described feminine suffering and went on to assert that "the circumstances in which woman has been placed are . . . powerfully calculated to develop and foster those Christian virtues which the Word of God specifies as the most important attributes of the renewed nature."[49] Elizabeth Oakes Smith described her countrywomen's view of suffering as transcendence. She wrote, "Suffering to a woman occupies the place of labor to a man, giving a breadth, depth, and fullness, not otherwise attained."[50]

In addition to diaries and advice literature, domestic fiction also contained feminine suffering and self-sacrifice as a theme. The women who wrote popular fiction in the early and mid-century period accepted suffering as part of woman's lot, even while they rebelled against it. Mary Kelley, in *Private Woman, Public Stage*, demonstrates that a central purpose of the writers was to make feminine suffering and sacrifice meaningful by writing stories in which those character-istics were a force for good.[51] Similarly, Nina Baym, in *Novels, Readers, and Reviewers: Responses to Fiction in Antebellum America*, notes that reviewers praised female characters for stereotypical rather than individual traits, and that "self-sacrifice, self-control, and self-denial" were the traits most often found and certainly most praised by critics.[52]

In advice literature, diaries, and popular fiction, women celebrated self-sacrifice to the point of suffering as part of true womanhood because this trait was seen as a necessary part of motherhood. The maternal script found in early-nineteenth-century popular literature defined women totally in relation to their children. It contained specific behavior advice to implement this child-centeredness, the central theme of which was female self-renunciation. The advisors described the mother-role as the major source of female power and as the necessary and sufficient condition for feminine happiness and fulfillment. By defining herself as a mother and consecrating her life to her child, a woman was assured of potency, transcendence, and the full experience of adult womanhood.

Writing in 1976, Adrienne Rich called the late twentieth-century version of the mother-role the "institution of motherhood," and defined the institution as an artificial cultural image of woman's reproductive capacity which serves an anti-female ideology.[53] While this judgment of the institution of motherhood as socially conservative could also be applied to the early-nineteenth-century maternal script, there are deep questions to confront about the mother-role then and now: how and why were women involved in the creation of the maternal script; and how and why did women participate in its perpetuation. Formed more generally, what is the relationship between the ideology surrounding motherhood and the women who are mothers at a given historical time and place? For a clearer vision of that relationship we need to look beyond ideology, beyond the institution of motherhood, to the complex process of human culture.

NOTES

1. The two most detailed discussions of the early-nineteenth-century mother-role as defined in popular literature are Ruth H. Block, "American Feminine Ideals in Transition: The Rise of the Moral Mother, 1785–1815," *Feminist Studies*, 4(1978), 101–125; and Mary P. Ryan, *The Empire of the Mother: American Writing About Domesticity, 1830–1860* in the series *Women and History*, Numbers 2/3, ed. Eleanor S. Riemer (The Institute for Research in History and the Haworth Press, 1982). Ryan uses the phrase "empire of the mother" and takes it from one early nineteenth-century source.

2. The helpmeet role is explained in Laurel Thatcher Ulrich, "Virtuous Women Found: New England Ministerial Literature, 1668–1735," *American Quarterly*, 28(1976), 20–40.

3. Linda K. Kerber, "The Republican Mother: Women and the Enlightenment— An American Perspective," *American Quarterly*, 28(1976), 187–205; Linda K. Kerber, *Women of the Republic; Intellect and Ideology in Revolutionary America* (Chapel Hill: University of North Carolina Press, 1980); Mary Beth Norton, *Liberty's Daughters: The Revolutionary Experience of American Women, 1750–1800* (Boston: Little, Brown, 1980).

4. Ruth H. Bloch, "Untangling the Roots of Modern Sex Roles: A Survey of Four Centuries of Change," *Signs*, 4(1978), 237–252, describes this shift from defining sexual difference in quantitative terms to defining it in qualitative terms.

5. Horace Bushnell, *Christian Nurture* (New Haven: Yale University Press, 1953). On changing ideas about childhood see: Philip Greven, *The Protestant Temperament* (New York: Knopf, 1977); Peter Slater, *Children in the New England Mind* (Hamden, CT: Archon Books, 1977); the path breaking study by Philippe Aries, *Centuries of Childhood: A Social History of Family Life* (New York: Alfred A. Knopf, 1967); Bernard Wishy, *The Child and the Republic* (Philadelphia: University of Pennsylvania Press, 1968); Monica Kiefer, *American Children Through Their Books* (Philadelphia: University of Pennsylvania Press, 1948); Anne Scott MacLeod, *A Moral Tale: Children's Fiction and American Culture* (Hamden, CT: Archon Books, 1975); Robert Sunley, "Early Nineteenth-Century American Literature on Child Rearing," in *Childhood in Contemporary Cultures*, ed. Margaret

Mead and Martha Wolfenstein (Chicago: University of Chicago Press, 1955), pp. 150–167.

6. Contemporary writers who commented on the absence of fathers and the subsequent increase in the parenting responsibility of mothers include: Sarah Josepha Hale, *Godey's Lady's Book*, 22(1841), 281; William P. Dewees, *Treatise on the Physical and Medical Treatment of Children* (Philadelphia: Carey, Lea & Blanchard, 1838), p. xiii; George Cook, "Mental Hygiene," *American Journal of Insanity*, 15(1859), 277; William Alcott, *The Young Mother* (Boston: Light & Stearns, 1836), p. 266. See also Sunley, "Early Nineteenth-Century American Literature on Child Rearing"; and Anne L. Kuhn, *The Mother's Role in Childhood Education: New England Concepts, 1830–1860* (New Haven: Yale University Press, 1947).

7. Hale, *Godey's Lady's Book*, 20(1840), 92; Ebenezer Bailey, *The Young Ladies' Class Book, a Selection of Lessons for Reading in Prose and Verse* (Boston: Lincoln, 1832), p. 26.

8. William Hosmer, *The Young Lady's Book* (Auburn: Derby & Miller, 1851), p. 232.

9. For examples of advice to pregnant women, see Mrs. T. Bakewell, *The Mothers' Practical Guide* (New York: G. Lane & D. P. Sanford, 1843), pp. 16–24; Lydia Huntley Sigourney, *Letters to Mothers* (New York: Harper & Brothers, 1839), p. 27; William A. Alcott, *The Physiology of Marriage* (Boston: J. P. Jewett & Co., 1856), p. 153; Henry Clarke Wright, *The Unwelcome Child: or the Crime of an Undesigned and Undesired Maternity* (Boston: B. Marsh, 1858), p. 21; Elizabeth Blackwell, *The Laws of Life, with Special Reference to the Physical Education of Girls* (New York: George P. Putnam, 1852), pp. 72, 73; Dewees, *Treatise*. pp. xii, xiii, 26, 27, 41–45.

10. Lydia Maria Child, *The Family Nurse; or Companion of the Frugal Housewife* (Boston: Hendee, 1837), p. 32.

11. Sigourney, *Letters to Mothers*, p. 26; Child, *The Family Nurse*, p. 35. Advice to mothers about nursing their infants was widespread. For example, see *The Maternal Physician*, by an American Matron (New York: Isaac Riley, 1811), pp. 8, 30, 140–144; Frances Parkes, *Domestic Duties; or Instructions to Young Married Ladies on the Management of Their Households, and the Regulation of Their Conduct in the Various Relations and Duties of Married Life* (New York: J. & J. Harper, 1829), p. 287; Bakewell, *The Mothers' Practical Guide*, pp. 31–34; *The Mother's Friend; or Familiar Directions for Forming the Mental and Moral Habits of Young Children*, no author (New York: Leavitt, Lord, 1834), p. 20; Charles Butler, *The American Lady* (Philadelphia: Hogan & Thompson, 1836), p. 243; William Beach, *An Improved System of Midwifery* (New York: Baker & Scribner, 1850), p. 259; Dewees, *Treatise*, pp. 48–62; Mrs. W. Maxwell, *A Female Physician to the Ladies of the United States: Being a Familiar and Practical Treatise on Matters of Utmost Importance Peculiar to Women* (New York: by the author, 1860), p. 82; Pye H. Chavasse, *Advice to Mothers on the Management of Their Offspring* (New York: Appleton & Co., 1844), pp. 32–43.

12. Alcott, *The Young Mother*, pp. 117, 118, 125.

13. Sigourney, *Letters to Mothers*, p. 17.

14. Child, *Godey's Lady's Book*, 25(1842), 248.

15. Eliza Farnham, *Woman and Her Era*, vol 1 (New York: A. J. Davis & Co., 1864), p. 70.

16. Sigourney, *Letters to Mothers*, p. viii.

17. The mother's role in "soul education" is elaborated in Bloch, "American Feminine Ideals in Transition," pp. 110–119.

18. Mrs. Marshall, *A Sketch of My Friend's Family* (Boston: Charles Ever, 1819), p.

15; *Hints and Sketches*, by an American Mother (New York: J. S. Taylor, 1839), p. 28; Hale, *Godey's Lady's Book*, 23(1841), 1. About the importance of mothers being home, see also Bushnell, *Christian Nurture*, p. 213; Louisa Caroline Tuthill, *The Young Lady's Home* (Boston: William J. Reynolds & Co., 1847), p. 94; Ann Taylor Gilbert, *Practical Hints to Young Females on the Duties of a Wife, a Mother, and a Mistress of a Family* (Boston: Wells and Lilly, 1820), pp. 125–127.

19. *Hints and Sketches*, p. 32.

20. *Woman's Influence and Woman's Mission* (Philadelphia: W. P. Hazard, 1854), p. 24.

21. Miss Coxe, *Claims of the Country on American Females* (Columbus, OH: Isaac Whiting, 1842), p. 45.

22. Mary Atkinson Maurice, *Aids to Development, or Hints to Parents; Being a System of Mental and Moral Instruction, Exemplified in Conversations Between a Mother and Her Children* (Philadelphia: Key & Bidden, 1834), p. 16. About mother as an example, see *Hints and Sketches*, preface; Parkes, *Domestic Duties*. p. 13. Kuhn, *The Mother's Role*, pp. 79–87, discusses the idea of maternal example as reflected in popular advice literature.

23. Lydia Maria Child, *The Mother's Book* (Boston: Carter and Hendee, 1831), p. 22.

24. Quoted in Bailey, *The Young Ladies' Class Book*, p. 82. About control of anger, see also John Abbot, *The Mother at Home* (New York: American Tract Society, 1833), p. 62; *The Mother's Friend*, p. 29; and Louisa May Alcott's description of Marmee's struggle to control her anger in *Little Women* (New York: Macmillan, 1962).

25. Sigourney, *Letters to Mothers*, pp. viii, 21, 22. See also Bailey, *The Young Ladies' Class Book*, p. 26; Hale, *Godey's Lady's Book*, 25(1842), p. 59.

26. Farnham, *Woman and Her Era*, p. 62.

27. Mary P. Ryan, *Cradle of the Middle Class: The Family in Oneida County, New York, 1790–1865* (New York: Oxford University Press, 1981), p. 219.

28. Farnham, *Woman and Her Era*, p. 62; Catharine Beecher, *A Treatise on Domestic Economy* (New York: Harper & Brothers, 1851), p. 115; Bailey, *The Young Ladies' Class Book*, p. 27. About suffering and motherhood, see also Bailey, *The Young Ladies' Class Book*, pp. 86, 90, 91, 146; Hale, *Godey's Lady's Book*, 20(1840), 268; Sigourney, *Letters to Mothers*, p. 22; Sarah Josepha Hale, *The Ladies' Wreath, A Selection from the Female Poetic Writers of England and America* (Boston: Marsh, Capen & Lyon, 1837), p. 243, Coxe, *Claims of the Country*, pp. 27–36.

29. *Woman's Influence*, p. 21. On motherhood as a mission from God and on mothers' power, see Joseph McDowell Mathews, *Letters to School Girls* (Cincinnati: Swormstedt & Poe, 1853), p. 247; Hosmer, *The Young Lady's Book*, p. 247; Mrs. L. Abell, *Woman in Her Various Relations* (New York: R. T. Young, 1853), p. 299; Hester Pendleton, *The Parent's Guide for the Transmission of Desired Qualities to Offspring, and Childbirth Made Easy* (New York: Fowler & Wells, 1856), p. 126; Sigourney, *Letters to Mothers*, p. 23; *Hints and Sketches*, preface; Hall, *Godey's Lady's Book*, 20(1840), 236; Lizzie R. Torrey, *The Ideal of Womanhood; or Words to the Women of America* (Boston: Wentworth, Hewes & Co., 1859), p. 39.

30. Sigourney, *Letters to Mothers*, p. 10; *Woman's Influence*, p. 21; Maurice, *Aids to Mental Development*, p. 19.

31. Hale, *Godey's Lady's Book*, 20(1840), 236.

32. Mrs. A. J. Graves, *Woman in America; Being an Examination into the Moral and Intellectual Condition of American Female Society* (New York: Harper & Brothers, 1844),

p. xix. On maternal power over future generations, see Abbot, *The Mother at Home*, pp. 152, 153; *Hints and Sketches*, pp. 20–30; Bakewell, *The Mother's Practical Guide*, p. 16.

33. Torrey, *The Ideal of Womanhood*, p. 19. On the power inherent in mothering sons, see also Sigourney, *Letters to Mothers*, p. 14; Hale, *Godey's Lady's Book*, 20(1841), 95.

34. *Woman's Influence*, p. 21. *Hints and Sketches*, pp. 29, 30. About the power of mothers over souls, see Sigourney, *Letters to Mothers*, pp. 10, 15; Abell, *Woman in Her Various Relations*, p. 301.

35. Carl Degler, *At Odds: Women and the Family in America from the Revolution to the Present* (New York: Oxford University Press, 1980) and Ryan, *The Empire of the Mother*, represent these two different arguments about women's relationship to family.

36. Sigourney, *Letters to Mothers*, pp. 1, 277.

37. *The Maternal Physician*, preface.

38. Hale, *Godey's Lady's Book*, 25(1842), 179.

39. Jane Grey Swisshelm, *Letters to Country Girls* (New York: J. C. Riker, 1853), p. 158. Torrey, *The Ideal of Womanhood*, p. 69. *Woman's Influence* devotes an entire chapter to "Maternal Love."

40. About the difference between mother-love and father-love, see Sigourney, *Letters to Mothers*, p. 47; Hale, *The Ladies' Wreath*, p. 278; Horace Mann, *A Few Thoughts on the Power and Duties of Woman* (Syracuse, NY: Hall, Mills & Co., 1853), p. 27.

41. Quoted in Bailey, *The Young Ladies' Class Book*, p. 148.

42. Sigourney, *Letters to Mothers*, p. 45; *The Young Husband's Book*, no author (Philadelphia: Lea & Blanchars, 1843), p. 44. See also Mann, *A Few Thoughts*, p. 27.

43. Sigourney, *Letters to Mothers*, p. 24.

44. Farnham, *Woman and Her Era*, pp. viii, 44. See also Hosmer, *The Young Lady's Book*, p. 232; *The Young Husband's Book*, p. 44.

45. Sarah Wentworth Morton, *My Mind and Its Thoughts* (Boston: Wells & Lilly, 1823). p. 219. See also: Farnham, *Woman and Her Era*, p. 62; Sigourney, *Letters to Mothers*, p. 125. Beecher, *A Treatise on Domestic Economy*, pp. 43, 44; Catharine Beecher, *Letters to the People on Health and Happiness* (New York: Harper & Brothers, 1856), p. 123; Anna Howard Shaw, *The Story of a Pioneer* (New York: Harper & Brothers, 1915), p. 21; Annie Adams Fields, ed., *Life and Letters of Harriet Beecher Stowe* (Boston: Houghton Mifflin & Co., 1898), p. 110; Emily C. Judson, *The Life and Letters of Emily C. Judson*, ed. A. C. Kendrick (New York: Sheldon & Co., 1862), p. 23; Caroline C. Briggs, *Reminiscences and Letters* (Boston: Houghton Mifflin & Co., 1847), pp. 19, 20.

46. Farnham, *Woman and Her Era*, p. 61.

47. Hale, *Godey's Lady's Book*, 20(1840), 268. See also: Lucretia Maria Davidson, *Poetical Remains of the Late Lucretia Maria Davidson* (Philadelphia: Lea & Blanchard, 1841), p. 192.

48. Elizabeth Oakes Smith, *Woman and Her Needs* (New York: Arno Press Reprint, 1974; reprint of 1851 edition), p. 83. See also Morton, *My Mind and Its Thoughts*, p. 221.

49. Coxe, *Claims of the Country*, p. 37.

50. Smith, *Woman and Her Needs*, p. 12.

51. Mary Kelley, *Private Woman, Public Stage: Literary Domesticity in Nineteenth-Century America* (New York: Oxford University Press, 1984), p. 308.

52. Nina Baym, *Novels, Readers, and Reviewers: Responses to Fiction in Antebellum America* (Ithaca, NY: Cornell University Press, 1984), p. 189.

53. Adrienne Rich, *Of Woman Born: Motherhood as Experience and Institution* (New York: Norton, 1976).

CHAPTER 3

The Material Roots of Ideology

At the core of feminine sexual ideology in the early nineteenth century was the imperial motherhood script. It offered middle-class American women behavioral guidelines for a new version of child-centered mothering and promised fulfillment and happiness as the emotional rewards of a good performance. While the mother-role did not determine action, it did provide a powerful set of socially approved rules and expectations, which assigned value and meaning to the central female life-experience.

Imperial motherhood grew out of social, economic, and cultural changes that affected the group of people who were beginning to call themselves a "middle class." The cult of domesticity and the belief in inherent differences between the sexes were ideological expressions that served the interest of this group. Various historians have pointed out the class function of sexual ideology. Mary Ryan argued that the private home/family became the "cradle of the middle class," a place to teach a new set of values and survival skills to children who would carry on their family's status through the change to urban-centered capitalist activity.[1] Karen Halttunen noted the utility of separate sexual worlds in easing the cultural vertigo of Jacksonian "boundlessness."[2] Other writers have emphasized how early-nineteenth-century sexual ideology was particularly useful to middle-class men.[3] Some historians have also pointed out that women were able to turn some aspects of the ideology to their advantage in spite of the fact that women were socially and economically disadvantaged relative to the men of their class.[4]

As part of the ideology of the middle class, imperial motherhood was related to changes that affected men and women as part of a class, and changes that affected men as men and women as women. Just as the generic "he" renders women invisible, too often descriptions of ideology which stress class dynamics make it impossible to see the women of that class as historical agents. In this chapter I am interested in the specific material conditions of women's lives that influenced the development of the mother-role so clearly outlined in early-nineteenth-century advice literature and woman-authored fiction. This is not to erase class as a factor or to argue that women created the mother script all alone, but it is to emphasize that sex as well as class is a significant historical category and that women actively respond to their sex- and class-specific "givens." Imperial motherhood reflected middle-class women's experience of the real conditions of their lives, translated into symbol or metaphor. The material conditions especially relevant to the mother-role included the choice involved in motherhood and the socioeconomic changes that defined the domestic space, on the one hand, and the physical and psychological changes associated with a new reproductive experience, on the other. By turning our attention to those material conditions we can begin to understand the significance of sex-specific experience in the formation of middle-class ideology.

Contemporary feminist thinkers such as Adrienne Rich, Nancy Chodorow, Rosalind Petchesky, and countless others have pointed out that motherhood is political as well as biological; that is, motherhood is a question of power, options, and autonomy and is a function of historical time and place.[5] The first step in describing the politics of nineteenth-century middle-class motherhood is recognizing the place of reproduction in women's lives. The maternal drama was the central, most universal life-experience for early-nineteenth-century American women. But how much of a choice was motherhood? At a time before reliable contraception, this question really concerns the choice of marriage.

As Lee Chambers-Schiller points out in her recent study of single women in the nineteenth century, many women were fearful of marriage and motherhood and wrote of "single blessedness" as an alternative. The trend of an increasing percentage of spinsters in the female population reflected a growing critique of marriage and a growing desire for independence among women. However, the percentage of spinsters was only 7.3 for women born between 1835 and 1838 and 8.0 for women born between 1845 and 1849.[6] Almost all of the women in the generation who wrote and read the imperial motherhood material were married. Marriage became more of an option for the daughters of these women, with mid-century spinsters accounting for 11 percent of women and the 1870s and 1880s witnessing the highest percentage of never-married women in American history. Most early-nineteenth-century women married and had children.

Although there was a beginning of ideological support for single blessedness, the economic structure did not offer a comfortable place to the woman outside of marriage. The lack of economic options for unmarried women was a significant factor in determining how much a choice marriage was. An unmarried woman from the middle class could be involved in female education or in elementary education; she could occupy herself as a domestic in the home of a relative; or she could attempt to support herself by her pen. Her earning power was limited in each of these possibilities. Indeed, one of the arguments Catharine Beecher used in her successful quest to open elementary education as an occupation for middle-class women was that women did not need to be paid as much as men. Even the women Chambers-Schiller concentrates on, women who actively chose to remain single for reasons of independence or work, reportedly had a difficult time economically.[7]

Women had few economic options to marriage and motherhood because they were not prepared to enter the new economic structure of the nineteenth century. Even the female academies that opened their doors in the early nine-teenth century assumed that domesticity would occupy their students, once graduated.[8] Middle-class women were prepared to do nothing but follow their feminine tasks outside the home. At first, in the mills of New England, this skill provided a way to earn a living for some young women. But by the 1840s, mill work was harder, dirtier, and done by Irish immigrant women.[9] An early-nineteenth-century woman's domestic training could not support her in middle-class style, unless she used it as a wife, in her own home.

The same reasons that made it difficult for women to resist marriage also made it difficult to leave a marriage. Divorce was rare not only because the law made it hard to end marriages, but also because a divorced woman, or a woman who deserted her husband as a kind of informal divorce, had the same problems of making a living as never-married women did. Recent studies of early nineteenth-century divorce indicate that severe financial hardship was the price women paid for living ouside of the conjugal unit. Robert Griswold, in his study of divorce in California, found that over 80 percent of divorced women ended up in menial occupations, mostly domestic service. In addition, divorced mothers had no legal right to their children, who, according to patriarchal law, belonged to the father.[10]

The early-nineteenth-century woman who resisted marriage, or who di-vorced, lived an economically and socially precarious life. Although there was some ideological support for single blessedness under some circumstances and although some divorced women found comfortable lives with their families of origin, being an unmarried woman was not a choice easily made or easily lived. The conditions surrounding the single life contributed to women's seeing mar-riage as natural and inevitable, even women who remained single. The most successful domestic fiction writers, many of whom lived outside the conjugal unit, continually wrote of their uneasiness about self-support and their ac-ceptance of domesticity as woman's true calling.[11] And even independent-minded single women were obliged (or obliged themselves) to be extremely involved in the domesticity of their families of origin, many times resulting in great disruption of their own work, indicating that they too saw the domestic role as a natural part of woman's life.[12] No early-nineteenth-century woman completely escaped the shadow of the domestic sphere.

Thus, within the economic structure of the early nineteenth century, the fact that most American women married and had children cannot be considered a "choice" in the same way as it is in the late twentieth century. In a social atmosphere still suspicious toward the single female, with no access to the political system except through men, and with limited opportunity for making a living, American women overwhelmingly "chose" marriage and motherhood. They then described mothering as "natural" and "essential" to a woman's nature. Within the material conditions of their lives they experienced marriage and motherhood as inevitable.

Whether a woman married or lived her life as one of the very few early-nineteenth-century spinsters, she occupied a sphere separate from men's. Her education, her possibilities for gainful employment, and her traditional up-bringing that associated woman with family, all emphasized life possibilities different from (and inferior to) her brother's. The social and economic changes associated with early industrialization provided a material base for the ideology of separate spheres. As men and productive labor left the home, women were stranded in the narrowing domestic realm by lack of education and training.

In an early study of sex and class in Jacksonian America, Gerda Lerner pointed out that accentuated separate spheres resulted in a loss of social status for women relative to men, because the male sphere was expanding while the female sphere was contracting.[13] During the early nineteenth century, the male sphere was teeming with economic and political opportunities for an increasing number of American men. Higher education and professional training were becoming available to more and more men and boys. New jobs and professions were blossoming, offering economic opportunities and social prestige. The franchise was extended to all white men 21 years and older, regardless of property or class. During this time of the most dramatic urban expansion in American history, the young men flocking to cities seemed almost dangerously filled with possibility.[14] Because this was a period of "boundlessness" for American men,[15] the home was relatively more confining for women than it had been a generation earlier. Physically separate spheres increased the discrepancy between male and female life-options, male and female education, and male and female expectations.

It was not only that women were kept from the expanding life-possibilities of their brothers, but that they were also kept in a realm of devalued labor. As factories took over an increasing number of feminine tasks, and as men's work began to be more commercial and centered outside the home, the social status and economic importance of female labor began to decline. Woman's work in the home, once a vital necessity, began to shrink in actual tasks and in significance. Although the housewife's job was extraordinary by modern standards, women in the early nineteenth century were less economically important than their grandmothers had been, because woman's work was not money-producing, and, therefore, was not a source of status, self-esteem, or survival in a market economy. Women's work produced "use value" but no surplus value. The factory system eroded women's economic power not because it left them taskless but because it shifted the emphasis from wife-labor to bought-labor, vested a new power in money-wages, and left women no access to this source of power other than marital dependency.[16]

The women who experienced the loss of status that accompanied economic change expressed disappointment, frustration, and sometimes rage about their new position relative to the men of their class. They described the work of the feminine sphere as necessary drudgery, as "domestic servitude" and a "double yoke of bondage."[17] They wrote with sadness or resentment about their brothers' educational opportunities, and they compared themselves unfavorably to their more useful mothers and grandmothers.[18] Some of these middle-class women even formed themselves into organizations to work for women's rights, certainly an indication that many were aware of the growing discrepancy between male and female power. Whether they quietly grumbled or wrote defiant "declarations of sentiments," middle-class women recognized the worlds of the sexes were not equally important or rewarding.

Not only were women kept from the education and economic opportunities of the male sphere, and not only was the home sphere less productive and satisfying, but the marital state itself was not a powerful one for women. Certainly most married women fared better than unmarried women in terms of economic status, but legally a married woman was much worse off than a single woman. In the early nineteenth century, the law still reflected the traditional patriarchal view of marriage. Wives belonged to their husbands, in terms of what little earning power they had and in terms of their actual bodies. Married women held no property in their own right and were not entitled to their own wages. Married women also were not legally exempted from mild physical chastisement or marital rape.[19] Motherhood within marriage was not a position of strength as far as the law was concerned, and in fact the entire empire of the mother was within the jurisdiction of the fathers.

The legal powerlessness of marriage was not a new condition for women, but it had a new significance during this time of economic transition. In an earlier, agricultural economy a wife had a right to one-third of her husband's estate, and she also contributed invaluable labor to their joint project. Her legal disability was partially offset by her economic clout, and the death of her husband would not leave her without provision. However, the women of the early nineteenth century who were most involved in the writing and reading of advice literature and domestic fiction were not in the same situation as their mothers and grandmothers. The new economic order left them without property and without wages, with no security against poverty except the labor of husbands willing to provide for their needs. Having no right to their own wages and performing no necessary home production, the early-nineteenth-century wife had nothing to offset the legal and economic power of her husband. Although the law itself had not changed, the new conditions of the time made the wife's legal position less powerful.[20]

The material conditions to which early nineteenth-century women had to respond presented a dilemma. On the one hand, lack of education and economic options made marriage a powerful choice; on the other hand, marriage rendered a woman economically dependent on a man who held real power over her and her children. The women in Chambers-Schiller's study clearly saw the fact that marriage robbed a woman of personal power. Early-nineteenth-century feminists also noted the powerlessness of the marital state and concentrated much of their energy before the Civil War to improving married women's property rights, divorce options, and rights to their own persons. Feminists and non-feminists, women who remained single and women who eventually married, also saw that marriage entailed a loss of personal autonomy for women. In the diaries of Michigan women, Marilyn Motz found repeated reference to women's fears of losing autonomy in marriage and being bound in household drudgery.[21]

For the most part, women responded to the dilemma posed by the structural constraints of their lives by attempting to transform marriage and domesticity into a power base. Because separate spheres created a new set of needs for men, women were very successful. Men's world of commercial activity was physically separate from the domestic world and superior to it in economic and social status, but men depended on the home-bound woman for the sentiment and warmth, selfless devotion and careful personal attention that were absent from the world of work. The sentimentalization of the home and the woman in the home was an expression of new male needs stemming from the separation of work and home. As non-participants in the male sphere of commercial activity, women and children were to occupy and animate a haven for the weary male worker. The home and the woman in the home were to offer the safety, unconditional love, and personal sentiment that were lacking in the work world.[22]

Considering women's social, economic, and political subordination, men's needs and expectations arising from separate spheres were important factors in defining the behavioral options of female life. However, that is not to say that men created the cult of domesticity and forced women to accept it. On the contrary, the new needs and expectations of men allowed women to assert their power in the home, and then outside the home into the schools and churches. The cult of domesticity must be seen as a joint creation of women and men. Male power in the home, although still an actual fact, was eroded by separate spheres as the companionate marriage began to replace the patriarchal style of marriage. Woman's "influence" grew throughout the century, as men gradually deferred to women in matters of religion, morality, and child-rearing.[23]

The influence women had over their husbands was based on the idea of innate differences between the sexes, an idea growing out of separate spheres. With male and female education and work so different, the belief that men and women also had naturally different personalities, strengths, and weaknesses seemed self-evident to most nineteenth-century people; it grew out of their experience. Although the new reality of separate spheres left them with few economic or social options to marriage, and although marriage itself entailed economic dependency and a loss of personal autonomy, middle-class women were able to transform the constraints of domesticity into a meaningful and powerful life-story by emphasizing their uniquely "feminine" qualities—self-sacrifice for the sake of others, heightened moral sensibility, gentleness and self-restraint—which they linked ultimately to their capacity to mother.

Motherhood was the central focus of the life-script middle-class women designed for themselves in response to their historical situation. Motherhood was the quintessential expression of femaleness at a time when celebration of innate sexual difference could augment women's power in the home. But there were other conditions within the home sphere that led women to turn their attention toward their children. Concentrating on motherhood as the measure of womanhood sidestepped the strain of relationships with husbands. By defining the mother-child bond as inherently more rewarding than the marital bond, women compensated for the lack of intimacy in their marriages.

There were many reasons that early-nineteenth-century marriages might not have been satisfying for women. Marriage was only recently a personal, rather than a family, choice, and the decision to marry a particular person was a life-defining one for a woman. Probably for her mother and certainly for her grandmother, marriage was a family decision and the young suitor was known, or known of, since childhood. And for those earlier generations of women, the personal relationship between husband and wife was expected to evolve over the years of their mutually essential economic activity on behalf of family. Early-nineteenth-century women, however, had different experiences of mate choice and different marital expectations. In a geographically mobile society and in a situation of separate spheres, young women had to attract and wed "promising" young men who would provide them support.[24] Separate spheres meant that women and men had little contact with each other and little opportunity to get to know each other. Likewise, it also meant that the sexes had little in common. Yet marriage was a choice to be made on the newly valued basis of romantic love! It is no wonder that women expressed such ambivalence in their diaries and letters about the decision to marry.[25]

The conditions under which early-nineteenth-century women married were not ones to encourage intimacy. Once married, the separate worlds of women and men likewise kept the sexes psychologically distant, with each regarding the other as a different kind of creature.[26] The female world of "love and ritual" described by Carroll Smith-Rosenberg was the locus of women's intimate relationships. As we shall see in the next chapter, sexuality was also a troubled area of the marriage relationship because of the perceived differences between the sexes and because of the desire to control fertility before reliable birth control techniques.

There were probably many personal reasons for marital unhappiness in addition to these structural ones, but, whatever the reasons, the theme of marital dissatisfaction appeared throughout early-nineteenth-century women's personal writings, advice literature, and domestic fiction. Mary Kelley, in her study of literary domesticity, found that women writers, in their fiction and in their personal diaries and correspondence, constantly referred to the numerous unhappy marriages around them. Catharine Sedgwick described marriages of "incurable and bitter sorrows," and others wrote of women uncomplaining in the face of marital wrongs.[27] Women who remained single and women who eventually married asserted that marital happiness was not the rule, but the exception.[28] Husbands disappointed women, or brought them psychological and physical pain, or did not understand them. This is not to say that there were no women who were satisfied in their marriages, but only that an intensely close spousal relationship was not a part of many marriages.[29] Instead, women created intimacy and relational meaning with their women friends and in their mothering.

Elaborating the mother-role was a way for women to accentuate their femaleness at a time when sexual difference could provide a basis for power in the home, and it was a way to compensate for an unhappy or distant marital relationship. Imperial motherhood also provided a meaningful rationale for women's newly intense childcaring responsibilities, another ramification of separate spheres. The simple presence of women and children in the home, in the absence of men, required that childcare be a major and exclusive female activity, which was not the case in an earlier time. When men's work was home-centered agriculture or artisan manufacturing, fathers and older brothers shared in the responsibility of caring for younger boys, although the care of infants and girl children was in the hands of mothers.[30] Another development of the early nineteenth century, the common school, may have actually made the childcare responsibilities of women even more intense. Toward mid-century schools were held suspect for younger children because the school was seen as depriving the young ones of maternal guidance and maternal love. Since the schools took older children out of the home, they were not as available as they had been in earlier times to care for younger siblings. There was little physical alternative to mother-care; a woman's young children were her constant companions.[31]

Because women had many children, their childrearing occupied much of their adult life. Although fertility rates began a gradual and steady decline just before 1800, over half of American mothers in the early nineteenth century gave birth to five or more children.[32] The estimates of women's fertility represent live-born children, they do not include stillbirths and late miscarriages and may not include some children born alive but dying in early infancy. These numbers indicate that for most American women pregnancy, birth, and childcare were almost continual activities during their adult lives.

The women who authored the imperial motherhood script experienced marriage and motherhood as "natural" to womanhood because the conditions of their lives offered few other options. Denied access to political power or the education and training necessary for middle-class economic positions, women accommodated themselves to their given situation by concentrating on domesticity. But the home sphere was not inherently powerful and was even losing its significance as the middle-class wife lost much of her productive role.

Finding themselves with less childcare help than their mothers had had, within emotionally disappointing marriages, and with their domestic power partially dependent on emphasizing the differences between the sexes, middle-class women elaborated the mother-role. Imperial motherhood transformed the material conditions of women's lives into a meaningful and powerful story.

Most aspects of the maternal script can be seen as women's response to conditions their mothers did not face. But because each woman first views herself through the lens of her mother's life, the women who wrote about imperial motherhood began with an inherited set of ideas about woman's role, a set of ideas their mothers, living in a different time, bequeathed to them.[33] The imperial motherhood script was an altered version of their own mothers' and grandmothers' life-scripts, changed to meet the new nineteenth-century conditions. The helpmeet role assumed woman's importance and centrality in the home was based on her economically valuable production. The republican mother-role extended that task to raising citizen-children. Imperial motherhood kept the woman central and essential in the home, but grounded her importance in emotional nurturance and influence of children and husband. To accommodate the new, nineteenth-century stage, the script was altered; but there was continuity between the new and old stories.

Imperial motherhood is a record of the adjustment, accommodation, and, as we shall see, ambivalence, of women responding to new socioeconomic conditions. Within the domestic sphere they created a mother-role that gave them emotional leverage with their husbands and that also gave them a sense of purpose and importance. Central to the mother-role was a blending of self and family and a celebration of self-abnegation as a source of strength. But there is another ingredient of imperial motherhood that is not completely explained by the material conditions outlined thus far. Suffering became an important characteristic of good mothering in the early nineteenth century. To understand this dimension of imperial motherhood we need to examine the most basic meaning of women's "material condition"—the body itself.

NOTES

1. Mary P. Ryan, *Cradle of the Middle Class: The Family in Oneida County, New York, 1790–1865* (New York: Oxford University Press, 1981).

2. Karen Halttunen, *Confidence Men and Painted Women: A Study of Middle-Class Culture in America, 1830–1870* (New Haven: Yale University Press, 1982).

3. David G. Pugh, *Sons of Liberty: The Masculine Mind in Nineteenth-Century America* (Westport, CT: Greenwood Press, 1983); Elizabeth H. Pleck and Joseph H. Pleck, *The American Man* (Englewood Cliffs, NJ: Prentice-Hall, 1980), the introduction and the article by Charles E. Rosenberg, "Sexuality, Class and Role in Nineteenth-Century America," pp. 219–254.

4. About the positive ways women used sexual ideology, see Daniel Scott Smith, "Family Limitation, Sexual Control, and Domestic Feminism in Victorian America," *Feminist Studies*, 1(1973), 40–47; Kathryn Kish Sklar, *Catharine Beecher: A Study in*

American Domesticity (New Haven: Yale University Press, 1973); Linda Gordon, "Voluntary Motherhood: The Beginnings of Feminist Birth Control Ideas in the United States," *Feminist Studies*, 1(1973), 5–22; Nancy F. Cott, "Passionlessness: An Interpretation of Victorian Sexual Ideology, 1790–1850," *Signs*, 4(1978), 219–236; Barbara Leslie Epstein, *The Politics of Domesticity: Women, Evangelism, and Temperance in Nineteenth-Century America* (Middletown, CT: Wesleyan University Press, 1981).

5. Adrienne Rich, *Of Woman Born* (New York: W. W. Norton, 1976); Nancy Chodorow, "Mothering, Male Dominance, and Capitalism," in *Capitalist Patriarchy and the Case for Socialist Feminism*, ed. Zillah Eisenstein (New York: Monthly Review Press, 1979), pp. 83–106; Rosalind Pollack Petchesky, "Reproductive Freedom: Beyond 'A Woman's Right to Choose,' " in *Women: Sex and Sexuality*, ed. Catharine R. Stimpson and Ethel Spector Person (Chicago: University of Chicago Press, 1980), pp. 36–61.

6. Lee Virginia Chambers-Schiller, *Liberty, A Better Husband: Single Women in America: The Generations of 1780–1840* (New Haven: Yale University Press, 1984), p. 3. A rising percentage of unmarried women does not necessarily mean that women felt marriage to be a real choice. See Nancy Cott, *The Bonds of Womanhood* (New Haven: Yale University Press, 1977); Marilyn Ferris Motz, *True Sisterhood: Michigan Women and Their Kin, 1820–1920* (Albany: State University of New York Press, 1983).

7. On Catharine Beecher see Sklar, *Catharine Beecher*. Chambers-Schiller, *Liberty, A Better Husband*, pp. 43–44.

8. I do not mean to dispute that female seminaries might have served as incubators of feminist values, especially for the women who organized them, as argued by Anne Firor Scott, "The Ever Widening Circle: The Diffusion of Feminist Values from the Troy Female Seminary, 1822–1872," *History of Education Quarterly*, 19(1979), 3–26. But the schools did not prepare young women to be wage earners in the new industrial economy; rather, they prepared their students for teaching and domesticity, even though the directors and teachers might have inspired new ideals of feminine possibility.

9. About the experience of women in the textile mills, see Caroline Ware, *The Early New England Cotton Manufacture: A Study of Industrial Beginnings* (New York: Russell & Russell, 1966, originally published in 1931); and Thomas Dublin, *Women at Work: The Transformation of Work and Community in Lowell, Massachusetts, 1826–1860* (New York: Columbia University Press, 1979).

10. Robert Griswold, *Family and Divorce in California, 1850–1890: Victorian Illusion and Everyday Realities* (Albany: State University of New York Press, 1982), p. 81. For a discussion of divorce and the general legal position of wives, see Cott, *The Bonds of Womanhood*, introduction; and Edward D. Mansfield, *The Legal Rights, Liabilities and Duties of Women* (Salem: John P. Jewett & Co. 1845), pp. 240–275. Motz, *True Sisterhood*, p. 112, also describes the plight of divorced and widowed women.

11. Mary Kelley, *Private Woman, Public Stage: Literary Domesticity in Nineteenth-Century America* (New York: Oxford University Press, 1984).

12. Chambers-Schiller, *Liberty, A Better Husband*, chapter 6.

13. Gerda Lerner, "The Lady and the Mill Girl: Changes in the Status of Women in the Age of Jackson," *American Studies Journal*, 10(1969), 5–15. Women's loss of status relative to men is also discussed by Barbara Berg, *The Remembered Gate: Origins of American Feminism, The Woman and the City, 1800–1860* (New York: Oxford Univeristy Press, 1978). The idea that separate spheres caused a status decline for women does not mean that women were powerless within the home sphere (as noted above).

14. Halttunen, *Confidence Men and Painted Women*, describes middle-class people's

perception of young men in cities as "in danger" because of the possiblities open to them and their own innocence.

15. The idea of the early nineteenth century as a time of "boundlessness" comes from John Higham, *From Boundlessness to Consolidation: The Transformation of American Culture, 1848–1860* (Ann Arbor: William L. Clements Library, 1969).

16. For a discussion of the change in women's economic productivity, see Dublin, *Women at Work; Carl Degler, At Odds: Women and the Family in America from the Revolution to the Present* (New York: Oxford University Press, 1980); Berg, *The Remembered Gate*. For a discussion of how this change relates to capitalism, see Eisenstein, *Capitalist Patriarchy*; and Eli Zaretsky, *Capitalism, The Family, and Personal Life* (New York: Harper, 1973).

17. Motz, *True Sisterhood*, pp. 17, 19. Kelley, *Private Woman, Public Stage*, found this view of domesticity throughout women's popular writing.

18. Women's perceptions of their "place" will be dealt with in chapter 5.

19. On women's legal position in marriage, see Cott, *The Bonds of Womanhood*; and Mansfield, *The Legal Rights, Liabilities and Duties of Women.*

20. On colonial marriage, see Laurel Thatcher Ulrich, *Good Wives: Image and Reality in the Lives of Women in Northern New England, 1650–1750* (New York: Oxford University Press, 1982); and John Demos, *A Little Commonwealth* (New York: Oxford University Press, 1970). Berg, *The Remembered Gate*, pp. 92–99, discusses the new economic conditions surrounding marriage.

21. Motz, *True Sisterhood.*

22. For a discussion of the new development of home as retreat from the world, see Mary P. Ryan, *The Empire of the Mother: American Writing about Domesticity, 1830–1860*, in the series *Women and History*, Numbers 2/3, ed. Eleanor S. Riemer (New York: The Institute for Research in History and The Haworth Press, 1982); Cott, *The Bonds of Womanhood*, pp. 64–75; Berg, *The Remembered Gate*, chapter 3; William Bridges, "Family Patterns and Social Values in America, 1825–1875," *American Quarterly*, 18(1965), 9–12. Recognition of this changed idea of home also appeared in children's stories. See Ann Scott MacLeod, *A Moral Tale: Children's Fiction and American Culture, 1820–1960* (Hamden, CT: Archon Books, 1975).

23. About the erosion of male power in the home, see Pugh, *Sons of Liberty*; Rosenberg, "Sexuality, Class and Role"; and Griswold, *Family and Divorce in California*, pp. 92–173.

24. About mate choice in the early nineteenth century, see Michael Gordon, "The Ideal Husband as Depicted in the Nineteenth-Century Marriage Manual," *The American Man*, pp. 145–158; Rosenberg, "Sexuality, Class and Role"; Chambers-Schiller, *Liberty, A Better Husband*, pp. 35–38.

25. Motz, *True Sisterhood.*

26. An exaggerated sense of sexual difference runs throughout early-nineteenth-century popular and serious writing. Kelley, *Private Woman, Public Stage*, finds it also in women's fiction. Likewise, women's private writings reflected this view. See Carroll Smith-Rosenberg, "The Female World of Love and Ritual: Relations Between Women in Nineteenth-Century America," *Signs*, 1(1975), 1–30; Motz, *True Sisterhood*; and Cott, *The Bonds of Womanhood.*

27. Kelley, *Private Woman, Public Stage*, pp. 239–246.

28. About women's perceptions of marriage as unhappy, see Ethel Peal, "The Atrophied Rib: Urban Middle-Class Women in Jacksonian America" (unpublished Ph.D.

dissertation, University of Pittsburgh, 1970); Motz, *True Sisterhood*, especially pp. 18–21; and Chambers-Schiller, *Liberty, A Better Husband.* Peal, "The Atrophied Rib," and Bryan Strong, "Toward a History of the Experiential Family: Sex and Incest in the Nineteenth-Century Family," *Journal of Marriage and the Family*, 35(1973), 457–466, argue that women focused on motherhood as compensation for the lack of intimacy in marriage.

29. Degler, *At Odds*, argues that spousal relationships were close, based on letters between husbands and wives. Some of the diaries Motz examined in *True Sisterhood* also indicated close marital relationships. Blanche Glassman Hersh, " 'A Partnership of Equals': Feminist Marriages in Nineteenth-Century America," in *The American Man*, pp. 183–215, maintains that feminist women had supportive husbands.

30. About colonial childcare arrangements, see Demos, *A Little Commonwealth.*

31. Ryan, *The Empire of the Mother*, stresses the point that women's childcaring responsibilities increased in the early nineteenth century. Although the home-bound mother and child was a middle-class experience and a middle-class value, reformers worked to impose this ideal on working-class families as well. See Christine Stansell, "Women, Children, and the Uses of the Streets: Class and Gender Conflict in New York City, 1850–1860," *Feminist Studies*, 8(1982), 309–336.

32. On American fertility, see Yasuba Yasukichi, *Birth Rates of the White Population in the United States, 1800–1860* (Baltimore: Johns Hopkins University Press, 1962); Robert V. Wells, "Demographic Change and the Life Cycle of American Families," *Journal of Interdisciplinary History*, 2(1971), 273–282; United States Department of Commerce, Bureau of the Census, *Historical Statistics of the United States* (Washington D.C.: Government Printing Office, 1975), Part I, pp. 41, 53.

33. Two important theoretical works about the importance of the mother in passing on feminine ideology to her daughter are Nancy Chodorow, *The Reproduction of Mothering* (Berkeley: University of California Press, 1978); and Ethel Spector Person, "Sexuality as the Mainstay of Identity: Psychoanalytic Perspectives," in *Women: Sex and Sexuality*, pp. 36–61.

CHAPTER 4

The Physical Roots of Ideology

The meaning women give to womanhood in any historical time and place is a blend of inherited ideas, the social and economic conditions defining women's place, and the somatic experience of being a female within this cultural setting. To understand women's role in creating feminine ideology, sex-specific physical experience must be considered along with the socioeconomic conditions of female life. Just as there was a relationship between the material conditions of women's lives and the imperial motherhood script, so too the physical experience of motherhood influenced women's collective sense of "true womanhood."

There is a fundamental reason for examining women's experience of motherhood as a clue to the social construction of femininity in the early nineteenth century. The biological phenomena of fertility control, pregnancy, birth, and lactation are never merely biological; they are experienced within the rituals, expectations, and technology of a particular historical time and place.[1] But they are also not "merely" social; they are most inherently female, specific to the female body. At a time when motherhood was not a real choice for women, and a time when the social conditions of reproduction were undergoing dramatic shifts, the experience of motherhood was a particularly significant condition of female life. Examining the changes surrounding fertility control and childbirth will enable us to see the connection between women's sex-specific physical experience and their definition of femininity.

Around the turn of the nineteenth century, American couples began to control fertility consciously.[2] Historians once assumed the change in fertility was confined to middle- and upper-class urban women and was caused by industrialization and urbanization. More recent research, however, has indicated that Black women as well as white women, ethnic minorities as well as native-born women, and rural Americans along with urban dwellers experienced fertility decline.[3] Diminishing land availability might have been an important factor in fertility decline for some people; the economic strain of children in an urban setting might have been the most relevant point for others; and the growing necessity of educating children in order to preserve middle-class status might have prompted fertility decline for still others. But no matter what "historical force" one chooses to stress as the root of fertility decline, the common denominator was the emergence of a new sense of human control over environment, of human choice as a factor in family size.[4]

The decision to have fewer children was made by couples in all the various living situations found in America, and it was made when birth control technology was primitive. Charles Knowlton, in his popular early-nineteenth-century book, *Fruits of Philosophy: or The Private Companion of Young Married People*, wrote of four methods of contraception: *coitus interruptus*, condoms, vaginal sponges, and douching with a sulfate solution. Knowlton is credited by Norman Himes in his *History of Contraception* as the first person to mention douching as a means of birth control. His suggestions for a sperm-sensitive douche included such ingredients as white oak bark, hemlock bark, red rose leaves, green tea, and baking soda. Another author included "tannin water" and "plain cold water" as possible spermicides and still another suggested opium, iodine, strychnine, or alcohol.[5]

Besides these common household spermicides, a cervical cap, the precursor of the diaphragm, was sold in the United States before the Civil War. The cap was a sponge with rubber pads to hold it tightly onto the cervix. It was not until 1880 that the modern diaphragm was invented, a revolutionary contraceptive device in that it was very effective. Before then, vaginal sponges, douching, and homemade condoms were the only available mechanical means of birth control. Since there were no laws against the distribution of such devices, they were available to the reading public.[6] However, the newly organized medical profession, in a spirit of moralism that sought to maintain the connection between sex and procreation, began a campaign to outlaw contraceptive devices in the mid-century period.[7] The doctors also argued against *coitus interruptus*, for health reasons, and against abortion.

Evidence suggests that most middle-class American couples in the early nineteenth century used abstinence as their primary contraceptive method, with abortion as a back-up.[8] The mood of the time reinforced the practice of infrequent sexual contact as more healthful for both sexes. The human body was described by popular medical writers as a closed energy system, such that any output of effort or vital juices was seen as a depletion of a limited supply of life force. Men were advised to engage in sexual intercourse only when "necessary," as a kind of safety valve of nervous energy. Women were warned to avoid intercourse during pregnancy and lactation, when their limited bodily vitality should be focused on the infant. Lectures on "voluntary motherhood" and "marital excess," very popular during this time, supported sexual abstinence as the key solution to the problem of birth control. One writer, Frederick Hollick, calmly suggested that men should absent themselves from their wives for three years between every two births as a means of spacing children.[9] And some middle-class women (notably Harriet Beecher Stowe) left home periodically for water cure establishments to insure sexual abstinence.[10]

Historians have pointed out the logical connection between the ideal of passionlessness and a lower birth rate, and between fertility decline and the domestic power of women to enforce abstinence.[11] But to understand the relationship between feminine ideology and female body, we need to explore how women experienced abstinence and what meaning they assigned to that experience. In spite of "feminine delicacy" making sexual subjects taboo, early- and mid-nineteenth-century women wrote a great deal about abstinence indirectly, and contemporary observers also provided clues as to the experience of abstinence in marriage.

For a woman to use abstinence as an effective means of birth control, she had to avoid sexual intercourse as much as possible.[12] This required that she deny or re-define whatever physical desire she might feel, that she distance herself from her body. It also required that she maintain her premarital coolness with her husband, and not be emotionally involved in his desire. The imperial motherhood ideal was one way women enforced and justified the goal of sexual abstinence. Within the maternal script, women defined themselves as child-centered and basically asexual, so that the child, not the husband, was to be the "good" woman's life-commitment. Embracing the maternal ideal, women could justifiably turn their attentions away from the sexual relationship and toward the child.

Women's writings indicate that this shift was indeed taking place. Passionlessness began to be seen as a necessary attribute of "true womanhood," and women wrote frankly that they had no sexual appetite.[13] Foreign and native observers began to comment about the "excessive maternal devotion" of American mothers, and about the growing tension in American homes.[14] Women wrote about the mother-child relationship as more rewarding and fulfilling than the sexual relationship.[15]

But if the maternal ideal provided women with a personal rationale for avoidance of sexual intercourse, it did not furnish a sure argument for convincing husbands. Early- and mid-nineteenth-century men had conflicting feelings about masculinity and sexuality, as Charles Rosenberg and David Pugh have described in different studies.[16] The ideal of the "Christian gentleman," who practiced self-denial and allowed his wife to dictate sexual interaction, was formulated by the 1850s; however, the practice of this ideal was not widespread until the last third of the century. Rosenberg points out that the men who created the ideal out of the new conditions surrounding manhood in the early nineteenth century lived with fathers who cherished an older, male-oriented ethic that encouraged sexual activity regardless of women's desire or lack of desire. Pugh argues that the ideas about masculinity created by men in the Jacksonian period helped them sublimate sex into non-sexual achievement areas, but at the expense of a healthy relationship with women. He describes the Jacksonian man as a blend of patriarch and eternal child, needing and rejecting women at the same time. Pugh and Rosenberg agree that men's conflict over masculinity in the early to mid-nineteenth century was not conducive to good marital relationships.

Women's writing about marriage and sex reinforces this view. Women wrote very matter-of-factly that marriage was not a blissful state, that men did not understand women, and that their husbands made too frequent sexual demands.[17] Advice books aimed at women counselled about unhappy marriages, and lecturers on "marital excess" enjoyed great popularity among married women.[18] Women frequently expressed the view that their husbands were overly interested in sex and that they themselves were not. One woman wrote of men, "I have found few who did not view marriage and a wife as my husband did, as a mere means of sensual gratification."[19] Women's interest in abstinence as a means of birth control was at the center of these sexual complaints.[20]

The attempt to limit fertility with sexual abstinence encouraged women to see men as creatures totally different from themselves. Women might have truly felt "passionless" in accordance with the ideology of the time and the type of sexual encounter they likely experienced; they might have used passionlessness as a justification for sexual restraint; or they simply might have exercised a great deal of self-control. But however they came to grips with abstinence, women were clear in their belief that men were almost incapable of such self-restraint. Women wrote that husbands had a sexual "right" in marriage because of their great sexual need. "I know that all would condemn me," wrote one woman, "if I felt to escape such an outrage [repeated sexual demands of her husband] as this was not considered a wrong to me, but his right."[21] Another woman wrote that most of her female friends believed that a woman who denied her husband sexual intercourse was morally responsible for his impure behavior. She went on to say, "The community of women... are educated to believe that God gave man such fierce passions that he cannot control them, that they must be gratified whenever excited, though at the expense of woman's health and happiness."[22] If by some accident or insistence her husband became sexually aroused, the early-nineteenth-century woman believed it her duty to submit to him. The experience of abstinence validated and encouraged the ideology of separate spheres by exaggerating sexual difference. Women believed male bodies required sexual intercourse while female bodies did not.

When abstinence worked at all, it worked by desensualizing the marriage relationship. The woman who wanted to control fertility had to be vigorously asexual and had to maintain a clear physical and psychic distance between herself and her husband. The experience of abstinence was one of self-control of female sexual energy, and avoidance or control of male sexuality by women. It was not an empowering experience, but a constant battle fought with uneven odds. Succcess depended on vigilance, coldness, and subtle manipulation. Because women felt no "right to themselves" in marriage (and indeed they had no "right to themselves" within marriage before the law), abstinence was always a request, not a demand—and a constant request. Any sexual encounter that included intercourse was a type of failure, a possible source of disappointment or disgust with her husband, an event producing anxiety.[23]

When abstinence failed, pregnancy was a possibility. Women frequently resorted to abortion to limit family size. Unlike contraceptive devices and information, abortion was a subject of law in all the states. The basis of abortion law was common law, in which the mother's life and health were the major concern. Fetal life legally began at "quickening" (the point at which movement could be detected *by the pregnant woman*, usually at about four months), and the willful abortion of such a fetus was a misdemeanor or felony, depending on the state. There was no provision in early-nineteenth-century law for protection of the rights of the unborn; instead, the laws were designed to protect mothers.[24]

In spite of the fact that abortion was illegal, the law was rarely enforced. Professional abortionists advertised their services in newspapers, and abortifacients were easily bought in stores. Mid-century abortion critics concluded that the public nature of abortionists and abortifacients testified to the frequency of the crime.[25] Although it is impossible to estimate the number of abortions in early-nineteenth-century America, the consensus among contemporary observers was that abortion was frequent and increasing. Pregnancies among unmarried women were historically considered to be the bulk of abortions, but in this period commentators described abortion as one of the birth control options employed by married women. James Mohr, in his study of nineteenth-century abortion policy, argues that a compelling reason for a mounting anti-abortion drive was the recognition that married women were seeking abortion in greater numbers.[26]

The first organized group to seek stricter, re-focused abortion laws was the medical profession. Physicians frequently publicized their collective horror at women's propensity to murder their unborn babies. One doctor, disturbed at what he saw as a breakdown of the motherly instinct, declared, "Physicians, medical men, must be regarded as the guardians of the rights of the unborn."[27] Accordingly, the medical profession was the first to champion the idea of legal redress in the name of the fetus, with one physician, Horatio Storer, leading the struggle. Storer published the most detailed account of abortion to come out of the mid-century period, *Criminal Abortion: Its Nature, Its Evidence, and Its Law*. He was convinced that abortion was a hideous crime, and set out to demonstrate empirically that it was very common. Based on comparative population increases, published records of stillbirths, numbers of arrests and trials for abortion, published numbers of immediate maternal deaths, pecuniary success of abortionists, comparative family size over time, and personal testimony by physicians, Storer concluded that American women were seeking abortion in greater numbers than in the past.[28]

Early-nineteenth-century abortion methods were numerous, with varying degrees of effectiveness and danger. Storer's list of the "instruments of abortion" included "knitting-needles, pen-handles, skewers, goose quills, pieces of whale-bone, and even curtain rods."[29] Although the introduction of sharp objects into the uterus was the surest method of abortion, women also tried other, less debilitating approaches. Extreme exercise carried on until exhaustion, patent medicines supposed to be abortifacients, and salves and lotions introduced into the vagina were commonly tried before resorting to the more lethal methods. Women also inflicted blows to their stomachs and loins attempting to abort an unwanted fetus. Physicians who performed abortions used surgical instruments and the various hooks and picks designed for use in difficult labors.[30]

Because of the crudeness of the methods, and because there was little knowledge even among physicians of the value of aseptic instruments, abortion was a high-risk operation. Death was a real possibility for the woman attempting abortion. Infection due to nonsterile procedure and bleeding due to puncturing the uterus were the primary causes of death in abortion attempts. Many abortion survivors suffered life-long chronic pelvic disease, including fistula (unhealed openings, vaginal and rectal), constant bleeding, incontinence, infertility, and future difficult labors. Frederick Hollick wrote in the 1850s of women coming to him after botched abortions:

Some of them have been almost torn and cut to pieces, and others so injured, that their lives hung as it were by a thread. Those who take drugs for this purpose are also equally exposed to risk, and suffer in their health to an equal extent, so that their lives become a positive burden to them.

He concluded, "There are no safe means of procuring abortion. . . . the chances are ten to one that death, or the evils above referred to, will follow."[31] Some doctors also attibuted cases of female insanity to abortion.

Although women had used the same dangerous abortion methods for centuries, the experience of abortion contained two new dimensions for early-nineteenth-century women. The first was its growing frequency as a birth control method among respectable married women. Contemporary observers asserted that at least 25 percent of American women had one or two abortions in their lifetimes, and Mohr, in his study of abortion, concurs that this is a reasonable estimate.[32] Because women (and men) wanted to limit fertility at a time when birth control technology was primitive, abortion was becoming a common experience of married womanhood, instead of an experience associated with illegitimate pregnancies. Moral women, "true" women (and their daughters) were likely to seek abortion during their married lives, or at least to know equally moral and true women who sought abortion. Therefore, the pain and danger of abortion could no longer be viewed as an unfortunate but just result of impurity or seduction; instead, such pain and danger had to be seen as an unavoidable (though lamentable) dimension of respectable womanhood. The new commonness of abortion encouraged women to perceive it as part of "woman's lot," and the pain and danger inherent in that early nineteenth-century abortion experience prompted women to associate "woman's lot" with suffering.

In addition to the growing tendency of married women to experience abortion, a second aspect of abortion new to the nineteenth century also affected its symbolic importance for women. As male physicians began to define abortion as an area of concern for the medical profession, abortion was transformed from a private female decision to a public male issue. This shift had immediate and long-term negative effects on women's power to obtain abortions and to "name" the experience in their lives.

The most straightforward result of medical interest in abortion was the eventual criminalization of abortion in all stages of pregnancy. By the 1870s and 1880s all states had reformed abortion law to eliminate the "quickening doctrine" and to define the woman seeking abortion as sharing in the criminal act of the abortionist.[33] Declaring that there was no scientific basis for viewing the pre-quickening fetus as different from the post-quickening fetus, male physicians asserted that no woman had the right to abort a fetus in any stage of pregnancy. This undercut women's reproductive choice not only in crimin-alizing abortion but more importantly in establishing the priority of male-dominated science over women's traditional decision-making process. Medical interest in abortion in the mid-nineteenth century was the first step in translating the issue from a question of personal choice to a question of medical technology and public interest.

A more immediate effect of the medical re-definition of abortion was the growing necessity for women to frame their arguments for abortion within a male-controlled discourse. In the beginning of the nineteenth century, most women who went to anyone for an abortion went to professional abortionists or to midwives; however, professional abortionists and female midwives became less and less available to middle-class women, as abortion was criminalized and as male physicians replaced midwives as childbirth attendants. Middle-class urban women began to see the male physician as a possible abortionist. If we look at the way physicians described women's reasons for seeking abortion, we can begin to understand the new meaning of the experience in women's lives.

In the eyes of the physicians who wrote about abortion, there were no "good reasons" for a woman to want to abort a fetus. Horatio Storer listed the reasons he and his colleagues had heard from women: ignorance of pregnancy, duress, impaired physical health, poor health of other family members requiring extra work of the woman, accident, fear of child-bed, hatred of the husband, and concealment of shame. Storer described these reasons as "excuses of little more value than those of extravagance or fashion."[34] Another male physician included "fear of labor ... and the indisposition to have the care, the expense, or the trouble of children" in women's common reasons for abortion, and called these "trifling and degrading."[35] Still another male physician complained that abortion and infanticide were frequent in all classes, and that women were frivolously deciding "whether or not to have children."[36]

There are several points worth noting in these physicians' accounts. Most obvious is the fact that women were consulting male physicians for abortions. Having accepted trained men as birth attendants in preference to midwives with no scientific training, middle-class women began to turn to male physicians for abortions also. However, physicians' accounts of women seeking abortion indicate that at least some doctors were extremely judgmental about abortion requests. Whether the woman's reasons were "selfish," individualistic ones (not wanting the trouble of more children) or reasons that fit into "true womanhood" and might prompt sympathy (fear, delicacy, the necessity of nursing sick family members), the doctors were not convinced that her motives were "right." Perhaps the women who went to male physicians for abortion ended up going elsewhere, or perhaps some of them convinced the doctors that their reasons were not "trifling" and that their cases were "special," but whatever the ultimate outcome, the women presented their requests to a judgmental outsider. It became necessary for women to learn to phrase their requests in the right way in order to merit the doctor's skills, especially as states began to criminalize abortion.

The growing power of physicians to dictate the public discourse on abortion altered the context of women's abortion experience, and therefore affected the meaning women gave to the experience. Although married women were using abortion as a means of birth control, as a conscious act to limit fertility, they described their abortions as experiences of victimization or loss of control. "Degrading," "humiliating," "repulsive," and "a crime against my womanhood" were the words women used.[37] There is no evidence that women felt guilt over abortion, but the little that women wrote about the experience suggests that they felt compelled to explain and justify abortion as prompted by selfless considerations or role requirements.

Being a "good" mother or a "good" wife meant that sometimes women might be forced to undergo abortion. Some women writing about abortion stressed the immorality of bringing forth unwanted children. One woman wrote of a doctor she knew who had been approached by six different women in his "little village" in one week for abortions. "They all insisted it was less criminal to kill children before they were born, than to curse them with an unwelcome existence," she explained.[38] These women were explaining and justifying their abortions using the general rhetoric of the imperial motherhood script. The emotional commitment of good mothering demanded that the child be wanted by the mother. Since good mothering was so important, if a woman couldn't be a good mother to her child it was better for the child not to be born at all. Within this point of view, the woman was not being selfish in wanting an abortion, but was instead undergoing abortion because she believed so strongly in the role she was to play.

Similarly, women explained their "degrading" experience of abortion as a consequence of sexual submission. If abstinence failed as a means of birth control because of the sexual demands of husbands, some women saw themselves as forced to undergo abortion as a last resort to limit fertility. One woman wrote of tolerating her husband's sexual demands for the sake of her first-born (to save the marriage), and settling on a course of frequent abortion. "For its sake [her child's], I concluded to take my chances in the world with other wives and mothers, who, as they assured me, and as I then knew, were, all around me, subjected to like outrages, and driven to the degrading practice of abortion."[39] With abstinence the only reliable means of birth control, many women associated abortion with the passive acceptance of their husbands' "sexual excess."

The new public nature of abortion and the use of male physicians as possible abortionists defined a discourse in which the woman had to explain her abortion within acceptable feminine boundaries. The necessity of explanation or justification altered the meaning of abortion by suggesting that a woman had no inherent right to abort. Confronted with this situation, women began to frame their reasons for abortion within an ideal of selfless, passive, suffering femininity. Abortion was "forced" on a woman because of a brutish husband or because of a duty to good mothering. And that "forced" abortion was inherently painful and dangerous. Woman's lot was to endure such pain and danger.

The biological/social experience of abortion had symbolic importance for women because it was both a "model for" and a "model of" femininity. The experience provided information about acceptable womanhood because the woman had to explain her reasons for abortion within the constraints of a male discourse. The experience also gave a clue as to the meaning of womanhood because it was a shared female experience (inherent to female body) among respectable women with honorable motives (fertility control). In both dimensions, as a model for and a model of femininity, the abortion experience symbolized the necessity of physical suffering and passivity for women.

Early-nineteenth-century middle-class women linked womanhood to suffering partially because their physical experience of fertility control and abortion was filled with pain and alienation. Further impetus to idealize suffering and passivity as feminine came from the new circumstances surrounding childbirth. By the second decade of the nineteenth century the babies of middle- and upper-class urban women were routinely delivered by male physicians. Historians have suggested that women might have chosen male doctors because they were status conscious and believed the more expensive physician must offer the better services, or simply because they sought the newest technology available to ease birth pain and insure a safe delivery and were impressed by the doctors' claim of superior education. Whatever their conscious or unconscious reasons for employing male physicians, for many of these women the physical surroundings of childbirth, the management of labor, and the paraphernalia and procedures associated with the birth attendant underwent a transformation.[40] Without romanticizing the earlier midwife-assisted birth or villainizing the professional physician, it is important to notice that the entrance of male physicians did alter women's experience of childbirth. We can get a sense of that change by looking closely at the training, attitudes, and childbirth practices of midwives and physicians.

Historians have noted that it is impossible to determine exactly how competent early American midwives were, but we do know something about their training and their most typical delivery practices.[41] It seems that midwives for the most part received no formal training, as professional physicians were quick to point out. Some women "drifted" into midwifery after successfully helping a neighbor or relative give birth. Others learned the skills of midwifery by apprenticing themselves to experienced midwives. Many midwives were really "occasional" midwives and did not consider themselves as having a specific occupation, and in fact many early American women felt capable of rendering midwifery services in an emergency and knew most of the regular procedures. This lack of formal training, coupled with the fact that much of midwifery was within the domain of "common knowledge," left midwives unorganized and vulnerable when professional physicians began to fight for obstetrical monopoly.[42]

But there is another side of this question of training that we should consider when thinking about women's perceptions of childbirth. With untrained midwives, knowledge of childbirth practices was shared knowledge and the knower and the known were the same. Unprofessional midwifery was truly an "empirical" science, with experience altering practice and with participant input as an essential element. One of the striking characteristics of early American midwifery was the attention given to the laboring woman's desires and self-reported feelings. Although most deliveries were (and are) "normal," there was enough leeway in midwives' practices to take seriously and to accommodate the variety of women's experiences. This sensitivity to the laboring woman as "subject" and major actor in the event was not due to a mysterious innate female quality, but was partially due to the lack of formal, canonized training and the fact that midwives had first-hand experience of the variety of childbirth (as mothers and as women). Furthermore, because of the "democratic" nature of midwifery knowledge, a woman giving birth with a midwife and female friends and relatives knew more or less what to expect in terms of possible procedures and their outcomes, and this foreknowledge might have been comforting in the face of the larger, uncontrollable questions of childbirth pain, injury, or death.[43]

Considering midwives' lack of formal training, it is not surprising that they thought of birth as a natural process and saw their role as "patient watchers" of nature. This attitude influenced not only the midwives' activity but also the atmosphere of labor. The warmed, well-lighted birth chamber was made as comfortable as possible. The laboring woman, surrounded by family and friends, was encouraged to move around during most of her labor. As the final stage approached, the children, her husband, and some of the women waited in another room while the woman, her midwife, and close female relatives or friends remained. The midwife as much as possible let nature do the work. Catherine Scholten described the midwife's role in the late eighteenth and early nineteenth century in this way:

They caught the child, tied the umbilical cord, and if necessary fetched the afterbirth. In complicated cases they might turn the child and deliver it feet first. . . . In all circumstances the midwife's chief duty was to comfort the woman in labor while they both waited on nature.[44]

There was no standard position for giving birth, no drugs available for pain (with the exception of alcohol), and no surgical procedures for assisting difficult live births.

The early-nineteenth-century woman who chose a midwife to assist her in childbirth could expect a familiar, patient watching delivery routine surrounded by participant/watchers, many of them women who had given birth or assisted at birth many times before. For the majority of women who had uncomplicated deliveries, childbirth with a midwife was a celebratory experience, a central ritual of the female community (as Carroll Smith-Rosenberg points out).[45] However, middle-class women more and more sought to control those aspects of childbirth which had always provoked fear and anxiety in women. By turning to male physicians, women hoped to have safer and less painful birth experiences. Ironically, for the first generation of women to choose male professionals, the childbirth experience was actually full of new dangers and new sources of pain and anxiety.

Although historians have had to piece together material and make some guesses about midwives' attitudes and practices, it has been much easier to trace the development of professional medical training, doctors' ideas about childbirth, and typical medical practices in the early nineteenth century. "Scientific medicine" was in its infancy in the early part of the nineteenth century, and medical education consisted of a few months of lectures with no clinical experience. Although medical education did include instruction in anatomy, students had no experience examining a live woman until they were practicing on their own patients after graduation. The "regulars," the doctors who would eventually establish the American Medical Association and would come to dominate medicine by the early twentieth century, received almost no midwifery training. In many early-century medical schools the course in midwifery was not required, and even the most advanced medical curricula gave the students no first-hand experience in actually witnessing (let alone assisting) a live birth. Indeed, the first attempt at "demonstrative midwifery" before the Civil War was denounced by the newly founded American Medical Association as indecent and unnecessary.[46]

Early-nineteenth-century medical students who attended institutions offering a midwifery course and who chose to attend the lectures received a kind of training midwives did not. Medical students were taught about forceps. It was the male physician's knowledge of forceps that convinced many women to abandon female midwives because women believed that forceps might eliminate the need for the hooks and scissors traditionally used (also by male physicians) in difficult labor. One physician, writing in the 1870s about forceps 100 years old, explained that the instruments were responsible for the immediate popularity of young physicians just beginning practice. "The introduction of an instrument by the use of which these death-dealing tools [sizzors and crochet hook] might be avoided, worked a revolution in the practice, and was the means of getting the young M.D. rapidly into business."[47] However, it is doubtful that physicians' training was at all beneficial to the laboring woman, and evidence suggests that it was harmful in many cases.

There was widespread consensus among early- and mid-nineteenth-century medical writers that forceps increased the danger of delivery and the pain of the woman. The possibility of severe laceration was great with the routine use of forceps, especially when we keep in mind that the "modesty" of the time required male doctors to work without actually looking at the woman's pelvic area. It is quite possible that the first gynecological surgery, the recto-vaginal fistula repair, as well as other birth repair procedures were developed to correct new problems resulting from the misuse or overuse of forceps.[48] Physicians wrote that forceps deliveries resulted in "lesions of the cervix and perforations of the vagina," "laceration of the vaginal parietes, bruising of the os uteri," "fractured pelvic bones," "disparted symphyses," "vesico-vaginal fistula," and "occlusion of the vaginal walls and the meatus urinarious." These were all cited as "common results" of forceps deliveries.[49] One physician reported, "In violent hands the long forceps . . . kills the child, bruises the soft parts, occasions mortification, breaks open the neck of the bladder, crushes the nerves." Another physician focused on the woman's experience, describing a "scene of harrowing agony" as "too often" occuring with forceps delivery.[50]

Physicians' experience with forceps is understandable considering their lack of visual knowledge of female anatomy. Medical students "practiced" applying forceps on a dummy, and they were unsure about the proper way to perform forceps delivery on a live woman. Dr. C.C.P. Clark, writing in favor of forceps, complained that the training was so bad that young practitioners always had a difficult time. "He is never sure that he is handling his blades rightly. This doubt is a constant source of embarrassment and hesitation, and often makes him withdraw and introduce a blade again and again."[51] One can imagine what pain and mortification this must have caused the laboring woman.

Young physicians and experienced physicians as well had difficulties with forceps because the textbook rules were complex, contradictory, and, by modern standards, totally incorrect. Most books instructed the doctors to apply forceps on the front and back of the fetus' head, regardless of presentation. This resulted in "very grave evils," according to Clark. He asserted that fetal presentation was not easy to know, even for the experienced doctor, and that ignoring the curve of the woman's vagina would do "violence" to the mother. Students were instructed to apply forceps in an antero-posterio position in some cases, and according to Clark (and modern medical knowledge), this position or a position approaching antero-posterio "involves straining back the perinaeum in a painful and injurious manner, and threatens harm to the soft parts that underlie the pubis."[52] Clark believed that forceps were useful and not dangerous when used properly, but he argued that the early- and mid-nineteenth-century textbooks and midwifery lectures gave wrong information about forceps. It was the misuse and overuse of instruments that Clark found to be widespread in the early- and mid-century period.

Although recent studies have indicated that female physicians in the 1870s were almost as likely to use instruments as male physicians, midwives did not have access to forceps.[53] In the first decades of the nineteenth century, because of the state of medical education and because forceps were used at a time before anesthesia was widely used in childbirth, it is reasonable to assume that physicians' overuse and misuse of instruments increased birth injuries and childbirth pain simply because physicians' technology outdistanced their knowledge and expertise for a time. In this respect, then, midwives' lack of scientific training was an advantage.

The general therapeutics of "regular" medicine in the early nineteenth century must also be considered when assessing the training of professional physicians. The scientific practice of the time consisted of bleeding and purging for almost any ailment and also of large doses of potentially dangerous drugs. Benjamin Rush, the most influential physician in the early nineteenth century, recommended bloodletting to ease labor pain, accelerate labor, and prevent problems. Bleeding laboring women was also approved of by William Dewees, professor of midwifery at the College of Pennsylvania from the mid–1820s to 1864 and the most respected doctor in American obstetrics at the time. Dewees recommended drawing 30 to 40 ounces of blood, until the patient fainted, and praised the anesthetic effect of the procedure. Thomas Denman, second only to Dewees as influential in American obstetrics, argued in his *An Introduction to the Practice of Midwifery* in 1821 that pregnant women have too much blood because of "retention of the menses" and that bloodletting relieves any complication of pregnancy. Physicians were also known to bleed for pregnancy complaints, including infection, convulsions, and hemorrhage.[54] Bleeding and purging a laboring woman might have been benign in some cases, but it might also have been extremely dangerous or even fatal in others. At any rate, physicians' training in this heroic therapy certainly did the laboring woman no good.

Finally, physicians' training in the early nineteenth century left them no better equipped than midwives to handle the disasters of childbirth. Although the medical profession argued that trained physicians should be birth attendants because they alone were capable of dealing with atypical deliveries, it is doubtful that medical training was useful in emergencies. The ability to control bleeding and to perform Caesarean delivery were not within the scope of scientific medicine in the early nineteenth century, and physicians could do nothing for women who developed eclampsia. Furthermore, the skill necessary to turn abnormal presentations was unlikely to come from medical training which included no visual or tactile experience with such emergencies. In terms of training, then, the physician in the early nineteenth century was actually less prepared than the midwife to offer the birthing woman a comfortable delivery free of complications, and in fact his training presented new dangers and new areas of possible pain.[55]

Physicians differed from midwives not only in their training, but also in their attitude about the nature of childbirth and the role of the birth attendant. Unlike midwives, most regular physicians believed that pregnancy and birth were precarious physical states always threatening to become pathological. Indeed, that was the basic medical argument in favor of trained physicians: that doctors possessed skills and knowledge necessary to deal with the abnormal physical state of pregnancy and birth.[56] Although this attitude was not unanimous among doctors, it was widespread enough to prompt non-regular practitioners to mount a campaign for the "naturalness" of childbirth to offset what they saw as scientific practitioners' successful attempt to dupe American women into dependence on the doctors' supposed expertise.

Because most physicians believed birth was a dangerous ordeal requiring medical supervision or intervention, they sought to control or "manage" childbirth according to scientific knowledge. Ideally, decisions about the atmosphere of the birth chamber, the presence of outsiders, birth position, bloodletting, instruments, and drugs were all to be made by the physician. However, physicians were not able to exert absolute control over birth until the early twentieth century, when childbirth moved out of the home and into the hospital. Throughout the nineteenth century, physicians "shared" authority with the birthing woman and her women friends. The medical writing of the early- and mid-century period indicates that physicians (many times successfully) demanded a solemn, dark atmosphere with a good hard bed and few onlookers. Physicians were especially disturbed about unmarried women in the birthing chamber and were upset by married women who wanted to "chat" about their own birth experiences. Women were very resistant to physicians' attempts to rid the birth chamber of women friends, but it is significant that doctors wanted this degree of privacy and were at least sometimes successful in imposing their ideas.[57]

In the early- and mid-nineteenth century, physicians had to share authority because medical knowledge was not yet totally removed from general knowledge. In addition, the childbirth situation physicians hoped to replace—the female midwife-attended birth—was a cooperative or community-participatory experience instead of a hierarchical one. Physicians had to strike a balance between being in complete control and being at the disposal of the laboring woman and her friends. If the physician asserted himself too strongly he might offend his patient/customer, but if he was not authoritative enough with his new tools and techniques he might damage his claim to superior expertise. The discovery of anesthesia in the 1840s accentuated this dilemma.

Although the European physician who first used ether in childbirth claimed it was harmless to mother and infant, anesthesia was not used routinely by American physicians until the 1870s. The question of safety was debated among American physicians in the mid-century period, with opponents of anesthesia arguing that birth pain was necessary for a safe delivery. Some physicians thought pain actually produced the contractions, while others pointed out that the intensity of pain was a kind of safety valve. Still others argued that birth pain helped establish a link between mother and infant, sounding very much like late twentieth-century advocates of "bonding" theory. Dr. Edward Mordecai wrote in 1849: "The associations connected with the pangs of parturition may play an important part in forming the indissoluble link which binds a parent to its offspring; in rearing the foundation upon which rests no inconsiderable share of the social happiness of this world." He went on to say that from birth pain mothers develop "that soul-stirring sympathy . . . that unremitted affection" that follows an infant "from the cradle to the grave."[58] A few physicians also saw birth pain as a punishment either for the sin of Eve or for modern women's disregard of the "laws of nature."

Although the issues of safety and the utility or nature of birth pain prompted debate, few physicians condemned anesthesia as absolutely uncalled for, and even physicians who were in favor of anesthesia resisted its universal use in childbirth. The real question was when and on whom to use it. By the last quarter of the nineteenth century there was growing consensus that "inflicted" pain, pain caused by instruments, should be controlled with anesthesia and that "refined" women suffered more pain in childbirth than other women.[59] These two conclusions about the use of anesthesia in childbirth were arrived at by physicians in relation to their middle-class private patients. Decisions about the use of anesthesia were ultimately the physician's, but he was influenced by his patient's (and her friends') demands. Gradually, physicians rationalized those demands into a "scientific" rule. This is not to say that women demanded and doctors complied, but instead that there was a struggle. Speculating about this struggle, we can sketch a possible explanation for the supposed increase in birth pain in the nineteenth century and about the increased "necessity" of instrument delivery in the mid-century period.

Women employed male physicians because they believed the doctors could provide a safer, less painful birth experience. Yet throughout the nineteenth century, as more and more urban women switched from midwives to male physicians, women associated pain with childbirth more often than in the eighteenth century.[60] Within the individual, pain is a psychosomatic phenomenon, an experience derived from physical and emotional/mental sources. But pain is not a totally "private" experience; instead, it is part of the on-going social construction of reality in which all of us participate. It can be argued that male

physicians increased childbirth pain in the mid-century period in both its physical and psychological dimensions. At first, male physicians used instruments
(and misused and overused them, by their own account) without anesthesia,
and this resulted in more physically based pain. But the struggle over when
and on whom to use anesthesia after the late 1840s, together with the simple
presence of male strangers as witnesses of birth, also affected women's experience of pain. Because physicians changed the very nature of the "audience"
of birth pain and introduced the possibility but not the promise of relief, their
presence and techniques were significant new factors in the socially produced
reality of childbirth pain.

Giving birth in an all-female group, with most of the women mothers themselves, was an important element in traditional childbirth. Giving birth under
the direction of a male physician, whose training and knowledge were limited
by his sex, was an entirely different event, especially at a time of exaggerated
female modesty.[61] The male physician was a different kind of "audience" for
childbirth and for birth pain than the female midwife. This is an obvious but
unappreciated point. From various perspectives early-nineteenth-century writers reported that the sex of the professional physician was the most significant
aspect of the midwifery controversy. Physicians arguing for the abolition of
midwives admitted that women preferred female attendants and worried that
if midwives were trained, women of the "better classes" would stop using male
physicians. Some opponents of male midwifery argued that it was immodest
for women to employ male physicians, while others stressed that men were
outsiders to "this sacred circle of experience" and that "the sympathy of one
woman with another" was the most important ingredient of an easy delivery.[62]
Having a male physician enter the birthing room reportedly stopped the contractions of one woman, and giving birth in the presence of a man was "the
severest part of her suffering" for another.[63] Doctors often complained of
waiting in the next room for hours before the woman would admit the man
into the birth chamber.

Although physicians argued for economic and professional reasons that men
should attend women in childbirth, doctors were not totally comfortable treating
women or witnessing birth. Physicians' writing indicates that they viewed the
female body as alien and a little disgusting. Medical writers described manual
examination of the vagina as a "painful duty," explained menstruation as the
"periodic discharge from the uterus and its appendages," and referred to the
placenta as "the foul excretions of the womb."[64] The professional discomfort
over "demonstrative midwifery," the desire of some physicians for darkened
birth chambers, and the fear expressed in medical journals that doctors could
not be trusted with anesthetized female patients all indicate that many physicians
saw themselves as their women patients did—as uneasy outsiders.

Having such an outsider witness and assist in childbirth could partially explain
why nineteenth-century women reported more birth pain than their mothers
and grandmothers had. Part of the psychological ingredient of pain is separation

of "self" and "body"—being able to contemplate the body as separate from the self.[65] Having a male attendant contributed to women's sense of separateness from their laboring bodies because the most important "point of view" was his and he was inherently separate from the somatic experience of labor in a way that a female midwife was not. His separateness contributed to her separateness, which heightened her sense of pain because it promoted the contemplation of physical sensation as a thing in itself. There is evidence of women's taking on the outside, male point of view of childbirth in women's fiction, evidence of women's seeing themselves give birth rather than seeing from the perspective of the birthing subject.[66]

The doctor was not only an outsider bringing a new and alien objective perspective into the birth chamber, but he was also the one to decide whether or not the woman should be relieved of the pain he witnessed. A woman had to convince her doctor of the necessity of anesthesia in her case. She had to appear in pain in order to merit this new technology. This does not imply conscious manipulation, but it does suggest that women's pain was being judged as "normal" or "terrible" by an outsider who had no first-hand experience by which to measure, and that the doctor's judgment of the "normality" of the pain was the criteria for deciding on anesthesia. Convincing male physicians that anesthesia was necessary in their case altered the birth experience for women of the middle and upper classes by accentuating the separation of self and body and by urging the contemplation and demonstration of pain. Out of women's performance came the compromise: anesthesia for instrument deliveries, especially for "refined" women.

Although this compromise indicates that physicians did not control childbirth but instead met resistence in their attempts at scientific managment, women's "victory" in insisting on anesthesia in special cases was actually a giant step toward physician control. Physicians who argued in favor of anesthesia for instrumental deliveries pointed out that patients who were anesthesized were completely under the doctor's control. One physician urged his colleagues to follow his example in using anesthesia to force women to undergo obstetrical surgery when they resisted their doctor's advice.[67] Obstetrical surgery dramatically increased after the introduction of anesthesia. We should not assume that most of this surgery was "forced" on women, but we likewise cannot ignore the fact that increased instrumental deliveries was the price women paid for anesthesia. Even if physicians did not totally control childbirth but instead shared authority with the woman and her women friends, the move towards scientific management steadily eroded women's power.

The differences in the training, attitudes, and childbirth practices of midwives and professional physicians were significant enough to alter women's birth experience. The poor state of medical education and scientific knowledge resulted in physicians with little or no midwifery training who practiced the heroic therapy of bleeding and purging on their maternity patients and who misused and overused forceps in a painful and sometimes dangerous way. The outsider "scientific" perspective of the physician, exaggerated modesty and embarrassment, and the power of physicians to use or refuse anesthesia encouraged women to objectify their experience and to feel pain more intensely. Regardless of the intention of women in employing male physicians—to establish more control over the pain and danger of childbirth—the male-assisted birth was less under female control and was more dangerous and pain-producing than the midwife-assisted birth.

In the 1820s and 1830s when urban middle-class women accepted professional physicians as birth attendants and thereby altered the biosocial experience of childbirth, passivity and suffering became central to the definition of "feminine" in women's writing. The social construction of female-specific experience—fertility control, abortion, and childbirth—together with other socioeconomic conditions defining women's place, inspired a paradoxical ideological expression: the "empire of the mother"—the domestic, maternal, woman-controlled home sphere—was held together by submission, impotency, and suffering. The idealization of feminine suffering, which ran throughout early-nineteenth-century woman-authored literature, reflected middle-class women's somatic and social experience of womanhood, translated into metaphor.

NOTES

1. I do not mean to imply that these are the only biosocial experiences. In a sense, all experience is biosocial. Also, the other female body experiences of menstruation, menopause, and sexual defloration are significant but not considered here.

2. Two general studies of American fertility are: Yasuba Yasukichi, *Birth Rates of the White Population in the United States, 1800–1860* (Baltimore: Johns Hopkins University Press, 1962); and Bernard Okum, *Trends in the Birth Rates in the United States Since 1870* (Baltimore: Johns Hopkins University Press, 1958). Carl Degler, *At Odds: Women and the Family in America from the Revolution to the Present* (New York: Oxford University Press, 1980), sees the "modern" family type as emerging around 1830 and as noticeably smaller in size than the pre-modern family.

3. Although fertility declined at different rates, the decline was apparent in all groups and in all regions studied. For example, see P. R. Uhlenburg, "A Study of Cohort Life Cycles: Cohorts of Native-Born Massachusetts Women, 1830–1920," *Population Studies*, 23(1969), 407–420; Stuart Blumin, "Rip Van Winkle's Grandchildren: Family and Household in the Hudson Valley, 1800–1860," *Journal of Urban History*, 1(1975), 293–315; Michael R. Haines, "Fertility Decline in Industrial America: An Analysis of the Pennsylvania Anthracite Region, 1850–1900, Using 'Our Children' Methods," *Population Studies*, 32(1978), 327–354; Richard A. Easterlin, "Factors in the Decline of Farm Fertility in the United States: Some Preliminary Research Results," in *The American Family in Social-Historical Perspective*, ed. Michael Gordon (New York: St. Martin's Press, 1978), pp. 533–545. Studies of Black fertility indicating patterns similar to those of whites include: Herman Lantz and Lewellyn Hendrix, "Black Fertility and the Black Family in the Nineteenth Century: A Re-examination of the Past," *Journal of Family History*, 3(1978), 251–261; Maris A. Vinovskis, "The Demography of the Slave Pop-

ulation in Ante-bellum America," *Journal of Interdisciplinary History*, 5(1975), 459–469. On Black fertility during the late nineteenth century, see Stanley L. Engerman, "Black Fertility and Family Structure in the United States, 1880–1940," *Journal of Family History*, 2(1977), 117–137.

4. For explanations of fertility decline, see Robert V. Wells, "Family History and Demographic Transition," in *The American Family in Social-Historical Perspective*, pp. 516–532; Robert V. Wells, "Women's Lives Transformed: Demographic and Family Patterns in America, 1600–1970," in *Women of America: A History*, ed. Mary Beth Norton and Carol Ruth Berkin (Boston: Houghton Mifflin, 1979), pp. 16–33; Tamara K. Hareven and Maris A. Vinovskis, *Family and Population in Nineteenth-Century America* (Princeton, NJ: Princeton University Press, 1978), the introductory essay; Nancy Osterud and John Fulton, "Family Limitation and Age at Marriage: Fertility Decline in Strubridge, Massachusetts, 1730–1850," *Population Studies*, 30(1976), 481–494.

5. See Norman E. Himes, *Medical History of Contraception* (New York: Gamut Press, 1963); James Reed, *From Private Vice to Public Virtue: The Birth Control Movement and American Society Since 1830* (New York: Basic Books, 1978); Linda Gordon, *Woman's Body, Woman's Right* (New York: Penguin Books, 1977). Contemporary sources on contraception include: Charles Knowlton, *Fruits of Philosophy; or the Private Companion of Young Married People* (London: J. Watson, n.d.); Frederick Hollick, *The Marriage Guide; or Natural History of Generation* (New York: T. W. Strong, 1859); A. Mauriceau, *The Married Woman's Private Medical Companion* (New York: by the author, 1854); Augustin K. Gardner, "The Physical Decline of American Women," *The Knickerbocker*, 55(1860), 49.

6. See Himes, *Medical History of Contraception*, pp. 211, 265; and Carroll Smith-Rosenberg and Charles Rosenberg, "The Female Animal: Medical and Biological Views of Woman and Her Role in Nineteenth-Century America," *Journal of American History*, 60(1973), 332–356.

7. Gordon, *Woman's Body, Woman's Right*; Smith-Rosenberg, "The Female Animal," pp. 344–351; Linda Gordon, "Voluntary Motherhood: The Beginnings of Feminist Birth Control Ideas in the United States," *Feminist Studies*, 1(1973), 5–22; John Paul Harper, "Be Fruitful and Multiply: Origins of Legal Restrictions on Planned Parenthood in Nineteenth-Century America," in *Women of America*, pp. 245–269; G. J. Barker-Benfield, *The Horrors of the Half-Known Life* (New York: Harper & Row, 1976), pp. 122, 204, 216, 269–272. Contemporary commentators on physicians and birth control include: Edward H. Dixon, *Woman and Her Diseases, Adapted Exclusively to Her Instruction* (New York: A. Ranney, 1857), p. 318; William A. Alcott, *The Physiology of Marriage* (Boston: J. P. Jewett & Co., 1856), p. 191.

8. About sexual abstinence as a birth control method see: Himes, *Medical History of Contraception*, p. 267; Mary P. Ryan, *Womanhood in America* (New York: New Viewpoints, 1975), pp. 120, 162; Gordon, *Woman's Body, Woman's Right*. pp. 101, 104, 105; Gordon, "Voluntary Motherhood"; Regina Morantz, "Making Women Modern: Middle-Class Women and Health Reform in Nineteenth-Century America," *Journal of Social History*, 10(1971), 497; Daniel Scott Smith, "Family Limitation, Sexual Control and Domestic Feminism in Victorian America," *Feminist Studies*, 1(1973), 40–57. Examples of contemporary writers urging control of sexual appetite include William Beach, *An Improved System of Midwifery* (New York: Baker & Scribner, 1850), p. 269; Alcott, *The Physiology of Marriage*, pp. 115–154.

9. Hollick, *The Marriage Guide*, p. 354.

10. Mary Kelley, *Private Woman, Public Stage: Literary Domesticity in Nineteenth-Century America* (New York: Oxford University Press, 1984), p. 281.

11. Smith, "Family Limitation, Sexual Control and Domestic Feminism"; Nancy F. Cott, "Passionlessness: An Interpretation of Victorian Sexual Ideology, 1790–1850," *Signs*, 4(1978), 219–236.

12. Although physicians knew by mid-century of woman's ovulation cycle, they held erroneous views about fertility. Even the latest scientific knowledge could not help a woman predict her fertile and infertile periods. Thus, abstinence was effective only if sexual intercourse were avoided at all times.

13. There were physiology texts describing female orgasm in the mid-century era, the most explicit of which was Frederick Hollick's *The Marriage Guide*, especially pp. 357–361. Even William Alcott spent a few paragraphs on nymphomania in *The Physiology of Marriage*, p. 170, and in *The Young Woman's Book of Health* (New York: Auburn, Miller, Orton & Mulligan, 1855), p. 215, although he described it as "extremely rare." The other evidence that female sexuality was a recognized phenomenon were the various books warning women about the evils of masturbation and a study of prostitution written by William Sanger, *History of Prostitution* (New York: Harper & Brothers, 1858). Of the 2000 New York City prostitutes interviewed by Sanger, 512 listed "inclination" as their reason for going into the business. However, most nineteenth-century writers saw female sexuality as procreative in impulse; medical writers seeking to describe and lay writers seeking to prescribe saw women as having very little pleasure-seeking sexual desire. For example, see Henry Clarke Wright, *The Unwelcome Child; or, The Crime of an Undesigned and Undesired Maternity* (Boston: B. Marsh, 1858), p. 35; Thomas Low Nichols and Mary S. Gove, *Marriage: Its History, Character and Results* (Cincinnati: V. Nicholson & Co., 1854), pp. 200, 201; Alcott, *The Physiology of Marriage*, p. 167. See also Gordon, *Woman's Body, Woman's Right*, pp. 98, 99.

14. On the tension in American marriages, see Wright, *The Unwelcome Child*, pp. 66, 104; William Alcott, *The Young Wife* (Boston: G. W. Light, 1837), pp. 69, 93, and a chapter on the necessity of wifely "cheerfulness" and cultivation of a spirit of "contentment" (p. 214); Charles S. Woodruff, *Legalized Prostitution; or Marriage As It Is, and Marriage As It Should Be* (Boston: Bela Marsh, 1862), pp. 99–105, 150. See also Ethel Peal, "The Atrophied Rib: Urban Middle-Class Women in Jacksonian America," Ph.D. diss., University of Pittsburgh, 1970, pp. 4, 106, 126, 130. About the excessive maternal devotion of mothers, see Peal, "The Atrophied Rib," p. 137.

15. The theme of the relative unimportance of men in women's lives and the great importance of children was apparent in Mrs. A. Graves, *Girlhood and Womanhood* (Boston: Carter, 1844), especially pp. 209–210; Ebenezer Bailey, *The Young Ladies' Class Book* (Boston: Lincoln, 1832), p. 148; Margaret E. Sangster, *From My Youth Up* (New York: Fleming H. Revell Co., 1909), p. 161; Caroline Howard Gilman, *Recollections of a New England Bride* (New York: Putnam, 1852), pp. 306, 308. See also Gordon, *Woman's Body, Woman's Right*, pp. 19, 22.

16. Charles E. Rosenberg, "Sexuality, Class and Role in Nineteenth-Century America," in *The American Man*, ed. Elizabeth H. Pleck and Joseph H. Pleck (Englewood Cliffs, NJ: Prentice-Hall, 1980), pp. 219–254; David G. Pugh, *Sons of Liberty: The Masculine Mind in Nineteenth-Century America* (Westport, CT: Greenwood Press, 1983).

17. Peal wrote in "The Atrophied Rib" that there was widespread marital unhappiness among New England women during the Jacksonian period. According to Peal's evidence, marriage was becoming a less satisfying institution because women's and men's marital

expectations and roles were changing. One of the areas of difference involved sexuality. Women wrote of unhappy marriages in various ways. They complained, they acquiesced, they suggested increased Christian involvement, and they spoke of "woman's lot." For contemporary examples, see Sarah Wentworth Morton, *My Mind and Its Thoughts* (Boston: Wells & Lilly, 1823), pp. 181, 219–221; Gilman, *Recollections of a New England Bride*, pp. 297, 298, 308; Elizabeth Buffum Chace and Lucy Buffum Lovel, *Two Quaker Sisters* (New York: Liveright Publishing Corporation, 1837), p. 46; Mary Ann Hubbard, *Family Memories* (Private circulation, 1912), pp. 39–41. See also Kelley, *Private Woman, Public Stage*.

18. On the advice books, see Peal, "The Atrophied Rib," chapter 6 (pp. 145–168).

19. Wright, *The Unwelcome Child*, p. 104.

20. Women frequently expressed the view that their husbands were overly interested in sex and that they themselves were not. Examples from women's letters can be found in Wright, *The Unwelcomed Child*, pp. 36, 66, 93, 101–102, 114. See also Nichols, *Marriage*, pp. 185, 196, 200–203; Alcott, *The Physiology of Marriage*, pp. 115, 116; Smith, "Family Limitation, Sexual Control, and Domestic Feminism," p. 50. Women's interest in abstinence was for reasons of birth control and body control, as the "right to oneself" argument illustrates.

21. Wright, *The Unwelcome Child*, p. 104. See also pp. 66, 102; and Nichols, *Marriage*, p. 201; Gordon, *Woman's Body, Woman's Right*, p. 102.

22. Wright, *The Unwelcome Child*, p. 104.

23. Peal, in "The Atrophied Rib," discusses the idea of sexuality as women's enemy, pp. 201–206. Wright, *The Unwelcome Child*, contained numerous examples of this view, such as: "Then my soul rebelled against having more [children], but my husband was deaf to my prayers and my tears, though he himself was opposed to my having any more children, and insisted it was my fault if I did, though he persisted in his right to his sensual indulgences" (p. 102). See also pp. 36, 76, 110, 118.

24. On abortion in nineteenth-century law, see Edward D. Mansfield, *The Legal Rights, Liabilities and Duties of Women* (Salem: John P. Jewett & Co., 1845), pp. 134–137; James Mohr, *Abortion in America: The Origins and Evolution of National Policy, 1800–1900* (New York: Oxford University Press, 1978). See also Hugh L. Hodge, *On Criminal Abortion: A Lecture Introductory to the Course of Obstetrics, and Diseases of Women and Children* (University of Pennsylvania, 1854–55 session), pp. 14–17; Horatio R. Storer, *Criminal Abortion: Its Nature, Its Evidence, and Its Law* (New York: Arno Press, 1974), pp. 1–10.

25. Storer, *Criminal Abortion*, p. 55.

26. See: Beach, *An Improved System of Midwifery*, p. 81; Hodge, *On Criminal Abortion*, p. 18; Gardner, "The Physical Decline of American Women," pp. 46–49; Hollick, *The Marriage Guide*, p. 333; Nichols, *Marriage*, pp. 225–245; Wright, *The Unwelcome Child*, p. 36; Mrs. W. Maxwell, A *Female Physician to the Ladies of the United States: Being a Familiar and Practical Treatise on Matters of Utmost Importance Peculiar to Woman* (New York: by the author, 1860), pp. 13, 14. See also Gordon, *Woman's Body, Woman's Right*, pp 53–55; Mohr, *Abortion in America*.

27. Hodge, *On Criminal Abortion*, p. 19. For similar views see: Dixon, *Woman and Her Diseases*, pp. 24, 25; Alcott, *The Physiology of Marriage*, p. 191; Hollick, *The Marriage Guide*, pp. 333, 334; Storer, *Criminal Abortion*, p. 97; Charles Meigs, *On the Nature, Signs and Treatment of Childbed Fever* (Philadelphia: Blanchard & Lea, 1854), p. 126. See also Barker-Benfield, *The Horrors of the Half-Known Life*, pp. 88, 122, 190, 204–

205. On male physicians and abortion legislation, see Barker-Benfield, p. 265; Mohr, *Abortion in America*; Sheila M. Rothman, *Woman's Proper Place: A History of Changing Ideas and Practices, 1870 to the Present* (New York: Basic Books, 1978), pp. 83, 84.

28. Storer, *Criminal Abortion*, pp. 24, 38, 57.

29. Storer, *Criminal Abortion*, pp. 84, 85.

30. About methods of abortion, see: Storer, *Criminal Abortion*, pp. 84, 85; Beach, *An Improved System of Midwifery*, p. 82; Hodge, *On Criminal Abortion*, p. 78.

31. Hollick, *The Marriage Guide*, p. 334. See also: Nichols, *Marriage*, pp. 225, 239; Storer, *Criminal Abortion*, p. 78.

32. Mohr, *Abortion in America*, p. 69.

33. Mohr, *Abortion in America*; R. Saver, "Attitudes to Abortion in America, 1800 to 1973," *Population Studies*, 28(1974), 53–67.

34. Storer, *Criminal Abortion*, p. 78.

35. Hodge, *On Criminal Abortion*, p. 18.

36. Gardner, "The Physical Decline of American Women," p. 47. See also Dixon, *Woman and Her Diseases*, p. 314.

37. Wright, *The Unwelcome Child*, pp. 63, 66.

38. Wright, *The Unwelcome Child*, p. 110. Other women writing to Wright expressed similar views about abortion, pp. 102, 114, 117. Although some women might have felt guilt over abortion, this feeling was not one they wrote about.

39. Wright, *The Unwelcome Child*, p. 66. That women viewed abortion as the only alternative after abstinence failed, and tied it to the excessive sexuality of their husbands, was apparent in Wright, pp. 66, 77, 101, 103, 112, 114, 117 and Nichols, *Marriage*, pp. 225, 239, 245.

40. On the transition from female to male midwives see Catharine M. Scholten, " 'On the Importance of the Obstetrick Art': Changing Customs of Childbirth in America, 1760–1825," *William and Mary Quarterly*, 34(1977), 426–445; Jane B. Donegan, *Women and Men Midwives: Medicine, Morality and Misogyny in Early America* (Westport, CT: Greenwood Press, 1978); Richard W. Wertz and Dorothy C. Wertz, *Lying-In: A History of Childbirth in America* (New York: Schocken Books, 1977). Donegan suggests the status motive, and Judith Walzer Leavitt and Whitney Walton, " 'Down to Death's Door': Women's Perceptions of Childbirth in America," in *Women and Health in America*, ed. Judith Walzer Leavitt (Madison: University of Wisconsin Press, 1984), pp. 155–165, argues that women turned to male physicians because they were searching for the safest, least painful birth experience.

41. Nancy Schrom Dye, "History of Childbirth in America," *Signs*, 6(1980), 97–108, points out that we have no way of knowing how competent early midwives were. However, we do have information about common practices in midwife-assisted births. See Scholten, " 'On the Importance of the Obstectrick Art' "; Donegan, *Women and Men Midwives*; Wertz, *Lying-In*; and Janet C. Bogdan, "Care or Cure? Childbirth Practices in Nineteenth-Century America," *Feminist Studies*, 4(1978), 92–100.

42. Donegan, *Women and Men Midwives*.

43. Leavitt and Walton, " 'Down to Death's Door,' " point out that the unpredictable and uncontrollable nature of childbirth added to women's anxiety.

44. Scholten, " 'On the Importance of the Obstetrick Art,' " p. 433.

45. Carroll Smith-Rosenberg, "The Female World of Love and Ritual: Relations Between Women in Nineteenth-Century America," *Signs*, 1(1975), 1–30.

46. Virginia G. Drachman, "The Loomis Trial: Social Mores and Obstetrics in the

Mid-Nineteenth Century," in *Health Care in America*, ed. Susan Reverby and David Rosner (Philadelphia: Temple University Press, 1979), pp. 67–83.

47. Robert P. Harris, "History of a Pair of Obstetrical Forceps One-hundred Years Old," *American Journal of Obstetrics and the Diseases of Women and Children*, 4(1871), 56.

48. Nineteenth-century writers who commented on doctors' overuse or misuse of instruments include: W. Beach, *An Improved System of Midwifery* (New York: Baker & Scribner, 1850), preface; Mrs. W. Maxwell, A *Female Physician to the Ladies of the United States* (New York: by the author, 1860), p. 44; Augustus K. Gardner, *The Modern Practice of Midwifery* (New York: Robert M. DeWitt, 1838), pp. 29–30. Historians who have written about physicians and forceps include: Donegan, *Women and Men Midwives*, pp. 87–89, 144; Wertz, *Lying-In*, pp. 63–64; Scholten, " 'On the Importance of the Obstetrick Art'," pp. 439, 444; Richard H. Shryock, *Medicine and Society in America, 1660–1860* (Ithaca, NY: Cornell University Press, 1962), p. 92; William G. Rothstein, *American Physicians in the Nineteenth Century: From Sects to Science* (Baltimore: Johns Hopkins University Press, 1972), p. 133.

49. C.C.P. Clark, "Management of the Obstetrical Forceps," *American Journal of Obstetrics and the Diseases of Women and Children*, 4(1971), 138–160. Clark is quoting several physicians about the use of forecps.

50. Clark, "Management of the Obstetrical Forceps," p. 140. Clark is quoting two different physicians.

51. Clark, "Management of the Obstetrical Forceps," p. 147.

52. Clark, "Management of the Obstetrical Forceps," pp. 148–150.

53. Regina Markell Morantz and Sue Zschoche, "Professionalism, Feminism, and Gender Roles: A Comparative Study of Nineteenth-Century Therapeutics," *Journal of American History*, 67(1980), 568–588, is a comparison of male and female physicians in terms of the treatment they prescribed for female hospital patients.

54. A. Clair Siddall, "Bloodletting in American Obstetric Practice, 1800–1945," *Bulletin of the History of Medicine*, 54(1980), 101–110.

55. Many historians already cited have concluded that male physicians were more dangerous birth attendants than midwives. In addition to the question of instruments, practical training, and heroic medicine, historians have pointed to the increased danger of infection in physician-attended childbirth before the widespread practice of aseptic technique. On this question, see also Paul Starr, *The Social Transformation of American Medicine* (New York: Basic Books, 1982); Henry Burnell Shafer, *The American Medical Profession, 1783–1850* (New York: Columbia University Press, 1936), p. 136; Shryock, *Medicine and Society in America*, pp. 15, 92, 123; James V. Ricci, *The Development of Gynaecological Surgery and Instruments* (Philadelphia: Blakiston Co., 1949), pp. 288, 313. Claude R. Heator, "Obstetrics at the New York Almshouse and at Bellevue Hospital," *Bulletin of the New York Academy of Medicine*, 16(1940), pp. 40–47, is an excellent summary of the childbed fever controversy in the United States.

56. On physicians' ideas about birth as disease, see Wertz, *Lying-In*, pp. 64–65 and introduction; Bogdan, "Care or Cure?"; and Shryock, *Medicine and Society in America*, p. 24.

57. Wertz, *Lying-In*. Probably much of this uneasiness stemmed from doctors' real lack of experience contributing to insecurity about their performance, and also from their embarrassment over the physical intimacy inherent in childbirth.

58. Quoted in Martin S. Pernick, *A Calculus of Suffering: Pain, Professionalism, and*

Anesthesia in Nineteenth-Century America (New York: Columbia University Press, 1985), p. 48.

59. On anesthesia and childbirth see: Pernick, *A Calculus of Suffering*; A. D. Fare, "Early Opposition to Anesthesia," *Anesthesia*, 35(1980), 896–907; Wertz, *Lying-In*, chapter 4; Erwin Ackerknecht, A *Short History of Medicine* (New York: The Ronald Press Company, 1968), p. 190. Contemporary writers include: Walter Channing, *A Treatise on Etherization in Childbirth* (Boston: William D. Ticknor & Co., 1848); Augustus K. Gardner, *The Modern Practice of Midwifery* (New York: Robert M. DeWitt, 1838), p. 26; Frederick Hollick, *The Matron's Manual of Midwifery and the Diseases of Women during Pregnancy and in Childbed* (New York: T. W. Strong, 1848), chapter "On Preventing Pain in Childbirth."

60. About increased pain in childbirth, see Mary S. Gove, *Lectures to Ladies on Anatomy and Physiology* (Boston: Saxton & Peirce, 1842), p. 219; Elizabeth Blackwell, *The Laws of Life, with Special Reference to the Physical Education of Girls* (New York: George P. Putnam, 1852), p. 21; Cecil K. Drinker, *Not So Long Ago* (New York: Oxford University Press, 1937), pp. 54, 55; George Gregory, *Medical Morals* (New York: by the author, 1852), p. 12; Wertz, *Lying-In*, pp. 94, 109, 113, 114.

61. Female "delicacy" in dealing with male physicians was a much discussed subject in the early nineteenth century. For example, see Horace Mann, A *Few Thoughts on the Power and Duties of Woman* (Syracuse, NY: Hall, Mills & Co., 1853), pp. 94, 95; Richard Reece, *The Lady's Medical Guide* (Philadelphia: Carey, Lea & Blanchard, 1833), introduction; Gregory, *Medical Morals*, pp. 4, 37; Mary A. E. Wager, "Women as Physicians," *The Galaxy*, 6(1868), 774; Maxwell, *A Female Physician to the Ladies of the United States*, p. 9. For historians' discussions of modesty and the male physician, see: Ricci, *The Development of Gynaecological Surgery and Instruments*, p. 313; Wertz, *Lying-In*, chapter 3. Although husbands may have been present in some early nineteenth-century births, women experienced the presence of a male physician—a relative stranger—quite differently.

62. Eliza Woodson Farnham, *Woman and Her Era*, vol. 1 (New York: A. J. Davis & Co., 1864), p. 41; Maxwell, *A Female Physician to the Ladies of the United States*, pp. 12, 45.

63. Quoted in Gregory, *Medical Morals*, p. 7. About women's reactions to men in the birth chamber see Scholten, " 'On the Importance of the Obstetrick Art,' " p. 433, 442; Maxwell, *A Female Physician to the Ladies of the United States*, p. 41; Gregory, *Medical Morals*, p. 28.

64. Dixon, *Woman and Her Diseases*, p. 19; Ricci, *The Development of Gynaecological Surgery and Instruments*, p. 313; Meigs, *On the Nature, Signs and Treatment of Childbed Fevers*, p. 229.

65. Donald M. Lowe, *History of Bourgeois Perception* (Chicago: University of Chicago Press, 1962), pp. 95–99.

66. Carol H. Poston, "Childbirth in Literature," *Feminist Studies*, 4(1978), 18–31. See also Wertz, *Lying-In*, p. 105; Bogdon, "Care or Cure?"

67. Pernick, *A Calculus of Suffering*, p. 230.

CHAPTER 5

Mothers and Daughters: Acculturation into "True Womanhood"

In 1882 Mary Terhune wrote of a "guild of suffering" among women, "known in its fullness of bitterness only to the initiated."[1] Terhune had very definite ideas as to how daughters were initiated into the guild, many of them having to do with socialization and physical restrictions, but she also revealed that the female body itself provided an early lesson about the requirements of adult femininity. The girl entering puberty "must be made to understand that it is cowardly to cringe or lament under her share of woman's appointed lot, or to shirk her given lesson in the practice of womanly fortitude," Terhune wrote.[2] The necessity of female self-sacrifice, womanly submission, and the equation of self with gender role was part of the gender script middle-class daughters of the mid-century period inherited from their mothers. In the mother/daughter relationship, within the structure of middle-class family life, daughters were initiated into their mothers' feminine guild.

Since the work of Sigmund Freud, neither clinical analysts nor social scientists have been able to ignore the centrality of family dynamics in gender formation. Family is the medium through which male and female are transformed into masculine and feminine; the physical body is given cultural meaning within the context of family. Freudians, neo-Freudians, and developmentalists agree that the primary caretaker is a pivotal character in the child's gender learning and that the mother/daughter relationship is different from the mother/son relationship. Nancy Chodorow argues in *The Reproduction of Mothering* that the nuclear family structure in which women have sole responsibility for child-rearing results in specific psychosexual consequences for daughters' gender learning.[3] The process of daughters' gender formation and the content of feminine gender are both affected by family structure. Since the childrearing situation common to middle-class nineteenth-century Americans is the family structure Chodorow describes, her analysis of female gender learning is relevant to the mid-century daughters' initiation into the "guild of suffering."

According to Chodorow, the process of female gender learning is defined by the fact that daughters are mothered by the same-sex parent. Because of this, a girl learns about being a woman in a more first-hand personal way than her brother learns about being a man. In learning what is womanly, a girl is actually learning her own mother's idea of womanliness. The mother's sense of femininity is totally accessible to the daughter through word and action, and the daughter defines her own sense of feminine in response to her mother's life.

Besides affecting the social process of a girl's gender learning, the structure of exclusive maternal parenting also influences the very content of femininity. Chodorow, Dorothy Dinnerstein, Adrienne Rich, and others have pointed out that the sexual division of labor in which only women parent produces over-identification and boundary-fuzziness between mothers and daughters and leads to over-relatedness as a feminine trait.[4] The mother experiences her daughter as an extension of self and a validation of her life as a woman. The daughter, likewise, over-identifies with her mother and experiences her mother as a larger version of herself. The boundary-fuzziness between mothers and daughters affects the content of feminine ideology because it prepares the girl for an over-related life, a life in which she defines herself only in relation to others. The structure of same-sex parenting contributes to the young woman's thinking that her relational social role is her entire identity.

If we keep in mind that the family structure of exclusive and intense maternal parenting developed among middle-class Americans during the early nineteenth century, this sociological insight about family and personality has historical importance.[5] Mid-century girls grew in such a family environment. In addition to the structure of the family, the entire life world of middle-class daughters further encouraged intense identification between mother and daughter. The separate spheres of women and men and the close community of women provided an excellent medium for mother/daughter identification and helped to infuse female body with symbolic significance.

The mid-nineteenth-century girl spent most of her time in the company of women. Her world was composed of and defined by her mother, her mother's friends and relatives, her sisters, and her own girl friends.[6] This was more than a "female community"; the daughter's world was primarily her mother's female community. Lydia Sigourney, a popular early-nineteenth-century writer, recognized this special physical closeness between mothers and daughters, and the resulting strength of maternal influence. "Our daughters . . . being more constantly with us, and more perfectly under our control . . . are emphatically our representatives, the truest tests of our systems, the strongest witnesses to another generation, of our fidelity, or neglect."[7] The mother/daughter relationship was the core experience of nineteenth-century feminine acculturation.

In their autobiographies and diaries, nineteenth-century women testified to the intensity of the mother/daughter relationship. Daughters wrote of their tremendous need of their mother and of their fear of being left without maternal counsel. The words used to describe mother were extremely affectionate and moving. Lucy Howard wrote in the 1850s, "I think I am in love with my beautiful mother . . . Sometimes in the streets we have been taken by strangers for sisters. This pleased me much."[8] Lucretia Davidson wrote poetry about her mother, and other women described their mothers with extreme tenderness and emotion.[9]

At the core of the mother/daughter relationship was a recognition of mutual confidence and friendship. "It seemed impossible to find a better stronger friend than my mother," Rachel Butts wrote.[10] Lucy Howard described the close friendship between her mother and herself: "I enjoy her society more than that of any gay companion. Our confidence is perfect. I tell her every plan and every thought."[11] Another daughter wrote of the "sister-like confidence and closer companionship" that developed between her mother and herself as she grew to maturity.[12]

Although the descriptions of nineteenth-century mother/daughter relationships found in diaries, personal correspondence, and popular literature are almost all positive, it is important to recognize that not all women had intensely close relationships with their mothers, that many women had close relationships with their fathers, and that birth order probably affected the closeness of mother/daughter relationships within a single family.[13] Among the mid-century daughters' generation there was even complaint of "lack of confidence" between some mothers and daughters. Grace Dodge (born in 1857) wrote: "Mothers and daughters are often not the friends they should be."[14] Stella Gilman (born in 1844) went so far as to say: "I believe it is as rare as it is beautiful for mothers and daughters to be confidential friends."[15] Whether or not all mother/daughter relationships were intense, sister-like friendships, the daughter still formed her primary gender identity within her mother's world. What went on between mothers and daughters, and between older women writers and younger female readers, provided the living model and the verbal cues essential for developing a sense of the "feminine."

The maternal generation, the women who formulated the imperial motherhood script from the material conditions of early nineteenth-century womanhood, passed on this feminine sexual ideology to their daughters. Self-denial for the sake of others and physical suffering as transcendence represented the heart of the maternal generation's synthesis. By accepting the physical suffering connected with motherhood, a woman transcended the limits of body and gained spiritual power. Her womanly suffering gave her sentimental influence in the lives of her husband and children and gave her status in the community of women. While denying the body, the idealization of suffering surrounded it with a new symbolic meaning. The pain itself—the physical manifestations of poorly assisted deliveries, the endless litany of "female troubles"—all became symbolic of the woman's devotion to others, the woman's claim to moral superiority.[16]

Women's literature in the mid-century period indicates that the telling of the suffering was almost as important as the suffering itself. A woman found audience in the feminine circle in which she lived and in the daughter who was her nearly constant companion. While communicating her suffering to her daughter, a mother also demonstrated the womanly method of handling the pain that accompanied role performance. The older woman provided the younger with a living model of total feminine role commitment by advocating a lifestyle while expressing unhappiness with it, by celebrating femininity while suffering through it.

Acculturation into womanhood demanded the equivalence of "woman" with "feminine," a self/role blur. If she were to become an acceptable woman a girl needed to define herself totally in relationship to man and family. To do this, it was essential that she realize that her dissatisfaction and unhappiness with the role was personal, her own personal failure, and was to be handled in a personal way. The role was not to be challenged; her commitment to role was not to be shaken. All difficulties, contradictions, and anguish associated with role must be accepted as part of "woman's lot," and handled in private discussions with female friends and relatives. Nineteenth-century daughters developed a belief in woman-as-role from mothers, and the female community in general, who "coped," "calmly endured," "suffered through" their feminine activities and glorified this self-abnegation. The maternal message of encouraging identification with role while admitting dissatisfaction with it helped solidify the self/role blur for daughters.

Nineteenth-century diaries and books written by adult women for the next generation contain evidence of this mixture of role-advocacy and admission of pain. In explaining to daughters the proper relationship between women and men and in teaching them the details of domesticity, mothers also communicated their personal disappointment. In the maternal message concerning the marital relationship and the specifics of domesticity, this blend of recommendation and dissatisfaction was a central theme.

The sexual ideology of the time, which dichotomized the roles and very "nature" of male and female, provided a setting, an outline for the maternal message. Proponents of separate spheres, from outright misogynists to domestic feminists, agreed that differing sexual roles were the result of differing sexual "natures." Ann Taylor Gilbert wrote of women's "minute discernment" and "intuitive penetration," making them able "to feel their way through the difficulties of the world." She added that all but the "superficial observer" recognized men's deficiency in this sensitivity.[17] The consensus among nineteenth-century writers was that men were emotionally distant and self-centered and that women were more moral, sensitive, and other-directed.[18]

With the sexes so diametrically opposed in terms of basic characteristics, what were daughters to expect of the marital relationship? The female writers of the time made it abundantly clear that emotional mutuality was one thing daughters should not anticipate. Elizabeth Oakes Smith asserted that men had no understanding whatsoever of women. She urged her readers to notice the way men wrote about women "as creatures, one would suppose, belonging to a different race."[19] Mrs. A. J. Graves wrote of men's "ignorance of the peculiar nature of woman's feelings and susceptibilities," and Caroline Howard Gilman more bluntly stated that men do not understand "the moral and physical structure of our sex."[20] Part of the message young women were given was that the sexes were so different from each other that communication and mutual understanding were rare between women and men.

For the sexes to co-exist, it was necessary to erect and maintain a bridge between the two spheres. Sexual hierarchy spanned the chasm created by sexual "complementariness." As daughters learned of the essential differences between women and men, they learned too that hierarchy was a defining characteristic of the sexual relationship. Although mother was more moral, sensitive, and religious, she submitted herself and her family to her husband's control.[21]

The direct experience of mother and father in their roles impressed young women with a personal sense of sexual dichotomy and hierarchy. The image of "man" found in nineteenth-century diaries, an image based on young women's experience of their parents, was not a complimentary one. It did, however, correspond to the popular notions about masculinity. Daughters described their fathers as distant, unemotional, and preoccupied, as psychically detached from the family unit. Neither mother nor children expected any form of emotional support from father. Anna Howard Shaw's father was totally insensitive to his wife's physical and psychic difficulties in making a home on the frontier. Shaw's mother never fully recovered from the emotional shock of having to deal with her husband's choice.[22] Catharine Sedgwick's father's winter departure for political service year after year caused "almost cruel" hardship for his wife and seven children. Sedgwick recorded that her mother had begged her father not to leave her so, "winter after winter, tottering under her burden of care." Her mother finally died at the age of fifty-four after two or three "turns of insanity."[23] Where fathers' distance and insensitivity were chronicled, daughters laid no blame on them. Indeed, they viewed the behavior as perfectly congruent with the male role. Even Sedgwick, who did describe her father's activity as "almost cruel," accepted his behavior as required by "self-devotion to his country's good."[24]

Young women learned, from the culture at large and from their own family situations, to expect little emotional support or understanding from men. The role of the male in the family involved work, or worldly orientation, and patriarchial control within the household. He was in the family, but he was not of the family. Absolute authority and emotional distance were essential elements of the masculine role. As Elizabeth Buffum Chace wrote in her diary, "In families the husband and father was the person not only to be held in the highest respect, but to be regarded with awe and a kind of fear by all the women."[25]

In their families young women witnessed a living demonstration of sexual dichotomy and sexual hierarchy. Father was distant and commanding. Mother was a "sympathetic nature in whom all around seemed to find comfort and repose," or "a very modest, quiet, unassuming woman, devoting herself exclusively to her family," or "a gentle, tender, loving woman, whose whole life was devoted to the happiness of those about her."[26] The image of "mother" found in women's diaries was that of a woman submerged in family, providing the emotional glue of the household while submitting herself to her husband's authority.[27]

Female advisors reiterated the theme of sexual polarity, and recommended to young women that they practice submission, emotional availability, and selfless devotion to others. According to Lydia Sigourney and Sarah Josepha Hale, mastering the art of physical and emotional caretaking was essential for young women. They, and others, also strongly recommended that mothers teach their daughters how to nurse the sick, so as to practice being of service to others.[28] Young women were urged to tame their spirits in relation to men by cultivating docility with their brothers. One advisor recommended that in arguments with brothers "sisters should exercise patience, and not endeavor . . . to convince them of the fallacy of opinion, in which vital interests are not involved." She added that "young females should also evince affectionate solicitude in regard to the physical comforts of their brothers."[29] Louisa Caroline Tuthill counseled young women to develop "self-denial" and "cheerful acquiescence to the will of others." She warned her young readers that "a young lady who is not an affectionate, docile daughter, a loving, kind sister, cannot make a good wife."[30]

Mothers and female advisors advocated in their lives and in their writing a very specific marital lifestyle. They added the weight of personal testimony to the ideology of sexual polarity and elaborated the specifics of sexual difference. Young women were presented with an image of marriage in which the emotionally nurturing, moral, and submissive wife devoted herself to the service and care of a distant, authoritarian man. This unconditional recommendation of sexual dichotomy was only one aspect of the intergenerational communication, however; women also admitted that the marital relationship brought pain and disappointment for wives. This blend of advocacy and acceptance of pain was the crucial element in feminine acculturation.

Women wrote in general about marital unhappiness, and also specifically about individual cases. Catharine Sedgwick described her older sister's marriage as "not a congenial one." She added that Eliza "endured much and heroically."[31] Elizabeth Oakes Smith observed that unhappy marriage was the rule and not the exception. "It is not enough to say that thousands are content under this state of things," she wrote. "There are tens of thousands who are not—who are degraded, oppressed, and miserable under it."[32] Foreign observers noticed a "coldness" between husbands and wives in early-nineteenth-century America, and commented on the lack of mutual fervor in the marital relationship.[33]

While young women heard their mother's generation sing praises of sexual dichotomy and hierarchy, they also were aware of widespread marital unhappiness. Within this contradiction was the important maternal message about men: the sexual relationship of polarity and inequality was essential and unchangeable; the "good" woman was one who could endure without complaint. Marilyn Ferris Motz, in her study of Michigan women's diaries, found that young women commonly associated marriage with suffering. One unmarried woman wrote of a woman about to be married as "full of hopes which are to be crushed" whose "fair brow would be lined with care and trial." Another wrote that she expected marriage to be "nothing but cares and forever after."[34] Caroline Howard Gilman's mother was a poignant example of women's association of marriage and pain. When she told her mother she wanted to marry, "My dear mother! She took me in her arms and wept—she to whom tears were so rare! All that day she drooped in her duties; her brow was thoughtful; she sighed often, and seemed like one struggling with a burden."[35] Many writers encouraged later marriages, so as to postpone the harsh realities of "woman's lot." None but the radical theorists, however, suggested the possibility that women should expect more from their relationships with men.[36]

Although a few mothers "cherished the decided wish, that their daughters should never marry," most women viewed marriage as an essential relationship a woman had to suffer through.[37] An early-nineteenth-century mother could recommend such a life to her daughter, without sadism or insensitivity, because she expected her to find solace and "place" in a female community that defined suffering as virtue. Men were relatively unimportant in women's lives; instead, women found emotional support and determined their sense of status in the company of children and other women.[38] For her humble submission to the sexual status quo, a woman was rewarded with the sympathy of her peers.

In addition to their double message about the marriage relationship, mothers communicated a similar idea about the domestic life. Just as women advocated sexual dichotomy while admitting that it involved a great deal of pain, so too they praised domesticity while asserting that it brought physical and psychological suffering. In so doing they impressed upon their daughters the necessity of blending the self into role, and introduced them to physical suffering as a means of feminine transcendence.

The most specific way mothers prepared daughters to fill their proper sphere was by teaching them domestic arts and advocating domesticity. As Carroll Smith-Rosenberg has pointed out, in the early nineteenth century there was a true apprenticeship system between mothers and daughters in learning domestic tasks.[39] Contemporary women agreed that a daughter's training for her feminine life's work took place "at her mother's fireside."[40] Mrs A. J. Graves wrote, "As the girl is the woman will be," and went on to give examples of mother/daughter training combinations and the effects on daughters as women.[41] Catharine Maria Sedgwick expressed it most succinctly, telling young women, "Nature has apprenticed you to your mothers."[42]

Besides preparing daughters for the life-activities of adult womanhood, mothers were also important in restricting girls' education to domesticity. Mrs.

Marshall wrote a book "primarily intended for daughters" in which she sketched an ideal mother/daughter apprenticeship. The mother taught the daughter "all the quiet duties of the female life ... calculated to contribute to the comfort of those around her." The mother would not allow her daughter to study art, telling her that any pursuits "not consistent with the performance of every relative duty, the acquirement of domestic habits, or the attainment of sound and useful knowledge ... are better not attempted."[43] Later the reader finds out that the mother herself had had scholarly aspirations she was forced to put aside when she married. She was trying to save her daughter from the disappointment she saw as inherent in any non-domestic ambitions. This idea was echoed by several diarists, one of whom wrote that her mother was totally unimpressed when she, the daughter, won academic honors during her two-year school experience, yet was elated beyond description when she made her first dress.[44] Although some women urged that a girl be trained in money-making skills, these were to be used in case the girl was unlucky in the marriage market or in case she was widowed. They were not meant to offer the girl an option to domesticity.[45]

Young women learned more than the specifics of domestic service from their mothers. According to the writers and diarists of the time, girls learned the arts of household management from a mother who considered the role distasteful, but part of the life-expectations of a female. Women writing essays and advice literature noticed that some mothers so dreaded household tasks that they purposely postponed training their daughters so as to give them more time to enjoy girlhood. According to Mrs. A. J. Graves, such mothers believed "girls should *enjoy* themselves while single, because, poor things, they will have *trouble enough* when they are married."[46] Implicit in this maxim is the idea that domesticity is a necessary aspect of adult femininity and one not meant to be fulfilling.

While mothers trained their daughters in the skills necessary to repeat the mothers' lives, they communicated their feelings of dissatisfaction with those same activities. Mothers taught their daughters that the essence of femaleness was absorption of self into role. It was unnecessary and unexpected that the daughters would like the role. Acceptance and faithful performance were the only requirements. No other activity, no personal interests, could take precedence or could interfere. Mothers taught their daughters to acquiesce to "woman's lot" by providing a living example of a dissatisfied woman faithfully performing her duties.

There was a deeper level involved also. Not only were daughters learning to curb their ambition and confine their activities within the narrow field of domestic service; not only were they learning the feminine necessity of internalizing anger and dissatisfaction in order to continue role-performance; they were learning also that the feminine sphere often destroyed the physical and mental health of its occupants. Their mothers were willing to pay such a price, and so daughters learned to exact it from themselves. They learned to expect physical fatigue and mental nervousness as indicators of faithful domestic service. They learned to view these symptoms of bodily and psychological distress as a measure of true womanhood.

Diarists and essayists continually noted the physical and psychological toll of domestic service. One woman wrote of women "overwhelmed with the pressure of domestic cares," and another observed that women must learn to "smile amid a thousand perplexities."[47] Harriet Johnson wrote in her diary of a married woman "tied to domestic servitude, a perfect slave to her children" and concluded, "Such, I suppose is woman's sphere."[48] Caroline Briggs described her mother as a woman "whose whole life was devoted to the happiness of those about her," and who "had a wonderful patience and endurance." She went on to say that her mother "never yielded to pain or weariness" though she was "overweighted with care and responsibility all the days of her life." Briggs praised her mother's domestic ability, yet observed that "to accomplish all this she gave her health, her strength, and her life," and added, "When old age came my mother was worn and weary."[49] In her diary, Catharine Maria Sedgwick spoke of her mother as "oppressed with cares and responsibilities," and of her older sister's marriage initiating her into "a life of toil, of patient endurance . . . of harsh trials."[50]

From various types of sources, the American woman in the early-and mid-nineteenth century emerges as an unhealthy, overworked, early-aging person. The female community described itself as progressively declining in health. In 1856, Catharine Beecher published a personal survey of middle-class women in *A Letter to the People on Health and Happiness*. In it she noted that women repeatedly told her that their mothers and grandmothers were physically stronger than they. Whether or not women's general state of health was actually worse is less important than the fact that women believed themselves to be declining in health. Young women were exposed to a female community that advocated domesticity while loudly proclaiming the physical cost of the domestic life.[51]

The psychological strain was also duly noted. In the beginning decades of the nineteenth century, women began to admit to a new level of unhappiness. Physicians documented this melancholy and began to write of female hysteria: a burst of sullenness, aggression, or tears with no apparent provocation. Dinah Marie Mulock Craik, writing in 1858, was aware of "a large average of unhappiness existent among women . . . not merely unhappiness of circumstances but unhappiness of soul." She also wrote that happiness in marriage was very uncommon.[52] Hester Pendleton asserted that "thousands of women are not happy wives and mothers," and Elizabeth Oakes Smith noted that middle-aged matrons were spoken of as "past all joy, and beauty, and hopefulness."[53] There was also notice taken by various observers that a large number of American women were resorting to strong tea, coffee, rum, or opium to ease their psychological distress.[54]

Mrs. A. J. Graves, in *Woman in America*, embodied the double message about domesticity: the combination of advocacy and admission of pain. She wrote in the preface that women should be stronger in the domestic sphere and that women's education should correspond to their domestic duties. She later asserted, "For a woman to be domestic is so consonant with every feeling of her heart, and so true to her nature, that where she is not so it must be the result of a training which has counteracted the design of Providence, and guided her contrary to her innate propensities." Less than ten pages later, she described a typical overworked wife, a woman settled into domesticity: "Cares eat away at her heart; the day presses on her with new toils; the night comes, and they are unfulfilled; she lies down in weariness, and rises with uncertainty; her smiles become languid and few."[55]

Mrs. Graves is an example of what the female community in general, and mothers in particular, were telling young women about womanhood. It is woman's nature to be domestic. It conforms to a great social law. Domesticity results in sickness, weariness, and unhappiness. Your life as a woman will be confined to this sphere, and will necessarily involve suffering and unhappiness. Your self-worth, fulfillment, and social significance are directly proportional to your faithful role performance. Thomas Low Nichols and Mary S. Gove summarized this attitude precisely. They wrote, "Women are everywhere instructed that it is better to endure everything than to attempt to change their position. It is for the good of society; for the sake of the children."[56]

The maternal generation demonstrated femininity by sending a double message about marriage and domesticity; they also instructed daughters on feminine behavior in the mother/daughter relationship itself. By facilitating a carefree adolescent lifestyle for daughters, mothers provided a lesson in motherly sacrifice for family and reiterated the expectation that adult womanhood would soon enough bring such sacrifice to daughters. Although changing socioeconomic conditions created the possibility of adolescence as a life phase for middle-class youth, mothers were responsible for designing or allowing an adolescent lifestyle for their daughters.[57] According to mid-century observers and late-century women who made up the daughters' generation, the female adolescent lifestyle was characterized by a certain educational experience, a great deal of leisure time for reading, parties, and courting, and the absence of domestic responsibilities.[58] This relatively frivolous adolescence can be seen as a mother's final gift to her daughter, a gift for which the mother sacrificed.

What daughters were not required to do with their time is revealing about the mother/daughter relationship. In the maternal generation, there were warnings and laments about mothers not training their daughters in domestic arts and about mothers not allowing their daughters to do any domestic work.[59] One older woman advising a younger one to avoid marriage as long as possible pointed out all the advantages of being a daughter: "[You] have no care, no trouble and have nothing to do but enjoy yourself."[60] The daughters' generation, while describing the period between childhood and womanhood as "the happiest part of her [the girl's] life," saw this respite as evidence of "mother-love, deep though misdirected," and mothers' "mistaken kindness." Daughters wrote of girls who never sewed or cooked or washed a dish, of girls "half-taught to do nothing," and of girls avoiding housework as they would the smallpox. One woman wrote of her mother teaching her "nothing" and making "no demands upon my time or service."[61] Women wrote of middle-class adolescence in the mid-century period as a time of leisure, late hours, and no housework.

In a household that still contained many children and still required many hours of maintenance-labor a day, allowing a young daughter leisure time cost a mother dearly. Women wrote of maternal sacrifice for daughters in various ways. Mothers were too "self-effacing," and mothers worked too hard. Mothers sacrificed for young girls' happiness, and mothers denied themselves in order to dress their daughters well. Mothers made themselves the "upper servants" of their daughters.[62] Mothers who allowed their daughters a carefree adolescence also taught them that adult womanhood required maternal self-sacrifice for the good (or simply the happiness) of family members.

Members of the maternal generation who felt that daughters would soon enough inherit "woman's lot" were willing to provide their girls with a few more years of relaxation and play, but they assumed suffering was a virtue daughters would emulate as they grew older. Helen Brown wrote a poem, "To a Daughter Just Entering Womanhood," in which she described her own life as full of "sorrow" and "grief." The suffering she had experienced she viewed as part of adult womanhood and wrote about it to the daughter as "the cross thou hast not lifted yet." Another popular poet, Felicia Hemans, wrote "Evening Prayer at a Girls' School," in which she sang praises of woman's willingness to suffer for others and also made it clear that daughters would one day inherit that feminine privilege.[63]

Daughters also perceived their mothers as having hard lives. One woman wrote of her "patient mother's hourly martyrdom," while another commented on her mother's "tottering under her burden of care."[64] A classic example of the subtle mother/daughter understanding about suffering appeared in a book *In Memory of Our Mother*. The eldest daughter remembered her mother as "burdened with a multitude of cares." The same volume contained a letter to that daughter from the mother, in which the mother described the duties and cares of her life ("I feel oppressed with an accumulation of the cares and anxieties of my years resting upon me") but ended by saying those cares would lead to salvation.[65] Still another daughter wrote of her mother's "patient service . . . a most willing and loving one, so unselfish that it made no demands for recognition or appreciation."[66]

From a carefree adolescence, daughters understood that they were to enter the tiresome duties of "true womanhood." The mother/daughter relationship that provided adolescent leisure also contained a lesson about the girl's feminine future. The self-sacrificial demands of womanhood, that would soon be the daughter's life, were evident in her mother's gift of a leisurely adolescence. By living within a female community that advocated a narrow, admittedly painful feminine lifestyle and elevated suffering to transcendence, the adolescent girl was introduced to a sanctified, womanly coping mechanism: the transformation of physical pain and the boredom of role performance to an avenue of spiritual release. By living with a mother who allowed a carefree adolescent lifestyle while paying for that gift with her own sacrifice, the daughter was given first-hand instruction on self-abnegation as a feminine trait. This became part of the gender script mid-century daughters were given.

The question to consider now is how adolescent girls took that maternal legacy into their adult lives. Keeping in mind that early nineteenth-century women, the maternal generation, had started with a feminine ideology stressing republican motherhood and had altered that script because of new physical and socioeconomic conditions of female life, how, then, did the daughters' generation transform their mothers' sense of the feminine to fit the new material conditions of late-nineteenth-century womanhood? And in light of the psychosexual characteristics of a close mother/daughter relationship—the self/other blur and over-identification described by Nancy Chodorow and others—how did daughters cope with life possibilities different from their mothers?

NOTES

1. Mary Terhune, *Eve's Daughters; or Common Sense for Maid, Wife, and Mother* (New York: J. R. Anderson & H. S. Allen, 1882), p. 7.

2. Terhune, *Eve's Daughters*, p. 100.

3. Nancy Chodorow, *The Reproduction of Mothering: Psychoanalysis and the Sociology of Gender* (Berkeley: University of California Press, 1978). See also: David B. Lynn, *Parental and Sex-Role Identification: A Theoretical Formulation* (Berkeley: McCutchen, 1969); Irene H. Frieze, et. al., eds., *Women and Sex Roles: A Social Psychological Perspective* (New York: Norton, 1978); Ethel Spector Person, "Sexuality as the Mainstay of Identity: Psychoanalytic Perspectives," in *Women: Sex and Sexuality*, ed. Catharine E. Stimpson and Ethel Spector Person (Chicago: University of Chicago Press, 1980), pp. 36–61; Carol Gilligan, *In a Different Voice* (Cambridge, MA: Harvard University Press, 1982).

4. Chodorow, *The Reproduction of Mothering*; Dorothy Dinnerstein, *The Mermaid and the Minotaur: Sexual Arrangements and Human Malaise* (New York: Harper & Row, 1976); Adrienne Rich, *Of Woman Born* (New York: Norton, 1976); Gilligan, *In a Different Voice*.

5. The weakness of Chodorow's theory is its lack of historical consciousness. The patriarchal nuclear family is assumed rather than explained in *The Reproduction of Mothering*. The book offers an extremely perceptive insight about the deep roots of femininity in the mother/daughter relationship, however, and can be useful to historians if the psychological dimension is put in historical context.

6. Carroll Smith-Rosenberg, "The Female World of Love and Ritual: Relations Between Women in Nineteenth-Century America," *Signs*, 1(1975), 1–30. Smith-Rosenberg has been criticized for romanticizing the female world. See Bari Watkins, "Woman's World in Nineteenth-Century America," *American Quarterly*, 31(1979), 116–127; Ellen DuBois, Mari Jo Buhle, Temma Kaplan, Gerda Lerner, and Carroll Smith-Rosenberg, "Politics and Culture in Women's History: A Symposium," *Feminist Studies*, 69(1980), 26–64. In spite of criticism, Smith-Rosenberg's description of women's ac-

tivities and women's concerns is important information about middle-class women's lives, regardless of how those activities are interpreted.

7. Lydia Sigourney, *Letters to Mothers* (New York: Harper & Brothers, 1839), p. 170. See also: *Hints and Sketches, by an American Mother* (New York: J. C. Riker, 1853), pp. 156–159; *Tribute to the Memory of Jane Porter Lincoln* (Baltimore: printed for private circulation by John D. Toy, 1855), p. 10; Sarah Josepha Hale, *The Ladies' Wreath, A Selection from the Female Poetic Writers of England and America* (Boston: Capen & Lyon, 1837), p. 278; Lucy Newhall Colman (born 1817), *Reminiscences* (Buffalo, New York: H. L. Green, 1891), pp. 12, 58; Julia Parker Dyson (born 1818), *Life and Thought*, ed. Miss E. Latiner (Philadelphia: Claxton, Remsen, Hafflefinger & Co., 1871), pp. 93–100. From the daughters' generation: Frances Willard, *A Great Mother; Sketches of Madam Willard* (Chicago: Woman's Temperance Publication Association, 1894), p. 270 (Willard wrote about her mother: "My nature is so woven into hers that I tremble to think what would become of me if the bond were severed. . . . I verily believe, I cling to her more than ever did any other of her children."). Christine Herrick, *A Home Book for Mothers and Daughters* (New York: The Christian Herald, 1897), p. 9. Mother/daughter closeness was also discussed in Barbara Welter, *Dimity Convictions: The American Woman in the Nineteenth Century* (Athens, OH: Ohio University Press, 1976), p. 7; and Smith-Rosenberg, "The Female World of Love and Ritual," p. 15; Mary Ryan, *Cradle of the Middle Class: The Family in Oneida County, New York, 1790–1865* (New York: Oxford University Press, 1981), p. 219.

8. Lydia Sigourney, ed., *Lucy Howard's Journal* (New York: Harper, 1858), p. 111.

9. Lucretia Maria Davidson, *Poetical Remains of the Late Lucretia Maria Davidson* (Philadelphia: Lea & Blanchard, 1841), pp. 191–192. See also: Margaret E. Sangster, *From My Youth Up* (New York: Fleming H. Revell Company, 1909). pp. 54, 55; Rachael Q. Butts, *A Hoosier Girlhood* (Boston: The Gorham Press, 1924), p. 31; Caroline C. Briggs, *Reminiscences and Letters* (Boston: Houghton Mifflin & Co., 1847), p. 19.

10. Butts, *A Hoosier Girlhood*, p. 39.

11. Sigourney, *Lucy Howard's Journal*, p. 112. For other examples of close friendship between mothers and daughters see: Mary A. Livermore, *The Story of My Life* (Hartford: A. D. Worthington & Co., 1899), p. 141; Lydia Howard Sigourney, *Letters of Life* (New York: D. Appleton & Co., 1867), pp. 241, 242.

12. *In Memory of Our Mother* (privately printed, 1882), p. 68.

13. On first daughters see: Sangster, *From My Youth Up*, p. 19; *In Memory of Our Mother*, p. 68. Mary Rossiter described her relationship with her father as very close and her relationship with her mother as distant in *My 88her's Life, The Evolution of a Recluse* (Chicago: Fleming H. Revell Co., 1900), pp. 31–37.

14. Grace Hoadley Dodge, *A Bundle of Letters to Busy Girls on Practical Matters* (New York: Funk & Wagnalls, 1887), p. 44.

15. Stella Scott Gilmore, *Mothers in Council* (New York: Harper & Brothers, 1884), p. 191. Other women who warned about a lack of confidence between mothers and daughters were Eleanor Donnelly, ed., *Girlhood's Hand-book of Woman* (St. Louis, MO: B. Herder, 1898), p. 123 ("Most of the grave mistakes committed by girls, come from a want of confidential relations with the mother"); Terhune, *Eve's Daughters*. p. 311; Sarah Bolton, *Every-day Living* (Boston: L. C. Page & Co., 1900), p. 22. However, these daughters seem to be commenting more about the young women they see around them in their older years than about themselves as daughters. A growing distance between mothers and daughters might have begun in the late nineteenth century. Harriet Paine

(born in 1845 but writing in 1890), *Girls and Women* (Boston: Houghton Mifflin & Co., 1890), pp. 219–220, wrote that education can create a gulf between mothers and daughters "in the present generation."

16. This idea of body denial will be an important concept when we consider the daughter's response to the maternal message.

17. Ann Taylor Gilbert, *Practical Hints to Young Females on the Duties of a Wife, a Mother, and a Mistress of a Family* (Boston: Wells and Lilly, 1820), p. 139.

18. See: Mrs. L. Abell, *Woman in Her Various Relations* (New York: R. T. Young, 1853), p. 299; Miss Coxe, *Claims of the Country on American Females* (Columbus: Isaac N. Whiting, 1842), p. 41; Eliza W. Farnham, *Woman and Her Era*, vol. 1 (New York: A. J. Davis and Co., 1864); *Godey's Lady's Book*, 25(July, 1842), 59 and (September, 1842), 155; Lucy Larcom, *A New England Girlhood* (Boston: Houghton Mifflin & Co., 1889), p. 198. Annie Adams Fields, ed., *Life and Letters of Harriet Beecher Stowe* (Boston: Houghton Mifflin & Co, 1898), p. 10. Eliza Spalding Warren, *Memoirs of the West* (Portland, OR: Marsh Printing Co., 1916), p. 22. See also Anne L. Kuhn, *The Mother's Role in Childhood Education: New England Concepts, 1830–1860* (New Haven: Yale University Press, 1947), p. 37. Nineteenth-century writers celebrating separate spheres and the different natures of women and men are almost too abundant to cite. Any issue of *Godey's Lady's Book*, the various gift books and advice books written by women and men, as well as more serious essays about the sexes, all contain profuse praise of dichotomizing male and female. See especially: Sigourney, *Letters to Mothers*, p. 13; Lizzie R. Torrey, *The Ideal of Womanhood; or Words to the Women of America* (Boston: Wentworth, Hawes & Co., 1859), pp. 80–81; Catharine Beecher, *A Treatise on Domestic Economy* (New York: Harper & Brothers, 1850); Dianah Marie Mulock Craik, *A Woman's Thoughts About Women* (Philadelphia: T. B. Peterson & Brothers, 1861), p. 20; Mrs. A. J. Graves, *Woman in America* (New York: Harper & Brothers, 1844), introduction, pp. 159–174. This praise was also found in children's literature, most of which was written by women. See Anne Scott MacLeod, *A Moral Tale: Children's Fiction and American Culture, 1820–1860* (Hamden, CT: Archon Books, 1975). On separate spheres and the natural differences between the sexes see also: David G. Pugh, *Sons of Liberty: The Masculine Mind in Nineteenth-Century America* (Westport, CT: Greenwood Press, 1983); Marilyn Ferris Motz, *True Sisterhood: Michigan Women and Their Kin, 1820–1920* (Albany: State University of New York Press, 1983); Barbara Berg, *The Remembered Gate: Origins of American Feminism, The Woman and the City 1800–1860* (New York: Oxford University Press, 1978), pp. 71–75.

19. Elizabeth Oakes Smith, *Woman and Her Needs*, excerpted in *Liberating the Home*, ed. L. Stein and A. K. Baxter (New York: Arno Press, 1974), p. 84.

20. Graves, *Woman in America*, p. 36; Caroline Howard Gilman, *Recollections of a Southern Matron* (New York: Putnam, 1852), p. 297.

21. On sexual hierarchy and the necessity of female submission see: Barbara Welter, "The Cult of 'True Womanhood': 1800–1860," *American Quarterly*, 18(1966), 151–174; Catharine M. Sedgwick, *Life and Letters* (New York: Harper & Brothers, 1871), p. 37; *Hints and Sketches*, p. 42; Graves, *Woman in America*, pp. 173–174.

22. Anna Howard Shaw, *The Story of a Pioneer* (New York: Harper & Brothers, 1915), p. 26.

23. Sedgwick, *Life and Letters*, p. 34–36. For more examples of daughters' descriptions of fathers see: Caroline Wells Healey Dall, *Alongside* (Boston: by Thomas Todd, 1900),

p. 31; Livermore, *The Story of My Life*, pp. 136, 144; Sarah Stuart Robbins, *Old Andover Days* (Boston: The Pilgrim Press, 1908), pp. 163–181.

24. Sedgwick, *Life and Letters*, p. 36. Of course, there must have been fathers who were caring and affectionate, but the image of father in women's nonfiction writing is one of distance.

25. Elizabeth Buffum Chace and Lucy Buffum Lovell, *Two Quaker Sisters* (New York: Liveright Publishing Co., 1937), p. 34. Another member of the daughters' generation, Martha Louise Rayne, *What Can a Woman Do, or Her Position in the Business and Literary World* (Detroit: F. B. Dickerson & Co., 1884), p. 445, described the typical middle-class father-child relationship: "The younger children get to regard him as a feature of Sundays, and perhaps associate him with the unpleasant slavery of sitting still in church." See also, *In Memory of Our Mother*, p. 45. Feminine submission also included sexual submission. See women's letters quoted in Henry Clarke Wright, *The Unwelcome Child; or, The Crime of an Undesigned and Undesired Maternity* (Boston: B. Marsh, 1858), pp. 66, 76, 95, 102, 104.

26. Fields, *Life and Letters of Harriet Beecher Stowe*, p. 9; Chace, *Two Quaker Sisters*, p. 25; Briggs, *Reminiscences*, p. 19.

27. For similar descriptions of mothers in families see: Warren, *Memoirs of the West*, pp. 14, 15, 22; Livermore, *The Story of My Life*, p. 76; Rebecca Latimer Felton, *Country Life in Georgia in the Days of My Youth* (Atlanta: Index Printing Co., 1917), pp. 29, 34; *In Memory of Our Mother*, pp. 68–96; Rossiter, *My Mother's Life*, pp. 15, 37–38.

28. Sigourney, *Letters to Mothers*, pp. 55, 125, 277; *Godey's Lady's Book*, 25(July, 1842), 58, 59 and (November, 1842), 247–248. See also: Abell, *Woman in Her Various Relations*, p. 303; Louisa Caroline Tuthill, *The Young Lady's Home* (Boston: William J. Reynolds & Co., 1847), p. 74; Catharine Marie Sedgwick, *Means and Ends; or, Self-Training* (Boston: Marsh, Capen, Lymon & Webb, 1840), p. 113. On nursing as feminine see also Motz, *True Sisterhood*, p. 107.

29. Coxe, *Claims of the Country*, p. 135. See also Abell, *Woman in Her Various Relations*, pp. 153–154.

30. Tuthill, *The Young Lady's Home*, p. 97. We don't know how seriously young women took this advice, but it was important in providing an image for proper feminine behavior.

31. Sedgwick, *Life and Letters*, p. 71.

32. Smith, *Woman and Her Needs*, p. 34. For other contemporary accounts of marital happiness see: Sangster, *From My Youth Up*, pp. 238, 246. Craik, *A Woman's Thoughts About Women*, p. 37; Briggs, *Reminiscences and Letters*, p. 98; Chace, *Two Quaker Sisters*, p. 46; Emily C. Judson, *The Life and Letters of Emily C. Judson*, ed. A. C. Kendrick (New York: Sheldon & Co., 1862), p. 23; Mary Ann Hubbard, *Family Memories* (Private circulation, 1912), pp. 39, 41. Ethel Peal, "The Atrophied Rib: Urban Middle-Class Women in Jacksonian America," Ph.D. Diss., University of Pittsburgh, 1970, pp. 128–130, 145–204; Nancy F. Cott, *The Bonds of Womanhood: "Woman's Sphere" in New England, 1790–1835* (New Haven: Yale University Press, 1977); and Robert Griswold, *Family and Divorce in California, 1850–1890: Victorian Illusions and Everyday Realities* (Albany: State University of New York Press, 1982), p. 58, discuss unhappy marriage in the early nineteenth century.

33. See: Arthur W. Calhoun, *Social History of the American Family*, vol. 2 (Cleveland: The Arthur H. Clark Co., 1918), p. 133; Peal, "The Atrophied Rib," pp. 8–11, 16, 17; Eric Dingwall, *The American Woman* (London: Gerald Duckworth & Co., Ltd.,

1956), pp. 72–73; Frances Trollope, *Domestic Manners of the Americans* (London: George Routledge & Sons, Ltd., 1927), pp. 127–128.

34. Motz, *True Sisterhood*, pp. 17, 18.

35. Gilman, *Recollections*, p. 255.

36. Some writers who encouraged later marriages were: Smith, *Woman and Her Needs*, p. 60; Elizabeth Blackwell, *The Laws of Life, With Special Reference to the Physical Education of Girls* (New York: George P. Putnam, 1852), p. 144. *Woman's Influence and Woman's Mission* (Philadelphia: W. P. Hazard, 1854), p. 23; Mrs. R. B. Gleason, "Hints to Women," *Water-Cure Journal* (July, 1853), p. 6; *Godey's Lady's Book*, 25(November, 1842), 234. Smith, *Woman and Her Needs*; and Margaret Fuller, *Woman in the Nineteenth Century* (New York: W. W. Norton & Co., 1971) both suggested that women should expect more from men.

37. Beecher, *A Treatise on Domestic Economy*, p. 44. See also Catharine Beecher, *Letters to the People on Health and Happiness* (New York: Harper, 1856), p. 121. Cott, *The Bonds of Womanhood*, pp. 78–81, quotes nineteenth-century diaries in which mothers express negative feelings over daughters' plans to marry. Carl Bode, *The Anatomy of American Popular Culture* (Berkeley: University of California Press, 1959), pp. 273–274, quotes Caroline Hentz's popular novel *Ernest Linwood* in which a dying mother tells her daughter: "Receive my dying injunction. If you live to years of womanhood, and your heart awakens to love,—as, alas, for woman's destiny it will,—then read my life and sad experience, and be warned by my example."

38. On the unimportance of men in the lives of women, see Cott, *The Bonds of Womanhood*; Calhoun, *Social History of the American Family*, p. 133; Helen Waite Papshvily, *All the Happy Endings* (New York: Harper & Brothers, 1956), chapters 7–9; Smith-Rosenberg, "The Female World of Love and Ritual." Carl Degler, *At Odds: Woman and the Family in America from the Revolution to the Present* (New York: Oxford University Press, 1980), argues that men were indeed important in nineteenth-century women's lives. He bases his conclusion on correspondence between husbands and wives. While admitting that there must have been some close marital relationships in the nineteenth century, both the nature of Degler's sources and the numerous sources to the contrary imply that distant marriages were more the norm. In letters one would expect to find overly sentimental endearments. Also, women's diaries, fiction, essays in periodical literature, advice books, and children's books all indicate that men were relatively unimportant within the female community.

39. Smith-Rosenberg, "The Female World of Love and Ritual," p. 16.

40. Tuthill, *The Young Lady's Home*, p. 97.

41. Mrs. A. J. Graves, *Girlhood and Womanhood* (Boston: Carter, 1844), introduction.

42. Sedgwick, *Means and Ends*, p. 69. See also: Sigourney, *Letters to Mothers*, pp. 125–126; Lydia Sigourney, *Letters to Young Ladies* (Hartford: W. Watson, 1835), pp. 28–29; Mrs. Marshall, *A Sketch of My Friend's Family* (Boston: Charles Even, 1819), pp. 50, 70–78; Lillie Savery, *Home Comforts*, in *Midcentury America: Life in the 1850s*, ed. Carl Bode (Carbondale, IL: Southern Illinois University Press, 1972), p. 67 (first published in New York in 1855).

43. Marshall, *A Sketch*, pp. 78–80. See also Sigourney, *Letters to Mothers*, p. 207.

44. Livermore, *The Story of My Life*, p. 124.

45. See: Judson, *The Life and Letters*, p. 26; Craik, *A Woman's Thoughts About Women*, pp. 11–12; Lydia Sigourney, *The Girl's Reading Book in Prose and Poetry for Schools*, 12th ed. (New York: Clement & Packard, 1841), p. 117; Sedgwick, *Means and Ends*, p. 18;

Hester Pendleton, *The Parent's Guide for the Transmisison of Desired Qualities to Offspring* (New York: Fowler & Wells, 1856), p. 111.

46. Graves, *Woman in America*, p. 38. This attitude was also expressed in Craik, *A Woman's Thoughts About Women*, p. 14; Coxe, *Claims of the Country*, p. 98.

47. Graves, *Woman in America*, p. 42; Gilman, *Recollections*, p. 297. See also: Coxe, *Claims of the Country*, p. 100; Blackwell, *The Laws of Life*, p. 145; Larcom, *A New England Girlhood*, p. 26; Judson, *The Life and Letters*, p. 23; Davidson, *Poetical Remains*, pp. 191–192.

48. Quoted in Motz, *True Sisterhood*, p. 17.

49. Briggs, *Reminiscences and Letters*, pp. 19–22.

50. Sedgwick, *Life and Letters*, pp. 28–29.

51. Beecher, *A Letter to the People*, pp. 130–132. The poor (and declining) health of American women was noticed by native and foreign writers. See: Sigourney, *Letters to Young Ladies*, pp. 39–40; Elizabeth Anthony Dexter, *Career Women of America, 1776–1840* (Clifton, NJ: Augustus M. Kelley, 1972), p. 42. Graves, *Woman in America*, p. 35; Beecher, *A Treatise on Domestic Economy*, preface and p. 43; Isaac Ray, *Mental Hygiene* (New York: Hafner reprint, 1968), p. 293; *Godey's Lady's Book*, 22(June, 1841), 281; Tuthill, *The Young Lady's Home*, p. 94. See also: Regina Morantz, "Making Women Modern: Middle-Class Women and Health Reform in Nineteenth-Century America," *Journal of Social History*, 10(1971), 490–507; Ann Douglas Wood, "The Fashionable Diseases: Women's Complaints and Their Treatment in Nineteenth-Century America," *Journal of Interdisciplinary History*, 4(1973), 26; Calhoun, *Social History of the American Family*, p. 82; Griswold, *Family and Divorce in California*, pp. 51–58, 115; Berg, *The Remembered Gate*, chapter 6.

52. Quoted in Peal, "The Atrophied Rib," p. 106.

53. Pendleton, *The Parent's Guide*, p. 111; Smith, *Woman and Her Needs*, p. 56.

54. About psychological stress and women using drugs see: Peal, "The Atrophied Rib," chapter 6; Blackwell, *The Laws of Life*, p. 30; Ray, *Mental Hygiene*, p. 293; Wood, "The Fashionable Diseases," p. 35; Graves, *Woman in America*, p. 38; Thomas Low Nichols and Mary S. Gove, *Marriage: Its History, Character and Results* (Cincinnati: V. Nicholson & Co., 1854), p. 86; Charles S. Woodruff, *Legalized Prostitution: or Marriage as It Is, and Marriage as It Should Be* (Boston: Bela Marsh, 1862), pp. 99–105, 150; Calhoun, *Social History of the American Family*, p. 231; Welter, *Dimity Convictions*, p. 59.

55. Graves, *Woman in America*, preface, pp. 24, 44.

56. Nichols, *Marriage*, p. 86.

57. There is some controversy over the beginning of adolescence as a phase of life in the United States. John Demos and Virginia Demos, in "Adolescence in Historical Perspective," *Journal of Marriage and the Family*, 31(1969), 632–638, argue that adolescence did not exist until the last two decades of the nineteenth century. They link the invention of adolescence to urbanization and to the work of G. Stanley Hall (1880s). However, Joseph F. Kett, in "Adolescence and Youth in Nineteenth-Century America," *Journal of Interdisciplinary History*, 2(1971), 283–299, argues convincingly that although the term "adolescent" was not used until the late nineteenth century, the concept of "youth" as a distinct period of life was recognized at the beginning of the nineteenth century. In my own reading of early-nineteenth-century advice literature I found that writers saw youth as a distinct period of life different from childhood and adulthood.

58. According to Smith-Rosenberg, "The Female World of Love and Ritual," most middle- and upper-class girls had some boarding school experience in the mid-century

period that was frequently the source of life-long friendships. For descriptions of the educational options of mid-nineteenth-century girls see: Thomas Woody, *A History of Women's Education in the United States*, vol. 2 (New York: Octagon Books, 1974); Cott, *The Bonds of Womanhood*, chapter 3.

59. For examples see: Graves, *Woman in America*, p. 26–27, 40–46; Abell, *Woman in Her Various Relations*, p. 268; Coxe, *Claims of the Country*, p. 100; Lizzie R. Torrey, *The Ideal of Womanhood: or Words to the Women of America* (Boston: Wentworth, Hewes & Co., 1959), p. 100; Sedgwick, *Means and Ends*, p. 70; Marshall, *A Sketch*, p. 88; Lydia Maria Child, *The Mother's Book* (Boston: Carter & Hendee, 1831), pp. 146–147; Graves, *Girlhood and Womanhood*, p. 82; Beecher, *A Treatise on Domestic Economy*, preface to the third edition, and in 1851 edition, p. 44; Hale, *Godey's Lady's Book*, 21(March, 1841), 142. See also Peal, "The Atrophied Rib," p. 100.

60. Quoted in Motz, *True Sisterhood*, p. 19.

61. Herrick, *A Home Book for Mothers and Daughters*, pp. 5, 8; Harriet Storer Doutney, *An Autobiography* (Cambridge, MA: by the author, 1871), p. 25; Margaret Sangster, *The Art of Being Agreeable* (New York: The Christian Herald, 1897), p. 106; Terhune, *Eve's Daughters*, p. 260; George Fisk Comfort and Anna Manning Comfort, *Women's Education and Women's Health* (Syracuse, NY: T. W. Durston & Co., 1874), p. 66; Rossiter, *My Mother's Life*, p. 31. See also: James Fernald, *The New Womanhood* (Boston: D. Lothrop Co., 1891), pp. 106–107; Gilman, *Mothers in Council*, p. 31; Jane Croly, *For Better or Worse (for Some Men and All Women)* (Boston: Lee & Shepard, 1875), p. 218; Anne Virginia Sharpe Patterson, *The American Girl of the Period: Her Ways and Views* (Philadelphia: J.P. Lippincott & Co., 1878); Eliza Bisbee Duffey, *No Sex in Education; or, An Equal Chance for Both Boys and Girls* (Philadelphia: J.B. Stoddart & Co., 1874), p. 71. One clergyman, Puchard Newton, in *Womanhood; Lectures on Woman's Work in the World* (New York: Putnam's Sons, 1881), wrote of daughters' time between school and marriage being occupied with "trivial pastimes," and these were "encouraged by parents" (p. 16).

62. Margaret Sangster, *Winsome Womanhood; Familiar Talks on Life and Conduct* (New York: F. H. Revell Co., 1900), p. 132; Eutocia Cook, *Easy Favorable Child Bearing* (Chicago: Arcade Publishing Co., 1886), p. 127; Dodge, *A Bundle of Letters*, pp. 44–46; Terhune, *Eve's Daughers*, pp. 290–291; Patterson, *The American Girl*; Lizzie Bates, *Woman: Her Dignity and Sphere* (New York: American Tract Society, 1870), p. 228; Mary Elizabeth Wilson Sherwood, *Amenities of Home* (New York: D. Appleton & Co., 1884), p. 11.

63. Appeared in Ebenezer Bailey, *The Young Ladies' Class Book; A Selection of Lessons for Reading in Prose and Verse* (Boston: Lincoln, 1832), pp. 90–91.

64. Robbins, *Old Andover Days*, p. 125; Sedgwick, *Life and Letters*, p. 36.

65. *In Memory of Our Mother*, pp. 68, 70, 73, 93. Interestingly, after her children were grown and the mother was experiencing the "empty nest" phase of life so common to twentieth-century women, she referred to this time as "her freedom" (p. 96).

66. Rossiter, *My Mother's Life*, p. 37.

CHAPTER 6

Daughters' Brave New World

Imperial motherhood, with its emphasis on suffering and self-abnegation, was the major feminine script the maternal generation passed on to daughters. Not only were young women exposed to their mothers' feminine ideology in popular literature and in general cultural norms, but they also encountered it from early childhood through adolescence in the mother/daughter relationship itself. Middle-class daughters' gender learning included living with a mother who advocated domesticity while admitting dissatisfaction with it and who modeled self-effacing womanhood by providing her daughter with a carefree adolescent lifestyle. The daughters' generation came to maturity with imperial motherhood as its core feminine ideal.

However, middle-class women who spent at least part of their girlhood in the mid-century period faced an adult world different from their mothers' in many important ways. In diaries, fiction, and popular essays and advice literature, this new generation recorded the continuity and change in the material reality of the female world. These personal documents of experience and response indicate that the mid-century daughter, as a late-century woman, took her mother's concept of femininity as the "thesis" or core idea of her gender consciousness. The differences in the physical and social realities of being a female in the late nineteenth century were antithetical to the daughter's inherited feminine thesis in many ways. In making meaning of her experience, the late-century woman amended her mother's synthesis significantly to arrive at a new understanding of "true womanhood" consistent with her new material conditions. In the late nineteenth century, female control replaced female suffering as the cornerstone of femininity. Instead of being a radical departure from the previous ideology of true womanhood, the celebration of control represented the daughters' interpretation of the new material conditions of female life, using the maternal world view as a starting point.

In the final third of the nineteenth century, urbanization, increased immigration, large-scale industrialization, and US continental hegemony altered the social, economic, cultural, and physical landscape of the country. Cities were large and congested; they contained ethnic and racial variation unsettling to native whites. The new wave of immigration during the 1870s and 1880s and the beginning of Black migration to southern and northern cities resulted in a very visible group of "other Americans" distinguishable both by racial or ethnic characteristics and social class membership. A maturing industrial economy unchecked by government regulation or powerful unions created an ever widening gap between middle-class comfort and working-class survival. A sense of uneasiness about the preservation of "American" values and institutions grew among native whites in response to these dramatic changes. The middle-class home, and the woman who managed it, found new importance as a symbol of the American way of life.[1]

The same forces that made middle-class people cling to home and family life as the measure of true Americanism also drew women out from home boundaries. The female world expanded as a by-product of the sweeping changes in American life during the last part of the nineteenth century, as middle-class women confronted the problems and possibilities of the time. Compared to the earlier maternal world, the stage for the daughter's adulthood was more spacious, contained more options, and involved less physical struggle. Thus, the daughter's material reality was different from her mother's.

By the late-century period the home was no longer the outermost boundary of proper feminine activity; the public space of the city was also womanly territory.[2] Brightly lit streets, public transportation systems, and large department stores welcomed women to participate in an emerging consumer economy as both window shoppers and buyers. One historian has suggested that the department store itself altered the socializing patterns of urban middle-class women by replacing the afternoon visit with the department store lunch as the mainstay of female companionship.[3] The city atmosphere also encouraged and made possible the development of women's organizations devoted to philanthropic, social, or political causes. The urban setting even provided reasons for getting together, from the recognition of sanitation problems or the awareness of working-class women's special needs to the desire for an improved municipal opera house.

Not only were the physical boundaries of womanly activity expanded in the late-century period, but the pre-marriage options were also more numerous for the young woman than they had been for her mother. Women's employment grew by 50 percent in the period 1880 to 1900, with the most striking increase among middle-class women. Technological and economic changes produced jobs, and some daughters occupied their late adolescence and early adulthood as salesgirls, stenographers, or typists. Although they were sex-segregated for the most part, the late-century jobs differed from the ones available for an earlier generation of women in that they were the creations of the new business economy. While some of their mothers had followed woman's work out of the home and into the weaving mills, schools, or hospitals, the daughters' pre-marriage jobs were world-oriented; instead of being asked to take their home work into the world, late-century women were invited to do the world's work. Although most of them only remained in the labor force until marriage, these young women's pre-marriage life experience was more expansive than their mothers' had been. The beginning availability of such jobs altered the social conditions of middle-class womanhood.[4]

Another important late-century change that widened the boundaries and increased the options of middle-class women's lives was the opening of higher education to women. This was important not because large numbers of women attended, but because the availability of university education challenged the idea of women's innately limited intellectual capacity and women's naturally constricted home activity. The eastern "sister schools" were founded between the 1870s and the 1890s, and in the 1870s eight states opened coeducational state universities. Nearly three-fourths of the late-century women who were educated attended coeducational state universities, institutions that were clearly different from the female academies and female seminaries of the time. Although only one in fifty women attended college in the late-century period, the women who did were the first to receive educations comparable to their brothers'.[5]

College-educated women were important beyond their numbers because they forced open new professional options for women and they offered role models for extra-domestic careers. Although many of the late-century women were involved in the home economics movement, some of them went into work that was less home associated. Occupational statistics for late-century women indicate that in 1910 one percent of the nation's lawyers, nineteen percent of university professors, six percent of doctors, seventy-nine percent of librarians, and fifty-two percent of social workers were women. With the opening of higher education to women, debates over serious female education and women's fitness for the professions were topics of public discussion that literate, middle-class women could not avoid. In spite of the fact that university education was still relatively rare for late-nineteenth-century women, expanded educational and professional options were part of the shared experience of the daughters' generation.[6]

In addition to social and economic change that invited women into extra-domestic space, other late-nineteenth-century developments relative to women's family roles reinforced female power in the home. Married women's property acts weakened the economic power of husbands over wives by giving women control over personal earnings and property. Divorce law reform also made it possible for women of the middle class to end unsatisfactory marriages for a variety of reasons. At the same time, the legal doctrine of "tender years" replaced the patriarchal assumption of father right regarding the custody of children in cases of divorce.[7] These legal changes altered the material conditions of womanhood by expanding the economic and social possibilities of married women.

The social and economic changes of the last third of the nineteenth century also lessened the psychological burden of motherhood for the daughters' generation. There was new enthusiasm for public education among the middle class by the 1870s, as women and men realized that it took more than maternal sacrifice to insure the success of their children in the new economic setting. While the common school movement in the early nineteenth century had made public education available, mid-century writers had urged mothers to educate their children's "hearts" by the home fires and had warned against accelerated mental development.[8] By the 1870s, however, public education was a popular middle-class concern. The first compulsory education laws were passed in the last quarter of the century to insure that all children would benefit from the educational and Americanizing effects of public education.[9] The kindergarten movement gained followers among middle-class women, as the age of entering institutions of instruction dropped to four or five years old. For middle-class women, this meant that children were occupied in classrooms for much of the day by the time they were five or six, leaving mothers with more free time. More significantly, widespread advocacy of public education at an early age meant that "good childrearing" and therefore "good motherhood" required neither suffering nor self-sacrifice.

These changes in the economic and social realities of middle-class women's lives increased the possibility for women to take a more public role than the cult of domesticity and suffering femininity allowed. However, new possiblities for women were necessary, but not sufficient, to change the ideology of "true womanhood." Middle-class women developed a new sense of self, and then a revised feminine synthesis, to fit the late-century world changes because they experienced change also at a more elemental level: the physical reality of womanhood was different for them than it had been for their mothers. Changes in the physical experience of being female enabled the daughters' generation to envision a more expansive womanhood, a sense of femininity wide enough to encompass the late-century options opening to them.

During the final decades of the nineteenth century, a new set of material conditions surrounding female body challenged the submission of women to nature and facilitated a sense of body control. The physical education movement illustrated the cultural foundations of feminine frailty, and medical advances made physician-directed birth less painful and dangerous and offered middle-class women the option of surgical treatment for physical repairs and psychological maladies. The common ingredient in these changes was an increase in female body-control[10] and a lessening of women's bondage to biologically determined suffering. Changes in women's physical experience accentuated the gap between the mothers' synthesis and the daughters' lives, a gap that allowed a new image of healthy femininity to emerge.

Since health is not an absolute but a relative term, women's perceptions of their physical experiences are as important as objective reports of mortality, hospital admissions, or numbers of operations performed. If women's perceptions are taken seriously, it is clear that the daughters had a different experience of female health than their mothers had had. Unlike the earlier generation, late-century women experienced the cared-for female body as naturally healthy, not feeble, and saw suffering as an aberration, not as an inevitable consequence of gender. Furthermore, the daughters as women viewed health and strength as essential to female beauty, a concept totally at odds with the earlier idealization of frail, pale, listless femininity, and the daughters attributed illness and weakness to socialization, not to nature. This change in perception came out of new conditions surrounding the female body.

The late-century physical education movment, concentrated in the colleges and universities, was one of the material changes contributing to this new sense of feminine health and new critique of femininity. Because the women who were directly involved became models of ideal womanhood and examples of the beneficial effects of physical training, the physical education movement had an impact on more than the relatively few women who attended institutions of higher education. Lida Rose McCabe, in *The American Girl at College*, painted an almost reverential picture of "the modern college girl, in Turkish trousers." She "crosses swords with a fencing master, vaults bars, climbs ropes, plays ball, rows and swims."[11] Although McCabe hoped that the college girl would not become competitive, she described the physical activity with unqualified approval. Other writers took that image and declared it a womanly goal. Mary Terhune, in a popular book "intended for the mighty middle class who are the heart of the nation," urged the non-college girl to make physical exercise and observance of the "laws of life" part of her daily routine.[12] The ways and means of physical education were popularized in books such as Mrs. John Baily's *Physical Culture*, Teresa Dean's *How to Be Beautiful*, and Mary Bissell's *Physical Development and Exercise for Women*, in which exercises were described and games and sports were encouraged.[13] Women pointed out enthusiastically that younger girls' physical habits were different from past generations of women, and that those differences produced healthier individuals.[14] "Modern young women," not just college girls, were said to possess "good physiques," and "the American girl" was described as "lovely, robust, paying no heed of bad weather."[15]

The mother's generation experienced the female body as weak and suffering, both on a personal level and collectively; they testified that they knew very few healthy women, and they described themselves as unhealthy. Physical education in the colleges and universities changed the next generation's perception of female body by proving that health was a possible and laudable goal for every woman. More importantly, physical training for the small group of American women who attended colleges indicated that health was a "natural" state of womanhood and disease or even weakness was unnatural.

Earlier reformers had urged women to adopt a more healthful style of dress and to let their daughters get plenty of air and exercise, and these ideas enjoyed some popularity. But physical education in the colleges offered an occasion to try both without appearing too radical or odd. Part of the standard curriculum and based on "scientific" ideas, physical education provided a proper feminine setting in which to remove corsets, alter the female costume, and engage in purposeful exercise. Although the ideas had been around for a while, physical education provided the material condition necessary to test the ideas without ridicule.[16]

The playing fields and gymnasia not only were arenas for testing reformers' ideas about female health; they were also incubators for a new image of feminine beauty. The late-century women who wrote of "American girls" and the possibility of female health were individually and collectively changing the image of a "womanly" female body. One self-conscious creator of the new feminine image, Mary Terhune, described the ideal woman of her own generation, the romantic maiden of the mid-century period: "The Representative American Woman of the period comprised between 1845 and 1875, should be painted with her hand on the lumbar region, eyes hollow and complexion chlorotic. *Prolapus uteri* became almost as common as toothache."[17] Helen Starrett, in *Letters to Elder Daughters, Married and Unmarried*, echoed Terhune's assessment of an earlier ideal, writing that "in days past" the notion of "lady" included "invalidism, pallor, small appetite, and a languid mode of speech and manners." It was especially fashionable to be "delicate," she added.[18] These two writers noticed "a turn in things" in the way women viewed their bodies. Unlike their own youth in which health was unladylike, in the late-century period women were asserting that health and strength were the essence of feminine beauty. "Health, Strength, Beauty—The Trinity of Happiness" appeared on one title page, and late-century books with such titles as *How to Be Beautiful, Talks with Homely Girls on Health and Beauty, Physical Beauty: How to Obtain and How to Preserve It*, and *The Potential Woman, A Book for Young Ladies* all connected feminine beauty to female health. The passive, suffering woman was no longer considered the ideal physical type.[19]

Underneath this dramatic change in image was an important change in attitude about body and self that became a root assumption in the late-century feminine ideology: the necessity and power of self-control. The body was no longer "constitutionally" weak, passively succumbing to natural inclinations of illness; instead, the body's well-being depended on the conscious control, the careful discipline of the woman. She alone determined her own health or sickness, by knowledge or ignorance of physiology and by observance or disregard of the laws of life. "*Nothing is more desirable* than a perfect body under perfect control," one woman wrote, expressing both the ideal of feminine health and the belief that self-control was essential to achieve that ideal.[20]

Thinking that health was not only possible and "womanly," but also dependent on knowledge and discipline, raised new questions about the origin of female frailty. Late-nineteenth-century women differed from their mothers' generation in their response to poor health or weakness among women. While the earlier generation was more inclined to blame frailty on "constitutional" problems, overwork, or the evils of civilization, late-century women pointed directly to feminine socialization as the source of female health problems. According to late-century women, young girls sometimes grew sickly as they entered adulthood not because they were improperly prepared for "new and untried duties" (as Catharine Beecher had suggested a generation earlier), but precisely because they were raised and educated for the female role. This awareness of the inherent "sickness" in femininity represents a major change in women's consciousness.

The physical repression that was a central part of feminine role training came under attack in the late nineteenth century, as writers criticized the dainty clothing and exercise prohibition for young girls. "The little girl not yet in her teens must not run, romp, and roll her hoop; she must play with her dolls in the house," one woman wrote. She went on to say:

When she goes out, it must be to show her fine spotless dress, her gaudy sash, and her dainty shoes; in her carefully gloved hand must be a delicate silk parasol; she must not let the sun light shine upon her pale cheeks, for it will tan her face or bring out the freckles; this ornamental, delicate child, is finally sent to school, where she fades and sickens, and the school receives all the blame.[21]

Along the same lines, Eliza Duffey wrote in 1874, "The boy is allowed to be natural, the girl is forced to be artificial." She explained:

While boys have their liberty more or less freely granted them, girls must stay at home and sew and read, and play prettily and quietly, and take demure walks.... The boy may strengthen his lungs by using them to his utmost power, the girl must always speak in mild and subdued tones.[22]

Elizabeth Blackwell pointed out the connection between physical training and enforced feminine passivity, and concluded that "the foundations of future invalidism are solidly laid before they [little girls] are ten years old."[23] Taking the argument to its logical conclusions, one writer asked her readers to imagine what effect a feminine upbringing would have on the bodies of boys. She implied that if boys were submitted to the physical repression common to girls, they too would be sickly and weak.[24]

According to late-century women, the little girl grew into the frail woman precisely because her early education led only in that direction. If girls were given a different sort of education, these women urged, they would grow into strong women. Socialization, not nature, was the source of feminine weakness and illness. This molding of the female body into weakness was apparent not only during early childhood in the restriction of girls' activity, but also during adolescence in the cultural requirements surrounding female coming-of-age. "A girl scarcely enters her teens before custom requires a change in her mode of dress," Helen Gilbert Ecob wrote in 1892. She went on to elaborate: "Her shoulder-straps and buttons are given up for a number of strings about her waist, and the additional weight of an increased length of skirt is added." The result of this, according to Ecob, was the prevention of healthy activity. "She is unable to take the proper kind or necessary amount of exercise, even if she were not taught that it would be unlady like."[25] In a book entitled *Health and Strength for Girls*, Mary Safford and Mary Allen reiterated this point about the adolescent lifestyle, saying that the activities to which young women were confined, such as novel-reading, no exercise, poor diet, and the necessity of dressing in a fashionable way, all contributed to feminine weakness.[26] Alice Stockham described little girls' and young women's socialization as consisting of "repression," as contrasted with the allowance of "expression" in boys and young men. She agreed with other late-nineteenth-century writers that this difference resulted in the physical debilities of womanhood. The general feeling expressed in various ways was that early learning and later cultural expectations were responsible for feminine weakness: the frail, weak woman was not born, but made.[27]

This insistence that physical frailty was culturally induced by socialization into the feminine role was especially significant because the most respected "scientific" writing of the time was positing just the opposite. During the late nineteenth century, Darwin was being interpreted as proof of innate superiority and inferiority based on physical characteristics, Herbert Spencer asserted that women were naturally inferior to men because reproduction thwarted the individual development of the female sex, and scientific medicine linked all of women's psychological problems to their reproductive organs. The intellectual mood of the time supported the idea that the female body determined proper feminine behavior, the natural inferiority of women's intellect, and the natural sensitivity and emotionality of women.[28] The women who wrote of feminine socialization as the root of female frailty were not echoing the dominant ideology of the time; instead, they were expressing an image formed partially out of a new experience of female body.

The political implications of seeing female frailty as culturally imposed and female health as a matter of conscious control were evident in the controversy surrounding Edward Clarke's *Sex in Education; or a Fair Chance for the Girls*. Clarke, a respected physican, argued that higher education was detrimental to women's health because nature demanded that young girls in adolescence devote their physical and mental energies to the reproductive apparatus.

Girls, between the ages of 14 and 18, must have sleep, not only for repair and growth, like boys, but for the additional task of constructing, or more properly speaking, of developing and perfecting then, a reproductive system—the engine within an engine."[29]

Clarke's book presented a classic argument for the idea that woman is body, confined to nature, and that any kind of activity or training which supposes otherwise will cause illness. Young women were frail, according to Clarke, because they sought to escape their feminine destiny.[30]

Sex in Education sparked a lively discussion about female health, feminine socialization, and politics. George Fisk Comfort and Anna Manning Comfort published *Women's Education and Women's Health* in reply to Clarke. They pointed out the class bias in Clarke's reasoning, noting that working women are required to do hard labor during those "crucial years" and are not frail because of it. They also noted the unscientific nature of Clarke's study, pointing out that he used no data but his own imagination and conservative views.[31] The writers in opposition to Clarke all maintained that feminine socialization, not higher education, was to blame for women's frailty. Eliza Duffey, in *No Sex in Education; or An Equal Chance for Boys and Girls*, presented a typical response. She asserted that the physical ills of women were not caused by "a man's education," but rather that

they first originate from, and are afterwards aggravated by, a course of life which recognizes an element of imagined feminine weakness and invalidism to which it is necessary to yield, and which forbids the wholesome active physical life led by the normally healthful man.[32]

Duffey was particularly critical of feminine dress which she saw as a requirement of femininity. She wrote that the young woman

must be put into corsets to give her a good shape. She must wear trailing robes to give her dignity. Her corsets pinch her and cramp her and prevent the full development and free play of her organs.... She gets dyspepsia and headache. Her face flushes.... she at once becomes subject to palpitations of the heart and hysteria."[33]

Caroline Dall pointed out another socialization-related reason for feminine frailty. She reminded Clarke and those who supported his ideas that women and girls do school work "in addition to their home cares," requiring double work of female students. If boys were required to make beds, take care of the baby, or help with meals, they too might be over-fatigued as students.[34]

While stressing the idea that socialization into the feminine role causes women to be weak, some writers also noted the stark politics involved in Clarke's argument. Julia Ward Howe, as editor of *Sex in Education: A Reply to Dr. Edward H. Clarke's "Sex in Education,"* called Clarke's book "a work of the polemic type, presenting a persistent and passionate plea against the admission of women to a collegiate education in common with men." Another writer in the collection noted: "This physiological scare is the most insidious form under which the opposition to the higher education of women has yet appeared."[35] Yet Clarke's argument was very much in keeping with the ideas of medical science about the female body. In pointing out the political nature of Clarke's position, Howe and her contributors argued that the real political issue was the primacy of women's experience over men's ideas of women. Elizabeth Stuart Phelps, a popular domestic novelist, was one of Howe's authors who angrily asserted that women's experience was relevant information in the debate. "The physician is not the person whose judgment can possibly be final," Phelps wrote. "The woman who is physically and intellectually a living denial of every premise and evey conclusion which Dr. Clarke has advanced, has yet a right to an audience."[36] Antoinette Brown Blackwell echoed this idea in *The Sexes Throughout Nature*, when she wrote: "Experience must have more weight than any amount of outside observation. We are clearly entitled on this subject, to a respectful hearing." She went on to offer herself as a living example of the falsity of Clarke's ideas.[37]

Other women too began to assert their experience as evidence of "truth" about female body and feminine socialization. There were testimonies from the University of Michigan, Mount Holyoke, Oberlin, Vassar, and Antioch offered as proof that Clarke was wrong about women's frailty being related to education.[38] The newly formed American Association of University Women went so far as to compile "Health Statistics of Women College Graduates" in which 705 women responded to questions about their general health and the effect of education on their bodies. The Association found that education did not contribute to feminine sickness.[39] More important than their findings was the assertion by all of these women that their physical experience be taken seriously, and that their experience was quite different from popular male ideas. In a similar vein, Mary Putnam Jacobi, a late-century physician, published a study entitled *The Question of Rest for Women during Menstruation* in which she used women's testimony about activity during their periods to argue that rest was not necessary, and indirectly that women's bodies would not be harmed by education. Jacobi's study, which was the Boylston prize essay of Harvard for 1876, was important in challenging by women's experience the prevailing medical view that the female body itself was "a pathological fact, constantly detracting from the sum total of health, and healthful activities."[40]

Going a step further in the argument that women's experience be considered in the debate about the side effects of education, Carolyn Dall asserted that college life was inherently good for women's health: "The regular studies, the early rising and retiring, the exercise in the gymnasium and the open air, the companionship with charming and cultivated women older than themselves, all tend to the most perfect health."[41] Taken together with women's outcry that feminine socialization was injurious to female health, this description of college life as healthful in itself was a bold challenge to the naturalness of domesticity. If indeed women were healthier going to college and associating with "charming and cultivated women" than they were when trained for domestic and child-rearing duties, then perhaps the female body was not "naturally" bound to home and family. Although this argument was not followed through, it indicates the radical possibilities of asserting that women's experience be taken seriously in the debate over the healthfulness of female education.

The controversy over Clarke's conclusions was one manifestation of women's altered self-consciousness. The changing material conditions of middle-class women's lives challenged the idea of innate feminine weakness by allowing some women to experience health and strength as natural and attainable. This created distance between the ideas of feminine frailty learned in childhood and the experience of female health as related to purposeful action. A shift in consciousness necessarily accompanied this dissonance, and many women began to look for sources other than "nature" to explain feminine weakness. Instead of accepting the idea that women were fated to sickness because of their femaleness, late-century women asserted that socialization rendered women weak and that active control was both possible and laudable in the area of female health.

The material conditions of late nineteenth-century middle-class womanhood opened up new life possibilities for daughters by expanding the boundaries of woman's sphere and by raising awareness of the social causes of female health or sickness. Unlike her mother, the daughter's life conditions did not require her to cultivate submission and self-denial. The late-century world encouraged instead a faith in self-control and healthy living, in self-direction and world-involvement. The daughters' world was not in harmony with the maternal script. As we will see, daughters' reproductive experience was also different from their mothers'. The combination of these differences resulted primarily in a new feminine synthesis, but secondarily in some daughters' ambivalence about impending womanhood.

NOTES

1. About the home and the woman as newly important symbols see: Clark E. Clifford, Jr., "Domestic Architecture as an Index to Social History: The Romantic Revival and the Cult of Domesticity in America, 1840–1870," *Journal of Interdisciplinary History*, 7(1976), 33–56; Gwendolyn Wright, *Moralism and the Model Home* (Chicago: University of Chicago Press, 1980); Elaine Tyler May, *Great Expectations: Marriage and Divorce in Post-Victorian America* (Chicago: University of Chicago Press, 1980). Although the late-century period was not the first wave of urbanization, it was the most significant in terms of disruption. Between 1880 and 1920 the country's cities nearly doubled in population, with immigration accounting for much of the increase. For a discussion of the late nineteenth century as a disruptive period for the middle class, see Anita Claire Fellman and Michael Fellman, *Making Sense of Self: Medical Advice Literature in Late Nineteenth-Century America* (Philadelphia: University of Pennsylvania Press, 1981).

2. Although early nineteenth-century women had several socially sanctioned avenues of activity outside the home (maternal associations, evangelical Christian organizations such as Sunday Schools), these extra-domestic options were temporarily held in suspicion during the mid-century cult of homebound domesticity. See Mary P. Ryan, *The*

Empire of the Mother: American Writing About Domesticity, 1830–1860, in the series *Woman and History,* Numbers 2/3, ed. Eleanor S. Riemer (The Institute for Research in History and The Haworth Press, 1982), chapter 4 on "Imperial Isolation."

3. This idea was suggested by Sheila M. Rothman, *Woman's Proper Place: A History of Changing Ideals and Practices, 1870 to the Present* (New York: Basic Books, 1978), pp. 20–21. About women in the urban environment, see also: Margaret Gibbons Wilson, *The American Woman in Transition: The Urban Influence, 1870–1920* (Westport, CT: Greenwood Press, 1979). Wright, *Moralism and the Model Home,* p. 124, also points out that city women bought many products their mothers had produced, such as bread, vegetables, canned goods, their husbands' clothing, medications, soap, and linen.

4. Wilson, *The American Woman in Transition,* chapter 6. May, *Great Expectations,* points out that the composition of the "middle class" changed as a result of changes in work, p. 50. She also notes that the average working woman in 1890 was single and under 25, with most of the middle-class women leaving work for marriage.

5. Susan Ware, *Beyond Suffrage* (Boston: Harvard University Press, 1981), pp. 22–25; Rothman, *Woman's Proper Place,* pp. 24–40.

6. Barbara J. Harris, *Beyond Her Sphere: Women and the Professions in American History* (Westport, CT: Greenwood Press, 1978).

7. May, *Great Expectations;* William O'Neill, "Divorce in the Progressive Era," in *The American Family in Social-Historical Perspective,* ed. Michael Gordon (New York: St. Martin's Press, 1978), pp. 140–151; Carol Brown, "Mothers, Fathers, and Children: From Private to Public Patriarchy," in *Women and Revolution,* ed. Lydia Sargent (Boston: South End Press, 1981), pp. 239–268.

8. Ryan, *The Empire of the Mother,* pp. 48–56.

9. See: Barbara Finkelstein, "Pedagogy as Intrusion: Teaching Values in Popular Primary Schools in Nineteenth-Century America," *Journal of Psychohistory,* 2(1975), 349–378; Karen Wolk Feinstein, "Kindergartens, Feminism, and the Professionalization of Motherhood," *International Journal of Women's Studies,* 3(1980), 28–38.

10. In the late twentieth century, "body control" is an important issue for the women's movement and is understood to include: the availability to all women of information and procedures relative to female body; complete freedom from constraints on women's decisions about sexuality and reproduction; freedom from work environments that can be hazardous to women's bodies; and, sometimes, female control of all technology and research having to do with women's bodies. Clearly, late-nineteenth-century women had no such body control. However, middle-class women's individual ability to "take control" of their bodies increased during the late nineteenth century in terms of reliable birth control, corrective gynecological surgery, and public permission to take charge of their health. It is this sense of body control that I mean throughout this chapter.

11. Lida Rose McCabe, *The American Girl at College* (New York: Dodd, Mead & Co., 1893), p. 15.

12. Mary Virginia Hawes Terhune, *Talks Upon Practical Subjects* (New York and Chicago: The Warner Brothers Co., 1895). introduction, p. 30. Other writers who urged young women to observe natural laws were: Harriet Eliza Paine, *Girls and Women* (by Eliza Chester; pseud.) (Boston and New York: Houghton Mifflin & Co., 1890); Puchard Haber Newton, *Womanhood; Lectures on Woman's Work in the World* (New York: Putnam's Sons, 1881); Eutocia Cook, *Easy Favorable Child Bearing; A Book for All Women* (Chicago: Arcade Publishing Co., 1886).

13. Mrs. John Baily, *Physical Culture* (New York: Press of J. J. Little & Co., 1892);

Teresa H. Dean, *How to Be Beautiful; Nature Unmasked, A Book For Every Woman* (Chicago: T. Howard, 1889); Mary Taylor Bissell, *Physical Development and Exercise for Women* (New York: Dodd, Mead & Co., 1891).

14. Mary Ashton Livermore, *What Shall We Do With Our Daughters* (Boston: Lee & Shepard, 1883), p. 33; Paine, *Girls and Women*, p. 24.

15. Caroline Hazard, *Some Ideals in the Education of Women* (New York: T. Y. Crowell & Co., 1900), p. 7; Amelia Barr, *Maids, Wives, and Bachelors* (New York: Dodd, Mead & Co., 1898), pp. 13–14.

16. On earlier health reformers see: Regina Morantz, "Making Women Modern: Middle-Class Women and Health Reform in Nineteenth-Century America," *Journal of Social History*, 10(1977), 490–507; Regina Morantz, "Nineteenth-Century Health Reform and Women: A Program of Self-Help," in *Medicine Without Doctors*, ed. Guenter B. Risse, Ronald L. Numbers, Judith Walzer Leavitt (New York: Science History Publications, 1977), pp. 73–94.

17. Mary Terhune, *Eve's Daughters; or Common Sense for Maid, Wife, and Mother* (New York: J. R. Anderson & H. S. Allen, 1882), p. 85.

18. Helen Starrett, *Letters to Elder Daughters, Married and Unmarried* (Chicago: A. C. McClurg & Co., 1892), pp. 132–133. See also Charles Fletcher Dole, *Noble Womanhood* (Boston: H. M. Caldwell Co., 1900), p. 13.

19. The title page quotation is from Terhune, *Talks Upon Practical Subjects*. Other expressions of this new idea of feminine health and beauty can be found in: Dean, *How to Be Beautiful*; Paine, *Girls and Women*; Martha Louise Rayne, *What Can a Woman Do; or, Her Position in the Business and Literary World* (Detroit: F. B. Dickerson & Co., 1884); Margaret Sangster, *Winsome Womanhood; Familiar Talks on Life and Conduct* (New York and Chicago: F. H. Revell Co., 1900); Prudence Saur, *Maternity: A Book for Every Wife and Mother* (Chicago: L. P. Miller, 1891); Jennie Willing, *The Potential Woman, A Book for Young Ladies* (Boston: McDonald, Gill & Co., 1886); Annie Jenness Miller, *Physical Beauty; How to Obtain and How to Preserve It* (New York: C. L. Webster & Co., 1892); Frances Smith, *Talks with Homely Girls on Health and Beauty* (New York: Burt, 1885). See also the first book-length study of the concept of beauty in America: Lois W. Banner, *American Beauty* (Chicago: University of Chicago Press, 1983).

20. Baily, *Physical Culture*, p. 12. See also: Paine, *Girls and Women;* Clarissa B. LeMoin, *The Uses and Duties of Life; A Series of Nine Lectures Delivered Before the Young Ladies of the Female Academy at Richmond, Texas* (Hartford, CT: Case, Lockwood & Brainard Co., 1882), p. 109; Alice Stockham, *Tokology; A Book for Every Woman* (Chicago: A. B. Stockham & Co., 1889); Alice Freeman Palmer, *Why Go to College?* (New York: T. Y. Crowell, 1897), p. 10.

21. George Fisk Comfort and Anna Manning Comfort, *Women's Education and Women's Health* (Syracuse, NY: T. W. Durston & Co., 1874), p. 100. See also Livermore, *What Shall We Do With Our Daughters*, p. 26.

22. Eliza Duffey, *No Sex in Education; or An Equal Chance for Both Boys and Girls* (Philadelphia: J. B. Stoddart & Co., 1874), p. 40. Similar ideas were expressed in: *Should Women Obey?* (Chicago: Loomis & Co., 1900), P. 9–10; Helen Gilbert Ecob, *The Well-Dressed Woman; A Study in the Practical Applications to Dress of the Laws of Health, Art and Morals* (New York: Fowler & Wells, 1892), pp. 29–30, 168; Mary Allen King, *Looking Backward; or Memories of the Past* (New York: Randolph & Co., 1870), pp. 15–16; Emma Stebbins, ed. *Charlotte Cushman: Her Letters and Memories of Her Life* (Boston: Houghton, Osgood & Co., 1878), p. 13.

23. Quoted in Terhune, *Eve's Daughters*, p. 41.

24. Lillie Devereaux Blake, *Woman's Place Today* (New York: J. W. Lovel Co., 1883), pp. 65–66.

25. Ecob, *The Well-Dressed Woman*, pp. 29–30.

26. Mary Safford and Mary Allen, *Health and Strength for Girls* (Boston: D. Lothrop & Co., 1884), pp. 7–8.

27. Stockham, *Tokology*, p. 153. See also: Mary Kavanaugh Oldham Eagle, ed. *The Congress of Women Held in the Woman's Building, World's Columbian Exposition, Chicago, 1893* (Chicago: International Publishing Co., 1894), p. 74; Antoinette Brown Blackwell, *The Sexes Throughout Nature* (New York: G. P. Putnam's Sons, 1875), pp. 113, 127, 171.

28. The nineteenth-century idea that women were definable as bodies is explored in: Carroll Smith-Rosenberg, "Puberty to Menopause: The Cycle of Femininity in Nineteenth-Century America," *Feminist Studies*, 1(1973), 58–72; Carroll Smith-Rosenberg and Charles Rosenberg, "The Female Animal: Medical and Biological Views of Woman and Her Role in Nineteenth-Century America," *Journal of American History*, 60(1973), 332–356; Ann Douglas Wood, "'The Fashionable Diseases': Women's Complaints and Their Treatment in Nineteenth-Century America," *Journal of Interdisciplinary History*, 4(1973), 25–52; G. J. Barker-Benfield, *The Horrors of the Half-Known Life* (New York: Harper & Row, 1976).

29. Edward Hammond Clarke, *Sex in Education; or A Fair Chance for the Girls* (Boston: J. R. Osgood & Co., 1873), p. 34.

30. Clarke's ideas were supported by many physicians, including: Henry Maudsley, *Sex in Mind and Education* (Syracuse, NY: C. W. Bardeen, 1884), and William Capp, *The Daughter; Her Health, Education and Wedlock* (Philadelphia and London: F. A. Davis, 1891), especially pp. 58–61.

31. Comfort and Comfort, *Women's Education*, pp. 20–21.

32. Duffey, *No Sex in Education*, introduction, p. 67. See also Anna Callender Brackett, ed. *The Education of American Girls* (New York: G. P. Putnam & Sons, 1874), pp. 128–133.

33. Duffey, *No Sex in Education*, p. 67.

34. Caroline H. Dall, in Julia Ward Howe, ed. *Sex and Education; A Reply to Dr. E. H. Clarke's "Sex in Education"* (Boston: Roberts Brothers, 1874), p. 94.

35. Howe, *Sex and Education*, pp. 14, 115.

36. Elizabeth Stuart Phelps, in *Sex and Education*, pp. 127–128.

37. Brown, *The Sexes Throughout Nature*, pp. 6–7, 165–167.

38. Brackett, *The Education of American Girls*, pp. 133, 141.

39. American Association of University Women, *Health Statistics of Women College Graduates* (Boston: Wright & Potter, 1885), p. 77.

40. Mary Putnam Jacobi, *The Question of Rest for Women During Menstruation* (New York: G. P. Putnam's Sons, 1877), p. 3.

41. Dall, in *Sex and Education*, p. 98.

CHAPTER 7

Science and Self-Control

Just as the material conditions of middle-class womanhood were changing in the late nineteenth century, so too were the conditions surrounding reproduction. Once again, this change was a possible source of dissonance for the daughters—a possible source of conflict between childhood expectations of adult role and actual adult role requirements. An expanded sense of self-control was the central new dimension of late-century reproduction. Technological changes, a different public attitude toward abstinence, and the illegality of abortion constituted new material conditions surrounding fertility for late-century women. The experience of these new conditions led women to challenge their inherited feminine thesis regarding the necessity of female submission and the inevitability of motherhood.

The late-century period was the first time in American history that a large group of women in the dominant middle class felt both able to control fertility and righteous about it. By late-twentieth-century standards, this control and self-direction appear tentative and awkward; technology had not yet provided the tools for bolder action. But for the women in the late nineteenth century, this consciousness shift was both a dramatic departure from their mothers' world view and a psychological foundation for a new definition of "true womanhood."

The most complete and most politically astute study of birth control in America is still Linda Gordon's *Woman's Body, Woman's Right*.[1] In her chapter on the "voluntary motherhood" movement, which was the central birth control development in the late-century period, Gordon describes the new "public" nature of the birth control question. Condoms, diaphragms, and vaginal syringes were available and even illegally advertised, although such advertisements could result in confiscation after the Comstock Laws were passed. The topic of fertility control was discussed and lectured about widely by radicals and straight-laced conservatives. And in the medical literature, for professional and lay readers, the mystery of women's ovulation cycle was pronounced "solved," as medical men and women advised the female population about the "safe" period for copulation without pregnancy. Ironically, the medical knowledge of the menstrual cycle was imperfect at best, since the "safe" period was thought to be mid-cycle immediately following the egg's release from the ovaries—the phase of the cycle actually most conducive to conception.[2] What was important about that advice was not its reliability, however, but its public nature. The voluntary motherhood people and the medical advisors and researchers proclaimed to the literate public that fertility was controllable and that control was both moral and desirable.

Late-century middle-class women were exposed to this debate as both participants and audience, an experience not shared by their mothers. According to one male physician, women sought birth control information in large numbers. "We know it to be a fact ... that physicians are daily beset for advice, as to the best means of preventing conception, by women who are the leaders both in society and philanthropy, and even by some, too, who are lights in the Protestant churches."[3] The idea of birth control and the "how to" of birth control were within the daughters' world.

But even more importantly, the daughters' consciousness of who should control fertility was different from their mothers'. Early- and mid-century women saw birth control, in the form of sexual abstinence, as a marital battle with uneven odds. They believed that submission was the feminine response to an uncooperative husband. Birth control was an uneasy bargain or an artful avoidance of sexual contact. Basically, it was the husband, not the woman, who was in control. The earlier consciousness surrounding birth control did not separate the woman from the destiny of her body; her individual self was still in service to species if her husband insisted on her sexual submission. Large numbers of the daughters' generation, on the other hand, were the first to assert that women should control their own fertility, that fertility itself was a specifically female power and a naturally feminine domain. In arguing for a woman's right to bodily integrity in marriage and in advocating mechanical as well as behavioral forms of contraception, late-century women separated the individual woman from biological determinism. This was a radical consciousness change made visible by women in various ways.[4]

Although the late-century woman was willing to accept her husband's opinions, preferences, and decisions in most matters, she was less and less willing to submit to his sexual demands without protest. The earlier generation fretted over male passion and endured it whenever necessary, but in the latter part of the nineteenth century women began to complain publicly of sexually abusive husbands, seeing frequency of intercourse, not specific sexual acts, as abusive.[5] Sex reformers, from advocates of free love to conservative champions of voluntary motherhood, vigorously denounced the ideal of female sexual submission. Isabella Hooker claimed in 1874 that it is scarcely an exaggeration to say that, so far in the history of our race, the unreasoning and inordinate indulgence of animal passion on the part of the man, and affectionate submission of the part of the woman, have had more to do with the continuance of the race than paternal or maternal instinct, or considerations of any other sort whatever.[6]

A popular birth control reformer, Edward Foote, received hundreds of letters from women telling of their personal struggles with sexual submission. One woman wrote of her husband: "Though he is a good man, there has not been a day in five years that I would not have felt it a glorious relief to have him brought to me dead. . . . Love is one thing and lust another."[7] While these writers indicated that sexual submission was still quite a problem, the public nature of the protest is significant. Women were beginning to feel more self-righteous in their refusals and less saintly in their acquiescence. Among radical and conservative writers and lecturers, a woman's "right to herself" was a common demand.[8]

The assertion of women's right to bodily integrity within marriage was reflected in more concrete ways as well. Because of late-century legal reform (fought for by feminists), divorce was a real option for middle-class American women for the first time. In her study of late-nineteenth- and early-twentieth-century marriage and divorce records, Elaine Tyler May found that women very commonly sought divorce because of too frequent sexual demands by husbands.[9] Although only a small number of women obtained divorce in the nineteenth century, the numbers were large by the standards of the time. A visible minority of women were willing to bring their husbands to court over the issue of sexual submission. The husbands still maintained that it was the wife's duty to submit to her husband, and most (male) judges agreed, but it is significant of a change in consciousness among women that sexual submission was brought into the public courtroom.

Another indication that women were asserting their rights to themselves within marriage was the continued dramatic decline in fertility in the late-century period, especially among native-born white women. In 1880, US fertility was lower than that in any other country in the world except France. The widespread public concern among men about population decline and race suicide reflected the belief that women were in charge of fertility. Male writers accused women of frivolous motives for not having babies, or, more correctly, for not having enough babies, but all the critics assumed it was a female decision.[10]

Even if public figures proclaimed women solely responsible for the lower birth rate, the new techniques of birth control as well as the standard means, abstinence and withdrawal, required cooperation on the part of the man. The voluntary motherhood crusaders and the sex radicals argued on behalf of a woman's right to herself, and that certainly gave women moral support in their struggle for fewer pregnancies, but marriage laws did not sanction a woman's right to herself. Middle-class women succeeded in their struggle for fertility control because men were willing to cooperate. Male attitudes about women and about their own sexuality formed a significant part of women's "given" situation in marriage. Late-century men were raised by what I have been referring to as the "maternal generation," and that experience influenced their ideas about sex and women.

Many writers have discussed male ideas about sexuality and women in the late-century period, but few have related those attitudes to childhood experience or to actual behavior with women. An early exception is Bryan Strong. In his article about sex and incest in the nineteenth-century family, Strong points out that the separate woman's sphere that boys occupied for the first years of their lives resulted in very mixed notions about women and sex.[11] Mother's sphere was not only "pure," religious, divorced from carnality, but mother also was a representative of chaste womanhood: sexless, good, moral, loving. Father, on the other hand, was a distant figurehead embodying the secular, exciting male world, which the boy's mother scorned yet respected. Such a childhood was bound to make adult life at least a little ambivalent for late-century men. Strong argues that men, forced into the sordid world and bereft of close male models, felt uneasy about sexuality and unsure about "manhood." This led them to split women into categories of "good" and "bad," the former to be enthroned in the home as wife/(mother) and the latter to be confined to the world as sex object/prostitute. The wife/(mother) was not to be pressed with sexual demands and was thought of as pure and sexless. In addition to this psychosexual dimension, late-century men were also beset with medical literature encouraging moderation in sexual matters and with a general cultural preoccupation with control (in architecture, medicine, government, business).[12] The late-century woman who asserted a "right to herself" with such a husband had a good chance of success.[13]

It is important to see women's experience of birth control in the late-century period as a rejection of physical submission on the one hand and as an assertion of self-control on the other. Although men idealized the sexlessness of women, at least some late-century women were indeed very sexual. In medical and lay writing, the erotic possibilities of the clitoris were discussed, and writers assumed women experienced pleasure in the sexual embrace. One medical writer described the clitoris as "the seat of special sensation," and explained that it becomes "somewhat enlarged and hardened when the passions are excited."[14] Elizabeth Blackwell, a conservative on sexual matters, maintained that women enjoyed sex as well as men, and medical writers also felt the need to caution women that they could become pregnant even when they did not feel "voluptuous sensations."[15] As Carl Degler found in his study of a small group of late-century women, sexual passion was an experience that at least some women expected.[16] Fertility control, when abstinence was used, was an issue of self-control for the woman, as well as a struggle to control her husband's sexuality by asserting a right to herself.

Although late-century women controlled fertility in basically the same ways their mothers had, mostly through abstinence, withdrawal, and abortion, their experience of birth control was very different from their mothers' in several important ways. As we have seen, they lived in a time when fertility was seen as controllable by both "natural" and mechanical means, they were less ambivalent about asserting their rights to bodily integrity in marriage, and they were more successful than the earlier generation partly because their husbands were more willing to cooperate. The daughters' experience of abortion was also different from their mothers' and involved a heightened sense of urgency about self-control.

In the 1870s and 1880s, through the efforts of the American Medical Association and one physician (Horatio Storer) who launched a personal crusade on behalf of the unborn, abortion was made a criminal offense. This new illegality of a once major means of birth control altered the material conditions of reproduction for the daughters' generation. To be sure, there were still abortions performed, but the competent, professional abortionists advertising their services in newspapers were no longer available to women. Instead, abortion became a dangerous, back-alley procedure for poor women and a relatively infrequent, physician-granted procedure for middle-class women and unmarried women of both groups. James Mohr, in his *Abortion in America*, reported that physicians performed abortion in the period 1880 to 1900 predominantly on unmarried women.[17]

Medical and lay writers, women and men, condemned abortion as a birth control procedure, just as similar writers had done in the early and mid-century periods. Abortion was considered a "crime" against the woman's body, a "risk of life and health."[18] Women were "victims" of abortion because of the unhealthful sexual indulgence of their husbands.[19] Among late-century writers on abortion, the necessity, health, and workability of abstinence or withdrawal was loudly proclaimed, and abortion was condemned as indicative of a failure in self-control.[20]

Although these views were very similar to those expressed in an earlier period, the growing difficulty of obtaining abortion made it more imperative that birth control succeed. To the late-century woman who wanted few children, wifely submission was no longer an "option" because, unlike her mother, the late-century woman had fewer reliable abortionists available to her. The criminalization of abortion made self-control and the control of husbands' sexuality more justifiable, and likewise made sexual submission less laudable or reasonable. The altered conditions of the daughters' adult world challenged a central tenet of early and mid-nineteenth-century "true womanhood."

Late-century women's experience of fertility control led some of them to question sexual submission and to praise self-control and bodily integrity as a necessary right. Likewise, in the experience of birth and late-century medical care, the daughters' generation came to challenge another physically based thesis of true womanhood: the necessity of feminine suffering. By the last two to three decades of the nineteenth century, anesthesia in the form of chloroform and ether became a common remedy for birth pain for middle- and upper-class women.[21] In this same time span, the gradual acceptance of antiseptic technique reduced the risk of puerperal fever, the leading cause of maternal mortality in childbirth.[22] Because of these two new practices, birth was physically easier and safer for the daughters' generation than it had been for their early- and mid-century mothers. Late-century women's challenge to the ideal of feminine suffering grew out of these new material conditions, but in a complicated way.

Historian Judith Walzer Leavitt has argued that the most significant change in childbirth practices was the hospitalization of childbirth which occurred in the early twentieth century.[23] Leavitt finds women's perceptions of birth also changed with the beginning of hospitalization. Whereas nineteenth-century women associated pain and danger with childbirth, twentieth-century women began to expect and demand a birth experience that was painless and safe. Although real change in women's experience of birth begins in the last quarter of the nineteenth century (routine anesthesia, beginning of antiseptic technique, and birth repair), women's expectations of childbirth did not change significantly until women gave birth in hospitals.

The apparent contradiction between women's expectations of childbirth and women's actual experience in the late nineteenth century eventually led to a change in women's expectations, but a generation later. Late-century women contributed an intermediate step to this consciousness shift: the recognition that female-specific pain and suffering were controllable. Only after one generation experiences the change can the next generation begin to expect a different experience.

The women of the late nineteenth century expected childbirth to be painful and dangerous partly because of their own mothers' birth experiences and partly because their birth attendants, male physicians, saw birth as "naturally" painful and dangerous. Most late-century male physicians and medical advisors took for granted that pregnancy and birth were traumatic experiences. One physician wrote of the sacrifices of motherhood as indicative of the intensity of a mother's love: "She . . . endures the pains of childbirth—many times suffering from the earliest period of gestation until long after delivery, to attain the joys of motherhood."[24] Another man called birth "that awful awful torture," while still another referred to delivery as "throes of agony, the days of prostration, of invalidism."[25] According to George Austin's *Perils of American Women: or, A Doctor's Talk With Maiden, Wife, and Mother*, after conceiving a child a woman was doomed to "labor and suffering" and "must bring it into the world in the midst of cruel pains."[26]

For women who employed male birth attendants, the common medical rhetoric of childbirth must have been influential. In addition, the medical attitude corresponded to what daughters had witnessed and been told of their mothers' birth experiences. According to popular sources and women's personal accounts, most middle-class women were convinced that pregnancy and birth were disease-like processes. Like their mothers, late-century women continued to hide during pregnancy, reflecting their belief in the inherent abnormality of their condition. They also were said to "prefer" the supine position of giving birth, a position introduced and eventually made mandatory by physicians.[27] It is not surprising that these women believed, with their physicians, that birth pain was natural.

Even if most women associated birth with pain, the fact that anesthesia was available to most middle-class women who were attended by physicians meant that women could "escape" their biologically natural pain. Thus, the connection between the suffering female body and the "femininity" of suffering and self-abnegation was not part of the daughters' experience in the same way as it was part of the mothers' experience. Although suffering was part of the daughters' expectation and part of the rhetoric of womanhood that they inherited, physical suffering was newly controllable for them. The female body could undergo pain in its most female function, birth, yet social intervention could eliminate that pain. If the earlier generation idealized suffering because it seemed so necessarily female, the daughters' generation had no direct experience to lead them to such an idealization.

Evidence that late-century women repudiated the ideal of feminine suffering is mostly negative: the absence of the rhetoric of feminine suffering. Unlike their mothers who constantly sang praises of feminine suffering and linked it to birth and motherhood, the daughters were either silent or contrary in their writings about suffering. In the late nineteenth century, there were no glowing descriptions of female pain as redemptive, no boasts of feminine suffering as the source of woman's power and influence. Some women went so far as to challenge the female necessity of suffering by asserting that birth pain and sickly pregnancies were *un*natural. Their arguments were along the same lines as those offered to prove frailty was unnatural. Socialization and feminine lifestyle were responsible for painful births and problem pregnancies, they claimed. Suffering, according to this view, was due to convention, not to nature.

Mary Terhune told her readers, "Pregnancy is no more a disease than is the ripening of a peach."[28] Alice Stockham bemoaned the fact that many women saw pregnancy as "one long nightmare" accompanied by "physical sufferings and mental agonies." But she related this physical difficulty to socialization into weakness and to the belief that reproduction is an ordeal. She claimed that suffering during pregnancy and birth was unnatural because suffering would be a "violation of nature's laws."[29] Stockham insisted that women would not suffer in pregnancy and childbirth if they took care of themselves and if they believed in their own wellness. Marie Dewing, in *From Attic to Cellar; A Book for Young Housekeepers*, agreed with Stockham. "Every one we see has been born," she observed. "If it were so difficult a matter some other way would have been found for bringing children into the world." Dewing blamed "the artificial life we lead, and conventional restraints of clothes and habits" for women's unnatural experience of pain.[30]

In a book entitled *Easy Favorable Child Bearing, A Book for All Women*, Eutocia Cook, a female physician, tied together many of the ideas expressed by her contemporaries about women and physical suffering. According to Cook, menstruation "should be as painless as digestion."[31] She maintained that nausea and dizziness during pregnancy were unnatural and that a woman should not even feel her pregnancy until quickening. Birth, too, was considered a natural, healthful experience by Cook, and she told of her own work delivering over two thousand babies: "One in thirty has had a so-called hard labor."[32] According to Cook, women could have "easy, favorable childbearing" if only they would learn about their bodies, take care of themselves, and employ female physicians. And Cook added that women's lives, full of monotonous, repetitive hard labor, compounded their physical problems. She suggested that women get angry and refuse to do their "duties."

Easy Favorable Child Bearing also contained a radically different view of the female body itself. Cook praised the female body as powerful and miraculous, calling the uterus "wonderfully strong and elastic" and noting that women's uteri were "as different in individuals as are their faces."[33] The uterus was described as an almost magical organ: "When empty the womb will not contain a tablespoonful, yet it will grow so as to contain twins, two after-births, and from a pint to a quart of water."[34] This was a definite break with male medical thought, which tied women to reproductive organs that were inherently sickly and somewhat disgusting. The idea that women's physical power of reproduction was awesome and beautiful led very easily to the idea that women were "naturally" superior because of their maternal function, a concept which became basic to turn-of-the-century feminine ideology.

Women who wrote about the possibility of painless childbirth or who claimed pain and suffering could be avoided by changing living habits were not new to the late-century period. Some health reformers had suggested similar ideas in the early nineteenth century. What makes the later writers significant is not the total originality of their position, but the altered nature of the discourse into which they fit. Earlier health reformers wrote as an alternative voice, competing with a popular literature, both fictional and advisory, which linked suffering to femininity. The later writers had no such opposition from women-authored literature. Certainly there were differences among the late-century health advocates; some urged the use of anesthesia to free women from pain while others stressed that pain itself was unnatural and women should avoid anesthesia and instead alter their living patterns. But neither group had to contend with the literature of suffering womanhood.

By the late nineteenth century advisors were no longer celebrating the femininity of suffering because a significant number of women no longer experienced physical suffering as inherently female. Because anesthesized, relatively safe childbirth freed late-century women of the biological necessity of female pain and eased the sense of female danger, these women began to repudiate the ideal of "feminine" suffering. Even if late-century women expected birth to be traumatic, as their mothers and birth attendants did, many found the experience to be manageable with the help of scientific medicine. Hence, as a generation, they were less inclined to write about womanhood as an ordeal and more inclined to write and read about ways to control or eliminate female pain.

In addition to making childbirth pain and danger more manageable, scientific medicine also brought female pain and debility more under control in the late nineteenth century with the development of gynecological surgery. Although many feminist historians see late nineteenth-century gynecology as anti-woman and late-century doctors as neurotic or even sadistic,[35] there were significant advances in surgical technique and in the safety of surgery that were beneficial to middle-class women. The operation to repair rectal-vaginal fistula, a debilitating birth-trauma injury, was perfected during the late-century period. Previously, women who suffered from this condition were permanent invalids. Episiotomy, a surgical incision in the perineum to prevent tearing during labor, can also be considered a positive innovation because episiotomy was more easily repaired than a tear. Caesarean section was also possible during the late nineteenth century, whereas previous cases requiring section either resulted in ruptured uterus (and death) or septic surgery (and death).[36] Even the sexual surgery of the time, clitorectomy and ovariotomy, must be assessed in terms of the women involved, and not in terms of armchair psychologizing as to doctors' motives or late twentieth-century horror over women's "victimization." Middle-class women sought sexual surgery, although certainly misguided and operating under assumptions most women today would find unbelievable and repulsive. For the women who went to doctors seeking a scientific solution to moodiness or unhappiness or the proclivity to masturbation, clitorectomies and ovariotomies were ways to assert control. No matter how we see these procedures today, late-century women believed in the efficacy of these cures and sought body-control, and therefore self-control, through gynecological surgery.[37] Because of these innovations, the female body was less subject to nature in the late nineteenth century than previously.

Women's lack of body-control and women's physical suffering in the early and mid-nineteenth century contributed to the idealization of submission and self-lessness as feminine characteristics. In the late nineteenth century, because women's physical experience changed in important ways, the body-as-symbol also changed. Health as natural and attainable, the female body as controllable, female reproduction as not necessarily painful—these experiences contributed to a new feminine synthesis, a new sense of what is natural to womanhood. Partially because of this late-nineteenth-century experience of body, the daughters were able to construct a powerful, active idea of "woman's nature" that provided a rationale for domesticating the public sphere. Before considering the daughters' new feminine synthesis, however, a final look at the mother/daughter relationship is in order.

NOTES

1. Linda Gordon, *Woman's Body, Woman's Right* (New York: Penguin Books, 1977), chapter 5.

2. This mistaken view of the "safe period" was common in nineteenth-century writing. See: William M. Capp, *The Daughter: Her Health, Education and Wedlock* (Philadelphia: F. A. Davis, 1891), p. 95; Prudence B. Saur, *Maternity: A Book for Every Wife and Mother* (Chicago: L. P. Miller, 1891), p. 24. Alice B. Stockham, *Tokology; A Book for Every Woman* (Chicago: A. M. Stockham & Co., 1889), p. 235; Ezra Harvey Heywood, *Cupid's Yokes* (Princeton, MA: by the author, 1877), p. 19; George Napheys, *The Physical Life of Woman: Advice to the Maiden, Wife and Mother* (Philadelphia: G. Maclean, 1870), p. 69.

3. George Austin, *Perils of American Women; or, A Doctor's Talk with Maiden, Wife, and Mother* (Boston: Lee & Shepard, 1883), p. 98.

4. Estelle Freedman, "Sexuality in Nineteenth-Century America: Behavior, Ideology, and Politics," *Reviews in American History*, 10:4(1982), 197–215, and Gordon, *Woman's Body, Woman's Right*, both consider this separation of sex and reproduction as representing major behavioral and ideological change.

5. See Elaine Tyler May, *Great Expectations: Marriage and Divorce in Post-Victorian America* (Chicago: University of Chicago Press, 1980).

6. Isabella Beecher Hooker, *Womanhood: Its Sanctities and Fidelities* (Boston: Lee & Shepard, 1874), p. 13. See also Mary Edwards Walker, *A Woman's Thoughts About Love and Marriage, and Divorce* (New York: Miller, 1871), pp. 25–26.

7. Edward Foote, *The Radical Remedy in Social Science; or, Borning Better Babies Through Regulating Reproduction by Controlling Conception* (New York: Murray Hill Publishing Co., 1886), p. 104. See also Eliza Barton Lyman, *The Coming Woman; The Royal Road to Perfection, A Series of Medical Lectures* (Lansing, MI: W. S. George, 1880), p. 207.

8. See: Saur, *Maternity*, pp. 168–169; Heywood, *Cupid's Yokes*, pp. 4, 17; James Caleb Jackson, *American Womanhood; Its Peculiarities and Necessities* (Danville, NY: Austin, Jackson, 1870), p. 88; Alonzo Newton, *The Better Way: An Appeal to Men on Behalf of Human Culture through a Wiser Parentage* (New York: Wook & Holbrook, 1875); John H. Dye, *Painless Childbirth; or, Healthy Mothers and Healthy Children, A Book for Women* (Silver Creek, NY: The Local Printing House, 1882), p. 28; Mary Elizabeth Sargent, ed. *Sketches and Reminiscences of the Radical Club of Chestnut Street, Boston* (Boston: J. R. Osgood & Co., 1880), p. 210; *Should Women Obey?* (Chicago: E. Loomis & Co., 1900); Lyman, *The Coming Woman*, p. 224.

9. May, *Great Expectations*, p. 105.

10. Gordon, *Woman's Body, Woman's Right*, chapter 7.

11. Bryan Strong, "Toward a History of the Experiential Family: Sex and Incest in the Nineteenth-Century Family," *Journal of Marriage and the Family*, 35(1973), 457–466.

12. See: Anita Clair Fellman and Michael Fellman, *Making Sense of Self: Medical*

Advice Literature in Late Nineteenth-Century America (Philadelphia: University of Pennsylvania Press, 1981); Clifford E. Clark, Jr., "Domestic Architecture as an Index to Social History: The Romantic Revival and the Cult of Domesticity in America, 1840–1870," *Journal of Interdisciplinary History*, 7(1976), 33–56; Robert Wiebe, *The Search for Order* (New York: Hill & Wang, 1967); see also the literature on the social purity movement: Gordon, *Woman's Body, Woman's Right*, pp. 116–126; David J. Pivar, *Purity Crusade: Sexual Morality and Social Control, 1868–1900* (Westport, CT: Greenwood Press, 1973); William Leach, *True Love and Perfect Union: The Feminist Reform of Sex and Society* (New York: Basic Books, 1980); Howard I. Kushnew, "Nineteenth-Century Sexuality and the 'Sexual Revolution' of the Progressive Era," *Canadian Review of American Studies*, 9(1978), 34–49.

13. See: Charles E. Rosenberg, "Sexuality, Class and Role in Nineteenth-Century America," in *The American Man*, ed. Elizabeth H. Pleck and Joseph H. Pleck (Englewood Cliffs, NJ: Prentice-Hall, 1980), pp. 219–254; David G. Pugh, *Sons of Liberty: The Masculine Mind in Nineteenth-Century America* (Westport, CT: Greenwood Press, 1983).

14. Saur, *Maternity*, p. 17.

15. Elizabeth Blackwell, *The Human Element in Sex* (London: J. A. Churchill, 1894), p. 51. See also: Austin, *Perils of American Women*, pp. 28, 87, 45; Stockham, *Tokology*, p. 326; Eutocia Cook, *Easy Favorable Child Bearing; A Book for All Women* (Chicago: Arcade Publishing Co., 1886, fourth edition), p. 67.

16. Carl Degler, "What Ought to Be and What Was: Women's Sexuality in the Nineteenth Century," *American Historical Review*, 79(1974), 1467–1490.

17. About the change in abortion laws, see: James Mohr, *Abortion in America: The Origins and Evolution of National Policy, 1800–1900* (New York: Oxford University Press, 1978); R. Sauer, "Attitudes to Abortion in America, 1800–1973," *Population Studies*, 28(1974), 53–67.

18. Stockham, *Tokology*, p. 246; Austin, *Perils of American Women*, p. 89. See also Mary Terhune, *Eve's Daughters; or Common Sense for Maid, Wife, and Mother* (New York: J. R. Anderson & H. S. Allen, 1882), p. 433.

19. Cook, *Easy Favorable Child Bearing*, p. 48. See also Lyman, *The Coming Woman*, p. 252.

20. Newton, *The Better Way*, pp. 19, 25–27. See also: Cook, *Easy Favorable Child Bearing*, p. 59; Jackson, *American Womanhood*, pp. 90–92; Mohr, *Abortion in America*, p. 105; Napheys, *The Physical Life of Woman*, pp. 98–99; Dye, *Painless Childbirth*, pp. 15, 28; Heywood, *Cupid's Yokes*, pp. 4, 17, 21; Foote, *The Radical Remedy*.

21. See: Richard Wertz and Dorothy Wertz, *Lying-In: A History of Childbirth in America* (New York: Schocken Books, 1977), chapter 4; and Martin S. Pernick, *A Calculus of Suffering: Pain, Professionalization, and Anesthesia in Nineteenth-Century America* (New York: Columbia University Press, 1985).

22. Wertz and Wertz, *Lying-In*, chapter 4.

23. Judith Walzer Leavitt, *Brought to Bed: Childbearing in America, 1750–1950* (New York: Oxford University Press, 1986). Wertz and Wertz make the same argument in *Lying-In*.

24. Dye, *Painless Childbirth*, p. 25.

25. Foote, *The Radical Remedy*, p. 104; Edward Hooker Dewy, *A New Era for Woman; Health without Drugs* (Northwich, CT: C. C. Haskell & Co., 1898), p. 323.

26. Austin, *Perils of American Women*, p. 33.

27. Dye, *Painless Childbirth*, p. 152; Stockham, *Tokology*, p. 177.

28. Terhune, *Eve's Daughters*, p. 441.

29. Stockham, *Tokology*, p. 174.

30. Marie Dewing, *From Attic to Cellar; A Book for Young Housekeepers* (New York: G. P. Putnam's Sons, 1879), p. 111. This idea was also expressed by Saur, *Maternity*, pp. 195–197.

31. Cook, *Easy Favorable Child Bearing*, p. 71.

32. Cook, *Easy Favorable Child Bearing*, p. 89.

33. Cook, *Easy Favorable Child Bearing*, p. 40, 42.

34. Cook, *Easy Favorable Child Bearing*, p. 43.

35. For expressions of this attitude see: G. J. Barker-Benfield, *The Horrors of the Half-Known Life* (New York: Harper & Row, 1976); Anne Douglas Wood, " 'The Fashionable Diseases': Women's Complaints and Their Treatment in Nineteenth-Century America," *Journal of Interdisciplinary History*, 4(1973), 25–52; Barbara Ehrenreich and Deirdre English, *Complaints and Disorders: The Sexual Politics of Sickness* (Old Westbury, NY: The Feminist Press, 1974). Leavitt, *Brought to Bed*, offers a more balanced view of the relationship between women and medicine; she argues that the various procedures surrounding childbirth were the product of women's and doctors' decisions. She also demonstrates the diversity of opinion within the medical profession on various procedures.

36. Wertz and Wertz, *Lying-In*, pp. 139–140; James V. Ricci, *The Development of Gynaecological Surgery and Instruments* (Philadelphia: Blakiston Co., 1949).

37. It is important not to underestimate these cures, even when twentieth-century medicine can demonstrate that they had no physical effect on the symptoms. A cure often has more to do with believing in the cure than with actual physiological cause/effect mechanisms, as recent scientific studies of placebos indicate. It is also important to understand that these women were seeking gynecological surgery to cure "diseases" that were themselves created by the time. Masturbation as a sickness and moodiness as ovary-induced were rooted in late nineteenth-century notions of sexuality and female body that were basically misogynistic. A woman who sought a "cure" was very much like the late twentieth-century woman who "cures" her depression with silicone breast implants. In both cases, the surgery is meant to physically correct a defect so that the woman can more closely approximate her culture's image of a "feminine" woman.

CHAPTER 8

Mothers and Daughters: The "Green Sickness" and Daughters' Ambivalence

As we have seen, both clinical observation and social-psychological theory indicate that the child-nurturing context of the privatized nuclear family produces definite consequences for mothers and daughters. The structure itself leads to an intensely close mother/daughter relationship and over-identification on the part of both mother and daughter. For the girl, gender is personified; the daughter's sense of femininity is fused with her sense of mother-as-female. We saw, too, that this structural feature of the middle-class family was accentuated in the nineteenth century by the woman's world Carroll Smith-Rosenberg has described. Not only were daughters raised in constant proximity to their female parent, but they were also part of their mothers' female community from infancy, through girlhood, to womanhood. They were constantly surrounded by live examples of their futures as women.

The feminine ideology that mid-century mothers passed on to daughters stressed suffering, self-abnegation, and submission as basic to "true womanhood," but the daughters' new experience as women made these "virtues" less relevant. Within the psychosexual structure of same-sex parenting and in a historical situation further encouraging intense mother/daughter identification, struggle between mothers and adolescent daughters would be avoidable only if daughters believed their lives would exactly replicate their mothers' lives. This is precisely what Smith-Rosenberg assumes to have been the case; supposedly, the daughter moved easily, without ambivalence, from girlhood into a womanhood like her mother's, and so mother and daughter felt no conflict and daughter was not concerned about her approaching womanhood.[1] But for daughters born in the mid-century period, this was not the story. The future included different possibilities. The necessity of feminine suffering, the propriety of non-domestic education, the assumption of self-denying motherhood as the natural and exclusive lifework of adult women—these were opened to question by the 1870s. Theoretically, the growing difference between their two worlds should have led to some degree of mother/daughter tension and to some uneasiness over the transition into womanhood.[2]

But how does the historian investigate intergenerational ambivalence? Letters between mothers and daughters surely would not indicate much tension or hostility, and, in fact, letters tend to sentimentalize the relationship between the correspondents.[3] It is possible to detect ambivalence in some women's diaries, by reading closely and between the lines, but failure to find ambivalence in diaries does not mean that it wasn't felt. A different kind of evidence is needed to explore possible mother/daughter conflict and uneasy transition from girlhood to womanhood.

One possible source of information about adolescent role conflict in the mid- to late-nineteenth century is psychosomatic illness. Many historians have argued convincingly that mental illness and psychosomatic illness can be interpreted functionally; that is, the illness can be viewed as an individual or group response to particular social conditions or cultural values. Carroll Smith-Rosenberg in her study of hysteria, Howard Feinstein in his study of neurasthenia in the James family, and Christopher Lasch in his study of narcissism argue that such illnesses are social phenomena and have wider significance than their individual sufferers.[4] The presence of mental or psychosomatic illness which is induced or aggravated by specific social or cultural conditions suggests that those conditions are also problematic in a less intense way for non-sufferers. Furthermore, the illness itself is merely an extreme response, an overreaction, that the healthy or the sane exhibit in less dramatic ways. In Lasch's words, "Pathology represents a heightened version of normality."[5]

Viewing psychosomatic illness as social commentary as well as individual malady can provide new information about nineteenth-century adolescence in what I have been calling the daughters' generation. Although women's letters to their mothers do not indicate hostility or tension and although there is little written evidence of difficult transitions into adulthood, some adolescent girls born in the mid-century period developed a psychosomatic illness known as chlorosis. Beginning around puberty and ending by age 25, chlorosis was an illness unique to adolescent women. Although the disease was reported as early as the sixteenth century, medical observers agreed that it was an increasingly widespread problem in the mid- to late nineteenth century, some even declaring chlorosis to be of epidemic proportions. By the beginning of the First World War, however, chlorosis had vanished as a commonly diagnosed medical problem.[6] Because it was directly related to adolescence and in fact was "cured" by physical maturity, and because it seemed to flourish in the 1870s and 1880s, chlorosis can provide information about the struggles of adolescent girls in that particular time.

Although chlorosis was named for the greenish color of its victims, medical historians believe this symptom was not actually characteristic. Besides the age and sex of its sufferers and the expectation of recovery, the most outstanding features of the disease were amenorrhoea (the absence of menses), a disturbed mental state, a pronounced disturbance of appetite, loss of weight, and a tendency to relapse in the third or fourth decades of life. Medical historians have puzzled over the nature and cause of chlorosis, but the most common explanation has been that chlorosis was a type of anemia. This explanation does not address the question of the special characteristics of the 1870s and 1880s that might have produced the anemia or made it more noticeable to medical writers. If we add a psychological dimension to the interpretation, a clearer image emerges. I. S. L. Loudon has argued in "Chlorosis, Anemia, and Anorexia Nervosa" that chlorosis was a functional disorder, psychologically rooted, which was closely related to anorexia nervosa: willful self-starvation accompanied by a distorted body image.[7] Loudon describes chlorosis in Great Britain and sees it as a manifestation of middle-class concerns over self-control at a time when such control was valued as a sign of middle-class status.

Although I will offer a different interpretation of the meaning of chlorosis, I agree with Loudon that the disease was another name for anorexia. Mid-nineteenth-century medical writers in the United States described chlorosis in terms very similar to twentieth-century descriptions of anorexia. Chlorosis was always associated with "young unmarried women" around the age of fourteen or fifteen, sometimes extending from fourteen to twenty.[8] "It never occurs except at or near the age of puberty," one physician noted.[9] Loss of appetite was a characteristic of chlorosis according to nineteenth-century writers. A "capricious appetite," "feeble appetite and digestion," and "eating little" were noted to accompany the disorder.[10] "One of the most frequent causes of the disease ... is *starvation*, as if the food prepared is at fault," one physician remarked.[11] In addition to appetite loss and age, a second commonly noted symptom of chlorosis was depression and a longing for solitude. Chlorotic girls were said to have "disturbing emotions," to be "low-spirited," and to "weep easily."[12] They also were described as having a "distaste for exertion and society."[13] Prudence Saur, a mid-century physician, described the chlorotic girl: "She is sad, subject to fits of weeping, and prefers to be alone."[14] These three characteristics (puberty related, appetite disturbance, depression) are also commonly associated with anorexia.

Further indication that chlorosis was what today would be diagnosed as anorexia is the nineteenth-century use of the term "anorexia." Physicians considered anorexia to be a symptom of physiological disorder, not as a disease in and of itself. They used the term "anorexia" to mean "loss of appetite."[15] Many physicians in the mid- to late nineteenth century explained the anorexia of chlorosis as related to the connection between the reproductive system and the digestive system. Some related the symptoms of chlorosis, including anorexia, to low hemoglobin. Even physicians who explained chlorosis as due to cultural or environmental factors, such as overeducation or overwork, believed the symptoms were physiologically induced. In an article entitled "Cases of Neurasthenia or Chlorosis," the physician-authors concluded that their cases were neurasthenia and not chlorosis because they displayed only psychological symptoms.[16]

Physicians did not see chlorosis as anorexia because they were looking for physical causes for the loss of appetite, refusal of food, and vomiting of food thought to be a symptom of chlorosis. Not until the twentieth century, with the growing influence of Freud and psychoanalysis, did "anorexia nervosa" become a popular diagnostic category and physicians begin to focus on psychological origins. At the same time, chlorosis began to disappear as a disease.[17]

Although most nineteenth-century physicians searched for a physical cause of the symptoms of chlorosis, many recognized the malady as a "nervous disorder" and some even identified malnutrition as the most significant symptom. A French physician quoted in an approving article in an American medical journal noted that "nervous troubles" were "extended," "profound," and "rebellious" in chlorosis.[18] An American physician, William H. Thompson, asserted that chlorosis was caused by a nervous disorder which affected the "nutritive organs." Thompson went on to say that a clear view of "anaemia, chlorosis, hysteria, et cetera" would only come with knowledge of the interrelationship of the "nerves" and the "organs concerned in nutrition."[19] For Dr. Thompson, anorexia and/or the rejection of food (vomiting) was the first manifestation of chlorosis.

The entire alimentary apparatus, from beginning to end, commences to act strangely. First of all, the nervous sensation of hunger disappears, to be replaced perhaps by the most curious and capricious manifestation indicative of perverted nervous transmission. The stomach frequently rejects food, or deals with it most uneasily.[20]

James McShane, a Baltimore physician, viewed chlorosis as "essentially a disease of the nervous system." He linked the malady to emotion, disappointment, city life, and a sedentary life, and described the psychological symptoms as "hysterical."[21] In "Cases of Chlorosis," the physician-author reported two cases of young women who were "afflicted with persistent vomiting" which left them weak and pale.[22] Each of these physicians described symptoms that today would be diagnosed as anorexia.

One nineteenth-century physician, Charles E. Simon of Baltimore, came closest to recognizing chlorosis as anorexia. Writing in the *American Journal of the Medical Sciences* of thirty-one cases of chlorosis, Simon reviewed the current theories as to the etiology of the disease and offered his own opinion based on case studies and reading other physicians' case studies. "The writer has been led to the conclusion," he wrote, "that in the great majority of cases chlorosis is essentially a disease of malnutrition, the result very frequently of abnormal feeding in early childhood."[23] He asserted that "every physician probably has seen cases of chlorosis in which body weight was 95 pounds or even less," and he noted that the "capricious appetite" of chlorotic girls is "proverbial." One of his own cases weighed 74 pounds. Simon thought that chlorosis was brought on by emotional or environmental, not physical causes, and he listed early habits of low protein eating, mental strain, sedentary habits, sexual excess (masturbation), worry, and grief as "causes" in his case studies. He also noted the pattern associated with the onset of anorexia by twentieth-century writers: the gradual elimination of various foods from the diet. "This and that article of food is thought to disagree and is abandoned, until finally a condition develops where the patient is practically starving."[24] It shouldn't be surprising that Simon treated chlorosis with a high protein diet (and a pint of dark beer daily).

If chlorosis was an early name for anorexia, what was the meaning of the malady for nineteenth-century girls? One possibility is that the chlorotic girl was simply trying to approximate the maternal generation's ideal of feminine beauty, and, like the modern anorexic, was displaying extreme behavior that was typical, in less dramatic forms, of young women in general. In the twentieth century, when most American women are either actively dieting or think they should be, the anorexic takes fashionable thinness to the point of absurdity. In the mid-nineteenth century, when paleness, fainting spells, and general "delicacy" were idealized as romantic and feminine, the chlorotic girl was the romantic heroine *par excellence*. Nineteenth-century writers noted that thinness was part of the ideal of feminine beauty: "invalidism, pallor, small appetite, and a languid mode of speech and manner" were considered fashionable in the mid-century period.[25] A foreign visitor noticed "too much thinness" among American girls.[26] And Jerome Smith, a mid-century physician, wrote: "No calamity is more dreaded than fat in an aspiring young lady." He went on to say that young women's "partial starvation" sometimes "degenerates into an insane determination to be the shadow, rather than the substance, of a live woman,"[27] a very apt comment about the deeper, psychological issues involved in chlorosis/anorexia. A British physician also interpreted the anorexia of chlorosis as prompted by cultural norms: "She thinks of her appearance and tightens her waist. Afraid of getting fat, she stints herself in food, and eats of only dainty things."[28] Like the twentieth-century anorexic, the nineteenth-century chlorotic girl can be interpreted as taking her culture's ideal of feminine beauty to its suicidal limits. Her pathology expressed an exaggerated normality.

While consideration of fashion might have prompted some cases of chlorosis/anorexia, there were deeper issues involved then as now. A 110-pound woman whose normal weight should be 125 could see herself as "fashionably thin"; when her weight drops to 85 pounds different questions must be asked. Both clinical psychiatrists and imagistic psychologists have described anorexia as an indication of acute anxiety over the adult feminine role expressed through rejection of the mature female body.[29] Both also view anorexia as a mother/daughter conflict. If applied to chlorosis, this explanation clarifies the meaning of the illness in the 1870s and 1880s adolescent world. Chlorosis was an exaggerated act of rebellion for the daughter, a temporary refusal to accept the dictates of "true womanhood" by rejecting maturity, resisting other-directedness, and declaring herself different and separate from mother—while at the same time never confronting mother directly, never specifically rejecting mother, and, in fact, imitating mother's own sickliness.

The chlorotic girl's rejection of physical maturity, and therefore the adult female role, was a dramatic acting out of a common adolescent fear carried to its extreme. In the mid-nineteenth century, when adult females continually described their lives in terms of suffering, even the healthy adolescent girl frequently experienced anxiety over her rapidly approaching maturity. Medical and lay observers testified that young women experienced puberty as a time of sickness.[30] Women also described it as a "crisis" and a "supreme emergency."[31] Girls' ignorance as to what was happening to them contributed to this healthy fear of maturity. Women wrote very frequently that mothers did not teach daughters about their bodies. More specifically, writers claimed that daughters were not taught about "the mysterious process of reproduction."[32] One woman wrote of her fear and ignorance on the eve of her mid-century marriage: "The problematic relations of marriage and its mysteries filled me with something akin to terror."[33] Another woman reported that girls commonly started their periods without knowing about menstruation.[34]

Puberty was dramatic not only because of the physical changes involved and because of body ignorance, but more so because the physical changes demanded that a girl think of herself as a woman. As her body began to resemble the mature female form and the onset of menstruation signified her physical readiness for reproduction, the cultural expectations of feminine gender became more acute for the growing girl. Associating puberty with its cultural manifestations, for example hair and dress style, young women often focused rage and disappointment on the symbols of womanhood. One wrote negatively of her dresses being let down and her curls "caught up and fastened with a matronly looking comb."[35] Another described "the traditional weight of an increased length of skirt."[36] Both viewed these womanly demands as a hinderance to activity and a cause of lament. Frances Willard gave a most revealing description of the outward changes demanded by culture to signify the girl was now a woman. She wrote in her diary:

This is my seventeenth birthday, and the date of my martyrdom. Mother insists that at last I *must* have my hair "done up woman fashion." She says she can hardly forgive herself for letting me "run wild" so long. We had a great time over it all, and here I sit. . . . My "back hair" is twisted up like a corkscrew; I carry eighteen hair-pins; my head aches, my feet are entangled in the skirt of my new gown. I can never jump over a fence again so long as I live. As for chasing the sheep down in the shady pasture, it's out of the question, and to climb down to my "Eagle's Nest" seat in the big burr oak would ruin this new frock beyond repair. Altogether, I recognize the fact that "my occupation's gone."[37]

The chlorotic girl was an exaggeration of this tension surrounding physical maturity. By reducing her food intake she became physically smaller, caused her menses to cease, and reclaimed maternal solicitude. In effect, she chose childhood over adulthood by refusing to allow her body to take on the characteristic curves and fullness of mature female form. The chlorotic girl expressed in extreme form what her more acquiescent sisters also felt: ambivalence about adult femininity.

This is especially clear when we consider physicians' case studies and the conclusions they drew from their cases. "Abnormal development of the sexual apparatus" and masturbation were cited as causes of chlorosis, indicating that adolescent awakening to sexual urges prompted some girls to stop eating.[38] One physician noted that "the process of sexual development is looked to as the time of most common occurrences of chlorosis."[39] Another noted that chlorosis was one of the most common disorders of women aged fourteen to twenty-four and concluded: "It is very natural, then, to attribute the disease to the effects of these processes which are going on in the bodies of young girls at the passage of puberty." The physician admitted, however, that no one understood the "physiological connexion" between puberty and chlorosis.[40] Many physicians, based on their experience with the disease, concluded that menstruation must in some sense "cause" chlorosis since physical maturity and chlorosis so often went together.

Physicians' interpretation of chlorosis as brought on by the physical changes associated with puberty should not be taken as necessarily "correct." However, the fact that girls were brought to physicians for chlorotic symptoms around puberty by mothers who saw their daughters as ill is significant. Girls were displaying these symptoms as their bodies were developing into women's bodies. Physicians who connected chlorosis with puberty were simply observing that chlorotic symptoms most often appeared during the transition to physical maturity.

The psychological strains of puberty, specifically the fear of womanhood, was noted by a New York physician, T. Gaillard Thomas. Thomas agreed with his colleagues that chlorosis was brought on by the changes of puberty, but thought that the emotional stress, not the physical stress, was most significant. He claimed that most chlorotic girls were brought to doctors by mothers who were concerned about their daughters' amenorrhea, obstinate constipation (a side-effect of anorexia), "or more or less rapid emaciation." Gaillard viewed chlorosis as caused by "some strong mental or emotional disturbance," and noted that "nostalgia" was regarded as "one of its most frequent causes."[41]

Some young women developed chlorosis after puberty, but several physician case studies indicate that these women, too, experienced adult femininity as threatening. Some of the older chlorotic women (between eighteen and thirty) developed chlorosis after being abandoned by lovers. In one case, a young woman developed chlorosis after being sexually aroused to the point of orgasm with her fiance. Another nineteen-year-old developed chlorosis after the wedding of a friend.[42] Like the younger girls, whose chlorosis was brought on by physical maturation, the older chlorotic young women also demonstrated ambivalence over adult roles.

Besides avoiding physical maturity, the young woman who developed chlorosis could also exert control and exercise self-direction over her life/body without rejecting her mother's world view. According to the maternal message, adult femininity demanded that a woman be passive and receptive. The "true woman" that the young girl was supposed to become was required to wait passively to be chosen in marriage, to endure patiently the physical trials of pregnancy and birth, to go quietly wherever her husband chose to live, to submit lovingly to her husband's wishes. Even in dealing with her own children, the "true woman" was not to be willful; she was to see herself as the transmitter of culture and the guardian of the young, always taking direction from husbands, clergymen, physicians, and counselors. The chlorotic girl, during the time of her illness, symbolically rejected this external control and asserted her will over her body and her environment.[43] She caused her body to diminish or grow according to her desire; she consumed indigestible substances (clay, pebbles, etc.) and elicited concern from her family; she became clinically ill (anemia was a side effect of chlorosis) and required medical attention. Like the twentieth-century anorexic, the chlorotic girl symbolically (and actually) controlled her world by controlling her body while never directly challenging her mother's world view.

The controlling aspect of chlorosis was clear in many case studies. One writer described the nervous symptoms of chlorosis as "rebellious" and another wrote that chlorosis brought on "hysterical and infantile paralysis."[44] A Baltimore physician presented case studies in 1876 in which chlorosis was said to change the "character." "The individual becomes morose, melancholic, or subject of various *whimsicalities* of disposition."[45] He hinted that such moodiness was manipulative, citing examples of chlorotic girls whose illness was cured by getting their way. A similar conclusion was drawn by a New York City physician whose chlorotic patient was "vomiting every day almost all the solids and fluids which she was prevailed upon to swallow"; the doctor treated her with a placebo and suggested that the girl's behavior was under her control and was manipulative like a hysteric's attack.[46]

The disturbed mental state accompanying chlorosis was described by many physicians as very similar to hysteria, a disease of more mature women that has been interpreted as a temporary release from role performance.[47] Like hysteria, chlorosis gave the young woman the opportunity to reject feminine other-directedness by giving her permission to be moody, infantile, and demanding. Instead of following the dictates of role that sometimes required her to provide care for others (younger siblings), to guard against angry or melancholy emotions, and to minister to the needs and desires of those around her (especially father and brothers), the chlorotic girl was freed by her illness to take, rather than give, and to express negative feelings, rather than hide behind a considerate facade.

Chlorosis put the girl in the center of the family and drew loving concern, patient understanding of moods, and gentle caretaking to her. Especially significant was the fact that the chlorotic girl received increased maternal attention in ways that she had as a very young child: motherly concern over diet and appetite, motherly pampering of fluctuating moods, motherly protection from the demands of household and household members. Regardless of the numerous theories as to what chlorosis actually was, physicians prescribed regimens that demanded increased maternal caretaking. Many recommended complete bed rest with very specific feeding routines. Almost all out-patient chlorotics were treated with some form of iron, administered by the mother. Also, since chlorosis/anorexia always involved constipation, most physicians prescribed some sort of laxative, thus making the girl's mother responsible for keeping track of her daughter's bowel movements in a way reminiscent of infancy. Instead of practicing other-directedness as "true womanhood" required, the girl suffering with chlorosis claimed the attention and concern of significant others, especially mother, without eliciting her mother's anger or disapproval.

The deepest mother/daughter questions involved in chlorosis/anorexia cannot be answered positively for the nineteenth-century malady. Although it seems logical to assume that the chlorotic girl was is some sense imitating her mother's "sickliness" or the sickliness the daughter associated with her mother's generation, physicians and therapists who work with twentieth-century anorexics see the mother's symbolic importance differently. For the twentieth-century researchers, mother is the symbol of adult femininity that daughter hopes to avoid. Anorexia maintains a distance between mother and daughter by preventing the daughter from becoming her mother, physically.

There's no way to prove this interpretation correct or incorrect for twentieth-century anorexia or nineteenth-century chlorosis, but it does provide a consistent and interesting summation of the mother/daughter dynamic in chlorotic behavior. While avoiding maturity, exerting self-control, and rejecting other-directedness, the chlorotic girl also expressed her difference from mother and her hope for a different future. The maternal body, with its curves, fullness, and fertility, represented the adolescent girl's destiny. In the feminine drama, the young woman was eventually to become her mother. But chlorosis established a physical boundary, albeit temporary, between mother and daughter, and thus hinted at different adult possibilities for the daughter. The chlorotic girl, with her slightly emaciated angularity and childlike, sexless contours, resembled her younger brother more than she did her mother. Perhaps, like him, she could escape the dictates of nature and female body. If her physical form were different enough from her mother's form, perhaps she was not predetermined to repeat her mother's life, but might, instead, have maternal permission for a different future.

Viewed within the context of the adolescent life world of the 1870s and 1880s, chlorosis can be seen as evidence that some daughters felt ambivalent about adult femininity and about their mothers as representatives of womanhood. Daughters at that time grew with a model of womanhood, an inherited feminine script, that was becoming obsolete in the transition to "modern" America. However, the structural and historical conditions defining a "female world of love and ritual" made it difficult for young women to express outright rebellion or to believe fully in a future different from their mothers'. Mother/ daughter tension and anxiety over impending womanhood surfaced in psycho-somatic symptoms. The nineteenth-century chlorotic girl was the embodiment of this tension and anxiety, but other girls who avoided the extremes of illness indicated similar feelings in their reluctant acceptance of the physical symbols of approaching womanhood, the dress and hairstyle changes that signaled the transition to a social status less free and more demanding. Although chlorosis only affected a small number of middle-class girls, it can be interpreted as an extreme form of a more pervasive, less intense adolescent response to a feminine ideology that was becoming out of touch with the changing material conditions of female life.

Faced with the female adolescent dilemma, the psychological impossibility and the experience-prompted necessity of going beyond the maternal world view, what was the response of "healthy," "normal" daughters? Most girls did not develop chlorosis; instead, as late-nineteenth-century women, they forged a new feminine synthesis from the contradictions of their mothers' world view and their own experience of a freer, less physically demanding womanhood. They created their own sense of proper femininity not by rejecting their in-herited sexual script and not by accepting it, but by amending it to express their acceptance of a world different from their mothers', while still remaining de-voted, uncritical daughters.

NOTES

1. Carroll Smith-Rosenberg, "The Female World of Love and Ritual: Relations Between Women in Nineteenth-Century America," *Signs*, 1(1975), 1–30.

2. Erik H. Erikson, *Childhood and Society*, (New York: W. W. Norton, 1963), argues that one "task" of adolescence is to test the parental world view against the experienced real world and that sharp discontinuity between the two produces anxiety in the ado-lescent.

3. Anne Boylan called my attention to this drawback in using letters as sources of information about the relative closeness or tension in relationships.

4. Carroll Smith-Rosenberg, "The Hysterical Woman: Sex Roles and Role Conflict in Nineteenth-Century America," *Social Research*, 39(1972), 562–584; Howard M. Fein-stein, "The Use and Abuse of Illness in the James Family Circle," in *Our Selves Our Past*, ed. Robert J. Grugger (Baltimore: Johns Hopkins University Press, 1981), pp. 228–242; Christopher Lasch, "The Narcissistic Personality in Our Time," in *Our Selves Our Past*, pp. 385–404.

5. Lasch, "The Narcissistic Personality in Our Time," p. 392.

6. I came across references to chlorosis in medical writings and in books dealing with health, such as: Edward H. Dixon, *Woman and Her Diseases* (New York: A. Ranney, 1857); Pye H. Chavasse, *Advice to Mothers on the Management of Their Offspring* (New York: D. Appleton & Co., 1844). William Beach, *An Improved System of Midwifery* (New York: Baker & Scribner, 1850), pp. 179–184, is the most detailed description of the "sickliness" of young women that did not name chlorosis (the writers were not physi-cians), but the descriptions coincide with the medical symptoms of chlorosis. See Samuel

Osgood, *The Hearthstone: Thoughts Upon Home Life in Our Cities* (New York: D. Appleton & Co., 1854), pp. 227–229; William A. Alcott, *The Young Woman's Book of Health* (New York: Auburn, Miller, Orton, & Mulligan, 1855), pp. 30–31, 201; George Sumner Weaver, *Aims and Aids for Girls and Young Women on the Various Duties of Life*; Caroline Louisa Tuthill, *The Young Lady's Home* (Boston: Wm. J. Reynolds & Co., 1847), pp. 74–78; Miss Coxe, *Claims of the Country on American Females* (Columbus, OH: Isaac N. Whiting, 1842), pp. 98–100; Catharine Maria Sedgwick, *Means and Ends, or Self-Training* (Boston: March, Capen, Lyon & Webb, 1840), pp. 34–51; Elizabeth Blackwell, *The Laws of Life, With Special Reference to the Physical Education of Girls* (New York: George P. Putnam, 1852), pp. 138–140; Mary S. Gove, *Lectures to Ladies on Anatomy and Physiology* (Boston: Saxton & Pierce, 1842), p. 227.

7. I.S.L. Loudon, "Chlorosis, Aneamia, and Anorexia Nervosa," *British Medical Journal*, 281(1980), 1669–1975. See also Paul B. Beeson, "Some Diseases That Have Disappeared," *The American Journal of Medicine*, 68(1980), 806–811; K. Figlio, "Chlorosis and Chronic Disease in Nineteenth-Century Britain: The Social Construction of Somatic Illness in a Capitalistic Society," *Social History*, 3(1978), 167–197. Recently chlorosis has attracted the attention of a women's studies scholar, Joan Jacobs Brumberg. In "Chlorotic Girls, 1870–1920: A Historical Perspective on Female Adolescence," *Child Development*, 53(1982), 1468–1477, Brumberg argues that chlorosis allowed daughters to share symptoms with their fashionably sick mothers and that turn-of-the-century changes meant less social approval for "sickliness" in general (thus the decline of chlorosis by World War I). While I am in basic agreement with Brumberg's explanation, I think she does not give sufficient attention to the mother/daughter relationship, and therefore misses the chlorosis/anorexia connection and the deeper psychological significance of chlorosis.

8. Prudence B. Saur, *Maternity: A Book for Every Wife and Mother*, (Chicago: L. P. Miller, 1891), p. 37; Eutocia Cook, *Easy Favorable Child Bearing: A Book for All Women*, 4th ed. (Chicago: Arcade Publishing Co., 1886), p. 331.

9. George Napheys, *The Physical Life of Woman: Advice to the Maiden, Wife and Mother*, (Philadelphia: G. Maclean, 1870), p. 27.

10. Cook, *Easy Favorable Child Bearing*, p. 331; Saur, *Maternity*, p. 43; George Austin, *Perils of American Women; or, A Doctor's Talk with Maiden, Wife, and Mother*, (Boston: Lee & Shepard, 1883), p. 189.

11. Napheys, *The Physical Life of Woman*, p. 31.

12. Saur, *Maternity*, p. 43; Napheys, *The Physical Life of Woman*, p. 27; Cook, *Easy Favorable Child Bearing*, p. 331.

13. Napheys, *The Physical Life of Woman*, p. 27.

14. Saur, *Maternity*, p. 44. Other writers described "case studies" of young women with chlorotic symptoms. See: George Taylor (M.D.), *Health for Women* (New York: American Book Exchange, 1879), pp. 290–298; Clarke, *Sex in Education*, pp. 105–106 (Clarke attributed the symptoms to too much "masculine" study); Ada Shepard Badger in *Sex and Education: A Reply to Dr. E. H. Clarke's "Sex in Education,"* ed. Julia Ward Howe (Boston: Roberts Brothers, 1874), p. 83 (Badger attributed the symptoms to the young girl's leaving school). One mid-nineteenth century woman described her mental state around age 12 when she was diagnosed as having chlorosis: "I became dyspeptic and nervous. I often awoke in the morning bathed in tears; and the most indescribable and horrible sinking of spirits was my portion." She also complained of headache and

dizziness. Gove, *Lectures to Ladies*, p. 227, in which the young woman was quoted, attibuted the girl's illness to masturbation as did the woman herself.

15. For example, William H. Thompson, "Chlorosis," *The Medical Record*, 1(1866), 161, wrote of the "first trouble" which brought girls and their mothers to the doctor as "persistent constipation, attended with anorexia."

16. Cherver Bevill and F. R. Fry, "Cases of Neurasthenia or Chlorosis," *St. Louis Courier Medicine*, 17(1887), 229–231.

17. In the first articles on anorexia nervosa, appearing in British medical journals, what is interesting to the authors is that the anorexia does not seem to be brought on by physiological causes but is instead brought on by "nervous" causes; hence the term "anorexia nervosa." See Sir William Gull, "Anorexia Nervosa," *Lancet*, 1(1888), 516–517; and in that same issue, W. S. Playfair, "Notes on the So-Called 'Anorexia Nervosa,' " 817–818. In the twentieth century, medical articles on anorexia nervosa multiply.

18. M. Nonat, "Reflections on Chlorosis, Especially in Children," *Cincinnati Lancet and Observer*, 3(1860), 706–713.

19. Thompson, "Chlorosis," p. 161.

20. Thompson, "Chlorosis," p. 162. Other physicians who saw appetite disturbance as the major characteristic of chlorosis include: J. A. Mayes, "Observations on Chlorosis, with a Case," *Southern Medical and Surgical Journal*, 6(1850), 513–522; Leon L. Solomon, "Chlorosis—Its Etiology, Diagnosis, and Treatment, Based Upon Constipation as a Causative Factor in the Production of the Morbid Condition," *The American Therapist*, 6(1897), 101–106. George A. Gibson, "On the Signs of Chlorosis," *Lancet*, 2(1877), 418–420 wrote that "pain in the epigastrium" after eating contributed to the "little appetite and enfeebled digestion" of the chlorotic patient.

21. James F. McShane, "Chlorosis," *Baltimore Physician and Surgeon*, 6(1876), 19.

22. James B. Burnet, "Cases of Chlorosis," *Medical and Surgical Reporter*, 17(1867), 71–72. On vomiting and chlorosis, see also William A. Hammond, "On Mental Therapeutics," 38(1878), 383–388.

23. Charles E. Simon, "A Study of 31 Cases of Chlorosis with Special Reference to the Etiology and the Dietetic Treatment of the Disease," *American Journal of the Medical Sciences*, 113(1897), 412.

24. Simon, "A Study of 31 Cases of Chlorosis," p. 417.

25. Helen Ekin Starrett, *Letters to Elder Daughters, Married and Unmarried* (Chicago: A. C. McClury & Co., 1892), p. 132.

26. Marie Therese Blanc, *The Condition of Woman in the United States, A Traveller's Notes*, trans. Abby Landdon Alger (Boston: Roberts Brothers, 1895), p. 26.

27. Jerome Smith, *The Ways of Women in Their Physical, Moral and Intellectual Relation* (New York: Jewett, 1873), p. 115.

28. Sir Andrew Clark, "Anaemia or Chlorosis of Girls, Occurring More Commonly Between the Advent of Menstruation and the Consummation of Womanhood," *Lancet*, 2(1887), 1004.

29. The medical (psychiatric and psychological) literature on anorexia is very extensive. For example, see: M. R. Kaufman, M. Heiman, eds., *Evolution of Psychosomatic Concepts: Anorexia Nervosa: A Paradigm* (New York: International Universities Press, 1964); H. Bruch, *Eating Disorders: Obesity, Anorexia Nervosa, and the Person Within* (New York: Basic Books, 1973); Salvador Minuchin, Bernice L. Rosman, and Lester Baker, *Psychosomatic Families: Anorexia Nervosa in Context* (Cambridge, MA: Harvard University Press, 1978); Alan Sugarman, Donald M. Quinlan, and Luanna Devenis, "Ego Boundary

Disturbance in Anorexia Nervosa: Preliminary Findings," *Journal of Personality Assessment*, 46(1982), 455–461; Paul E. Garfinkel and David M. Garner, *Anorexia Nervosa: A Multidimensional Perspective* (New York: Bruner/Mazel, 1982); A. H. Crisp, *Anorexia Nervosa: Let Me Be* (London: Academic Press, 1980). For a feminist explanation of anorexia, see Marlene Boskind-Lodahl, "Cinderella's Stepsisters: A Feminist Perspective on Anorexia Nervosa and Bulimia," *Signs*, 2(1976), 342–356. See also Robert Avens, *Imagination Is Reality* (Dallas, TX: Spring Publications, 1980); James Hillman, *The Myth of Analysis* (Evanston, IL: Northwestern University Press, 1972), especially part 3, "On Psychological Femininity"; Peter L. Berger and Thomas Luckmann, *The Social Construction of Reality: A Treatise on the Sociology of Knowledge* (London: Allen Lane, 1966).

30. Mary Terhune, *Eve's Daughters; or Common Sense for Maid, Wife, and Mother* (New York: J. R. Anderson & H. S. Allen, 1882), p. 85; Jane Croly, *For Better or Worse; For Some Men and All Women* (Boston: Lee & Shepard, 1875), p. 23; Anna Callender Brackett, ed., *The Education of American Girls* (New York: G. P. Putnam & Sons, 1874), p. 124.

31. Terhune, *Eve's Daughters*, p. 97; Frances Willard, *A Great Mother; Sketches of Madam Willard, by Her Daughter* (Chicago: Woman's Temperance Publishing Association, 1894), p. 145.

32. Anna Callender Brackett, *The Education of American Girls* (New York: G. P. Putnam & Sons, 1874), pp. 61–64. Writers who pointed out that mothers did not teach their daughters about their bodies included: Croly, *For Better or Worse*, pp. 216–218; Eliza Barton Lyman, *The Coming Woman; The Royal Road to Perfection*, a series of medical lectures (Lansing, MI: W. S. George, 1880), pp. 177, 178; George Fisk Comfort and Anna Manning Comfort, *Women's Education and Women's Health* (Syracuse, NY: T. W. Durston & Co., 1874), p. 60; Catharine Beecher, *Woman's Profession as Mother and Educator, with Views in Opposition to Woman Suffrage* (Philadelphia: George Maclean, 1872); Mary Studley, *What Our Girls Ought to Know* (New York: M. L. Holbrook & Co., 1878), p. 10; Margaret E. Sangster, *Winsome Womanhood; Familiar Talks on Life and Conduct* (New York: F. H. Revell Co., 1900), p. 27.

33. Mary Rossiter, *My Mother's Life, The Evolution of a Recluse* (Chicago: Fleming H. Revell Co., 1900), p. 72.

34. Terhune, *Eve's Daughter*, pp. 79–84. Since this is also true for some twentieth-century American girls, it is probable that it was more common in the nineteenth century when feminine "modesty" was held to be extremely important and when many women were ignorant of female physiology. It is also probable that many mothers did not have the language with which to describe menstruation (or intercourse) to their daughters, since female medical writers still referred to women's genitals as "the mysterious organs of generation."

35. Martha Jay Coston, *A Single Success, An Autobiography* (Philadelphia: J. B. Lippincott Co., 1886), p. 22.

36. Helen Gilbert Ecob, *The Well-Dressed Woman; A Study in the Practical Application to Dress of the Laws of Health, Art and Morals* (New York: Fowler & Wells, 1892), pp. 29–30.

37. Frances Willard, *How to Win: A Book For Girls* (New York: Funk & Wagnalls, 1888), pp. 16–17.

38. William B. Neftel, "Chlorosis," *Medical Record*, 8(1873), 98–99; Simon, "A Study of 31 Cases of Chlorosis."

39. Frederick P. Henry, "Relations Between Chlorosis, Simple Anaemia, and Pernicious Anaemia," *Medical Record*, 36(1889), 353.

40. Willoughby Francis Wade, "Clinical Lecture on the Relation Between Menstruation and the Chlorosis of Young Women," *British Medical Journal*, 2(1872), 35.

41. T. Gaillard Thomas, "Clinical Lecture on Chlorosis," *Boston Medical and Surgical Journal*, 103(1880), 389–390.

42. Simon, "A Study of 31 Cases of Chlorosis," p. 418; McShane, "Chlorosis," p. 19; Burnet, "Cases of Chlorosis," p. 71.

43. Control is also a very important aim of the anorexic. See Crisp, *Anorexia Nervosa*, p. 65; and Minuchin, et al., *Psychosomatic Families*.

44. Nonat, "Reflections on Chlorosis," p. 708; Neftel, "Some Recent Researches in Pathology," p. 98.

45. McShane, "Chlorosis," p. 19, my emphasis.

46. Hammond, "On Mental Therapeutics," 386–388.

47. On hysteria, see Anne Douglas Wood, " 'The Fashionable Diseases': Women's Complaints and Their Treatment in Nineteenth Century America," *Journal of Interdisciplinary History*, 4(1973), 25–52; Smith-Rosenberg, "The Hysterical Woman"; Ilza Weith, *Hysteria: The History of a Disease* (Chicago: University of Chicago Press, 1965); Maria Ramas, "Freud's Dora, Dora's Hysteria: The Negation of a Woman's Rebellion," *Feminist Studies*, 6(1980), 472–510. Physicians who used the term "hysteria" to characterize chlorosis include: Bevill, "Cases of Neurasthenia or Chlorosis"; Hammond, "On Mental Therapeutics"; McShane, "Chlorosis"; Thompson, "Chlorosis"; Neftel, "Some Recent Researches in Pathology."

CHAPTER 9

A New Feminine Synthesis

American women who were adolescents or young adults during the middle part of the nineteenth century were raised with a feminine ideology that stressed that suffering and self-abnegation necessarily accompanied the domestic life and willingness to suffer was the feminine avenue to fulfillment. But by the late-century period the material conditions of womanhood, which had inspired the ideal of feminine suffering, began to change. Just as their mothers' physical experience of womanhood became the root metaphor of femininity in the early nineteenth century, the daughters' different physical experience became the basis of a new feminine synthesis. The daughters' synthesis involved a re-definition of domesticity and motherhood; it was an alteration, not a rejection, of their mothers' world view.

Three themes in late-nineteenth-century women's writing illustrate both the body/culture connection and the generational dynamic involved in the formation of sexual ideology. Although late-nineteenth-century women echoed their mothers' belief that motherhood was woman's highest calling, they also revised the meaning of motherhood to fit their own experience. As women came to doubt that feminine frailty was innate, the naturalness of domestic inclination and motherly instinct was newly questionable. As suffering was recognized to be unnecessary and undesirable in physical mothering, self-abnegation was seen as a dubious virtue for the mother-role. And as physical submission to males came under attack, the possibility and righteousness of psychological independence was proclaimed. Late-nineteenth-century women transposed natural motherhood into professional motherhood, necessary suffering into chosen altruism, and submission to male authority into devotion to public-spirited maternal superiority. But these were variations of a theme, not an entirely new composition. Like their mothers, late-nineteenth-century women remained committed to separate spheres and a revised version of "natural" womanhood. The feminine score was altered, but not re-written.

Amid all the changes in women's material conditions in the late nineteenth century, there was generational continuity in women's high valuation of motherhood. Women who wrote for female audiences in the period from 1870 to the late 1890s described motherhood in terms similar to early and mid-nineteenth-century women. "As wife and mother, woman fulfills her destiny," one woman wrote in 1893. Another woman called motherhood "noble," and still others described "mother-love" in sentimental superlatives.[1] Even women who acknowledged the right of girls to work in "the world" praised motherhood as the highest calling and true vocation of woman. Mary Elizabeth Sherwood, after asserting that girls should be able to work, went on to advise her readers that "the happiest women are those who can lead the ordinary life ... be early married to the man of their choice, and become in their turn domestic women, good wives, and mothers. There is no other work, no matter how distinguished, which equals this."[2] In a book entitled *The Business Girl in Every Phase of Her Life*, Isabel Mallon assumed her young readers were typewriters, clerks, and saleswomen, but she opened her discussion of the realities of working life with this wish for the business girl: "The greatest happiness that can come to a woman—a loving husband, a happy home, and a group of affectionate children."[3] One group of working girls, the 38th Street Working Girls' Society, echoed Mallon's wish as an expectation: "We all ... hope to have some day homes of our own, where as wife and mother we can be queen of some larger or smaller place and center."[4] Another writer, Eleanor Donnelly, after acknowledging women's right to work, went on to write of "woman's true sphere" as the domestic one. "God made her to be queen of the Home. When she is driven out of it ... she is in a state of violence, her life is out of joint."[5] To Donnelly, no work could possibly compare to childrearing in terms of importance.

While late-nineteenth-century women saw motherhood as woman's true calling, they did not believe domesticity was "natural" to women. On the contrary, they described the desire to marry and maintain a home as the product of socialization and lack of options. According to Laura deForce Gordon, young women married because they were subjected to the "conservative, repressive training of the home."[6] Mary Walker emphasized that the social expectation that the girl should marry was as strong an influence as early training. "Grown girls are almost turned out of doors into marriage, by having their destiny as somebody's wife constantly preached," she wrote.[7] Responding to early role learning and social expectation, young girls were said to be unprepared for any other life choices but marriage. "To be 'engaged' is the triumph and secret object of the young girl's life," Jane Croly wrote in 1875. She went on to say that young women were unprepared for any other occupation and so they rushed into marriage.[8] This same idea was expressed by Grace Dodge, who wrote that young girls are brought up to think of "getting married" as "the one necessary thing in the world." Speaking personally, she testified that marriage "is our aim and desire from young girlhood up, and we are so afraid we won't get a husband, we take the first man who pays us attention."[9]

Although late-nineteenth-century women wrote of motherhood as woman's highest calling, they recognized that girls were prepared for the mother-role just as they were prepared to desire marriage: through socialization. Stella Gilman, in *Mothers in Council*, wrote of sex-typed toys (especially dolls for girls) as vehicles for role learning.[10] Other writers pointed out that the detailed role instruction and desperate insistence that women's natural motherly function would be easily polluted by education or any kind of individual freedom indicated just how unnatural and undetermined woman's mother-role actually was. According to one writer, the necessity of role definition and of confining women to the home sphere by social and economic force demonstrated "that woman is a most rebellious subject."[11] Taking a different approach to the same idea, Caroline Dall asked her readers to consider the reasons girls are over-prepared for motherhood while no one thinks of "preparing" boys for fatherhood. Dall indicated her belief that motherhood was a natural function surrounded by social convention:

Nothing is so absurd as to press upon a young woman's thought the idea that she is to become a mother. What if she is? Let her make herself a healthy, happy human being. ... People should live out their young and happy days, unconscious of this issue, as the flowers take no thought of seed.[12]

This distinction between the biological experience and the social role of motherhood was an important addition to feminine consciousness. In essence, some women were saying that biological femaleness did not necessarily entail a particular life pattern for women. Instead, the meaning of female body and the definition of women's reproductive role were seen as socially produced.

Believing that marriage and motherhood were social functions instead of biological "givens," late-nineteenth-century women asserted that "single blessedness" should be an option for every girl. In a book "for young ladies," Jennie Willing wrote of a popular joke that illustrated young women's feeling that marriage was a social necessity: A father comes to his daughter on her wedding day and says, "My dear child, it is an awfully solemn thing to get married." The young woman responds, "I know that. But it is an awfully solemner thing not to."[13] Amelia Barr accurately observed that her generation was the first to remain unmarried "from desire or from conviction," noting that such a life was considered more "respectable and respected" than in days past.[14]

The late-century generation was indeed the least married group of women in United States history, with a record thirteen percent remaining single.[15] There were two dimensions to women's support for the single life. Some writers, reflecting the idea that marriage and motherhood should be a conscious choice, urged young women not to marry merely for convention's sake. Criticism of marriage as a way to "make a living" was a popular late-nineteenth-century theme. Charlotte Perkins Gilman, in *Women and Economics*, emphasized this idea in her theoretical discussion of women's status, and other writers from less intellectual vantage points voiced the same criticism.[16] In addition, some late-nineteenth-century women argued for the positive virtues of the single life. Harriet Paine was typical of that point of view. She told her readers that increased freedom, better physical conditions, and new educational opportunities made unmarried women of the late nineteenth century different from those of past generations. She regarded the single state as an opportunity to fulfill ambitions or do something meaningful in the world.[17]

Women who viewed the single life as valuable in itself and women who saw it as simply a viable option when marriage was not offered were careful not to suggest that remaining unmarried was, or should be, a typical "first choice" for women. However, in defending the possibility of single blessedness, late-nineteenth-century women also urged that young girls be given non-domestic training as a matter of course. This was a bold departure from earlier female writers. Adult women in the late-century period expressed their conviction that girls should have training to permit wider life options, even as they claimed domesticity was the best life. This indicates that they did not believe in the "naturalness" of gender. From practical to idealistic perspectives, late-nineteenth-century women argued that young girls should be given job training and public permission to enable them to fill non-domestic roles. This was precisely the training and permission that they themselves had *not* received, and their arguments reveal feminine consciousness in the process of change.

A conservative expression of women's argument for economic training for girls was Lizzie Bates's *Woman: Her Dignity and Sphere*, published by the American Tract Society in 1870. Bates pointed out that the uncertainty of the American situation made it imperative that young women be trained for work other than domesticity. "Fortunes are unstable," Bates wrote. "Farmers become merchants; artisans become lawyers; laborers become judges and divines; rich men's daughters become the wives of poor men, and the reverse." From the instability of the time, Bates concluded that "for herself should a girl be educated . . . to render her a strong, wise, sensible woman . . . ready for every duty."[18] Mary Terhune expressed the same idea, noting that "the terrible fluctuations of American fortunes is a continuous object-lesson, enforcing the need of preparedness in the women themselves to meet reverses and override poverty."[19] Along these same lines, women argued that girls should be educated in a trade or profession in case they were not asked to be married or in case their marriages failed in some way. One woman even suggested that a "majority" of girls would some day have to support themselves.[20]

The positive value of non-domestic work was also praised by many late-nineteenth-century writers in various ways. One woman wrote approvingly of young women "challenging tradition" and "asking questions" about the naturalness of domesticity.[21] Other women argued, with Charlotte Perkins Gilman, that young girls should be trained for extra-domestic options so that marriage could be a real choice or so that "opportunities" would be equally opened to them. As a matter of life-training, one woman suggested that "every girl, as well as boy, should have a trade and a profession, and should be able to play one musical instrument."[22] Etta Taylor asserted that it was "the influence of the age" that prompted women to desire "to control an income of their own and to enjoy consequent independence in planning their expenses." She was in favor of greater education for girls and self-improvement plans for all women who wanted extra-domestic options.[23] Another writer described paid work as making life worth living, in contrast to women's domestic labor, which "lies so largely in the care, rather than in the production, of objects."[24] Although she was quick to point out that women have always "worked," she maintained that "the important thing for women to do to-day is to learn how to get money, and use it."[25] Adeline Whitney also expressed unqualified approval of extra-domestic training and options for girls, linking her ideas about training to middle-class women's shrinking domestic role. She wrote,

Women must have something to do. Our grandmothers and great-grandmothers used to spin, and weave, and distill, and knit, and stitch. We do not. Everything is machine-made, chemically compounded; there is comparatively no home manufacture. . . . women's energies have been set adrift.[26]

Whether they saw training for the "world's work" as a wise preparation in case of bad luck in the marriage market, as a positive value contributing to women's greater choice, or as a necessary response to a changing economic situation, late-nineteenth-century women expressed approval of non-domestic training for girls. In advocating female education for trades and professions, they took a position supported by only the radicals of their mothers' generation. They were able to do this not because they were rebellious, but because physical and social change prompted an alteration of their original feminine script. Domesticity was no longer seen as physically "natural" or socially necessary for all women. Unlike their mothers, late-nineteenth-century women experienced physical self-control and socioeconomic choice as real possibilities.

In reality, however, physical self-determination was more possible than socioeconomic self-determination. Body control was translated into the notion of life-control, so that the late nineteenth century seemed much more full of opportunity and choice than it actually was. Just as their mothers had experienced suffering as a necessary part of women's physical life and had used that body experience to construct the meaning of "femininity," so the daughters translated their experience of body to the social realm. Late-nineteenth-century women experienced the female body as released from the constraints of biologically determined pain, illness, and unwanted pregnancies; and womanhood to them appeared newly unfettered. This attitude was particularly apparent in women's descriptions of the opportunities and challenges facing girls in "the world."

A common incorrect assumption made by late-century women was that girls had hundreds of ways to make a living, as compared to "fifty years ago." Etta Taylor was optimistic about women's possibilities in numerous occupations, claiming that "practically she [woman] is today the recognized equal of man."[27] Jane Croly wrote of the "changing times," and reminded her readers that early-nineteenth-century women had no opportunity for education, training, or power, unlike young women of the late-century period.[28] Martha Rayne, in *What Can a Woman Do; or, Her Position in the Business and Literary World*, referred to Harriet Martineau's observation in the early part of the century that only seven industries were opened to women. Now (in 1884) in Massachusetts, Rayne observed that women could work in 284 different occupations.[29] Eleanor Donnelly echoed this optimism: "Almost all avocations, all to which there exists no insuperable physical ban, are now open to women; and the universities and professions receive them, so that liberty is unrestricted."[30] Gertrude Aguirre similarly pointed out: "Less than half a century ago, the only occupations in which she [woman] could engage, with her own and the public's consent, were teaching, housework, sewing and nursing." In a statement reminiscent of Margaret Fuller's early-nineteenth-century demand that women be able to be "sea captains" if they wanted, Aguirre boldly proclaimed: "Now she [woman] can be anything from lecturer to a steamboat captain."[31]

Although young women in the 1880s and 1890s did have greater opportunities for education and gainful employment than women had had twenty years earlier, the optimism expressed by late-nineteenth-century women reflected wishful thinking more than actual conditions. The common denominator in women's perceptions of changed conditions was the emphasis on choice, individual choice, as a new dimension of female life. Women's sense of physical choice, body control, was projected onto social reality, and women were convinced that girls could train for, and work in, non-domestic fields just by choosing to do so. Irene Hartt announced in 1895 that almost all fields were opened to girls. She reminded her young readers that the "battles" to open the fields were "fought and won for you, girls!" She went on to say: "Now girls may choose any profession and study it," and noted that the modern girl's choice was limited only "by her powers of endurance."[32] Sallie White expressed this same sense of limitless choice in *Business Openings for Girls*. She wrote: "To-day the young woman pauses to consider which of the many roads she will take . . . it is largely a question of choice."[33] Frances Willard, the energetic Women's Christian Temperance Union (WCTU) crusader, had a similar message for young women. She contrasted her own girlhood in the mid-nineteenth century to late-century girlhood in *How to Win: A Book for Girls*. "I had aspiration; you have opportunity, I breathed an atmosphere laden with old-time conservatism, . . . you are exhilarated by the vital air of a new liberty."[34]

A crucial thing to notice about these statements is the generational element.

Women who were girls and young adults in the mid-century period wrote of teeming opportunities for women who were girls and young adults in the late-century period. Mary Livermore put it bluntly, saying that the "woman question" was really the question: What shall we do with our daughters? She explained that equal rights would not affect adult women: "Their positions are taken, their futures are forecast; and they are harnessed into the places they occupy ... by invisible, but omnipotent, ties of love or duty." She went on to say: "It is for our young women that the great changes of the time promise the most: it is for our daughters."[35] The words written about the tremendous opportunities of the time were there to inspire younger women with a sense of "what should be done" or "what could be done" with a woman's life. Their belief in their daughters' potential to surpass domesticity was implicit in late-century writing. "If I required so little of myself, it was because the world required so little of me," Frances Willard wrote to her young readers. The hidden message was: "The world offers you more and expects more of you."[36] Adeline Whitney pressed her own sense of mission onto her adolescent readers, saying: "Now a girl is confronted from the beginning with some personal necessity and some vague accountability to all things.... 'What am I to do in the world.' "[37] These women wrote from their own personal perspectives, as adult women, of what they imagined the world would offer to them had they been seventeen instead of forty or fifty.

In their writing about the option to remain single and the possibilities for non-domestic work, late-nineteenth-century women were reporting actual conditions, sharing girlhood experiences of pressure to marry and frustration in life choices, and advising the next generation of girls. This combination, within a unified point of view, makes women's popular literature a rich source of information about changes in feminine consciousness. The internalized maternal (and cultural) message about true womanhood is present, the realization of new conditions is evident, and the altered feminine script that will be passed on to the next generation is also clear. When physical and social conditions changed so that mothers' precepts about femininity were severed from their experiential roots, daughters revealed ambivalence about their mothers' lives, cautious adoption of a new self-concept, and brave abandon about the future of womankind.

Late nineteenth-century women's recognition that domesticity was not biologically determined freed them to make bold pronouncements about single life, preparation of girls for non-domestic choices, and the wide-open world that they believed young women encountered. But late-century women were not ready to repudiate the domestic life or even to give it equal weight with other life choices. Marriage and motherhood was still considered the most important vocation for women. Late-nineteenth-century women believed that most girls would choose marriage and motherhood no matter what the options, but they also believed that these young women would not have instinctive knowledge about correct homemaking or childrearing.

It is important to notice that late-nineteenth-century women's new ideas about domesticity were new interpretations of an experience they shared with their mothers. The "naturalness" of domesticity could be challenged because of changes in body experience; however, the domestic life itself changed very little from the mid- to the late-nineteenth century. The tasks and responsibilities of the middle-class housewife were only slightly altered from one generation to the next. Even in the urban areas, the late-century housewife still made most of her own and her children's clothes, and the technology surrounding laundry and house cleaning was almost as primitive as it had been a few decades earlier. One area of housewifery that had improved since the Civil War was food preparation, with the daughters' generation the first to abandon the wood-burning stove for the gas range. In spite of the fact that canned foods were available for the first time, the housewife still did a great deal of individual canning and storing, as the huge pantries and food cellars of late Victorian architecture indicate.[38] In general, the late-century woman performed the same jobs her mother had performed.

Late-nineteenth-century women also shared their mothers' dislike of the domestic role. As Helen Gilbert Ecob wrote: "Housework . . . is despised by all classes of women. Those who are obliged to do it usually chafe under the drudgery."[39] Since less than 25 percent of women had even one servant in 1880, most middle-class women were "obliged to do it" themselves.[40] Amelia Barr wrote in 1898 that most women found housework "hard and monotonous and inferior," and Jane Grey Swisshelm, writing in 1880, compared housework to a kind of involuntary servitude that "no woman had gotten out of."[41] As in the earlier period, late-century writers also noted that domestic service was injurious to women's health. Maria Elmore asserted that marriage for women was "a regimen which imposes more duties, responsibilities, trials, burdens, cares, and sorrows than any other can, . . . which taxes health, strength, blood, and nerve."[42] Another woman wrote: "Almost every woman with whom you come into confidential discourse feels her life is loaded with problems."[43]

Mothers and daughters may have had common sentiments about their very similar domestic activities, but their different body experiences led them to different conclusions about the meaning of domesticity in a woman's life. Whereas early and mid-century women suffered through the housewife/mother role as a distasteful but "naturally" feminine task, late-nineteenth-century women "professionalized" domesticity as a necessary but socially learned feminine work. The late-century home economics movement and the popular cry to professionalize housework and motherhood were more than new attempts to make an old job less odious; they were bold redefinitions by women of women's work. While the professionalization advocates did not challenge the sexual division of labor, they did assert that women's work was socially valuable labor, significant to community as well as family. The envisioning of domesticity as professional activity was a renaming of women's work as complicated and worthy of respect, and as essential to the other professional and non-professional work of society. It was an ideological bridge between home and world not attempted a generation earlier.[44]

The professionalization idea implied a new feeling of role distance on the part of late-nineteenth-century women. Instead of seeing domestic service as something a woman naturally disliked and suffered through, late-century women viewed domesticity as a complex role demanding preparation.[45] Although one writer described domestic service as a "sacrifice ... on the altar of love," she was out-of-step with most of her contemporaries who viewed housewifery more as a tiresome and complicated job that one could learn to do efficiently for the sake of order.[46] Women no longer saw themselves in a strictly functional way, as suffering quietly through a naturally feminine duty.

For some women, this sense of role distance grew out of their experiences as untrained housewives. Harriet Storer Doutney wrote in 1871 that her mother did not teach her household skills "through mistaken kindness."[47] She expressed angry resentment toward her mother for this lack of preparation, recognizing as an adult that domesticity was not a natural feminine trait. As described earlier, the adolescent lifestyle of middle-class girls in the mid-century period included a great deal of free time and relatively little domestic work. Late-nineteenth-century women reached adulthood less prepared for the domestic role than their mothers had been, and therefore more able to see domesticity as learned and not innate.

Like domestic service, motherhood also was viewed as a complex "professional" job by the late nineteenth century. Although women wrote of maternal feelings as "natural," they saw the mother role as learned. One woman wrote of "an inborn fondness for babies" as innate in womankind, but she went on to give detailed instructions on child nurture, assuming her readers would not know instinctively how to care for a baby.[48] Another woman wrote of child care as natural to woman's life, but included a chapter on "Professional Motherhood" full of instructions and ideals.[49] Still another writer asserted that the care and teaching of children was the "nature" of the "mother-sex"; she too noted that women need preparation for this "naturally" feminine job.[50] Other women who also saw motherhood as natural nevertheless urged mothers to train their daughters in the specifics of child nurture.[51] There seemed to be widespread consensus that the mother role was not innate to womanhood.

Central to the late-nineteenth-century feminine synthesis, professional motherhood continued the earlier emphasis on reproduction as the focus of women's lifescript, but altered the meaning considerably. Early-nineteenth-century women saw their motherhood as a physical expression of femininity and blurred body and role to arrive at a sense of suffering as likewise naturally feminine. Late-nineteenth-century women also saw motherhood as an expression of femininity, but their experience of body as controllable and separate from self led them to disconnect the mother role from its biological roots. Motherhood, like health and fertility, was no longer naturally determined; instead, the activity of mothering must be learned and could be elevated to professional status. Sim-

ilarly, late-nineteenth-century women's experience of suffering as not necessary
to female body led them to reject passive suffering as the hallmark of the mother
role. In its place, the daughters urged active, altruistic service to family and
active, generous service to community as the basis of the mother role. From
the early to the late nineteenth century, the meaning of motherhood shifted
while retaining its place as the most important feminine life function. From a
passive, suffering expression of femininity and the source of womanly "influence," motherhood became an active, difficult profession and the source of
feminine power.

In the early part of the century, women were confident that the power of
motherhood was the influence the mother exerted over children and husband.
This influence resulted not from positive action, but from the mother's willingness to suffer and deny self for the sake of others. Even early-century writers
who stressed mothers' power to mold the immortal soul believed the molding
was accomplished by influence, and the influence was based on mothers' Christ-
like self-sacrifice. The mother inspired, and therefore influenced her family. By
the late nineteenth century, however, there was a subtle but important shift in
the definition of maternal power. As control of health and conquest of birth
pain became part of women's physical experience, the mother role was reshaped
to include a more active, less innate sense of good mothering. Instead of saintly
influence, the late-century mother determined her child's character and future
by intelligent control of the childhood environment. Active socialization replaced
passive goodness as the source of maternal power.

For late-nineteenth-century women, maternal control of socialization came
"naturally" with motherhood, but women needed skills to deal effectively with
that position. One woman wrote of the "early years" as "the most important
of life," and another called the power of motherhood "unquestioned" and
"absolute."[52] Mary Terhune reminded her readers that "to the child 'mother'
is authority, conscience, Bible." Because the child "dwells and develops under
her [mother's] shadow," Terhune reasoned that the mother's teachings were
lifelasting.[53] But late-century women were more interested in instructing mothers about the proper use of their position than in convincing them of the power
they held. Caroline Lefavre assured her readers that intelligent motherhood
could "wipe out in a few generations the feebleness of body, mind, and morals
that has resulted from the low estimate placed on the office of motherhood."[54]
Echoing this idea, another woman wrote: "The mother who has her own
children in her own care is the mother who, with intelligence, can do the most
for the race."[55]

Complementing this emphasis on intelligent socialization was a new version
of the malleable child. Horace Bushnell had argued that the child was a kernel
of possibilities, a delicate bud to be nourished to maturity with tender, loving
care. But late-nineteenth-century women offered a more environmental, less
romantic idea of childhood. While the early-century child was thought to possess
a certain disposition that the mother could influence by pious caretaking, the

late-century child's only innate characteristics were those of a young animal: curiosity, lack of self-control, love of play. It was up to the mother to form a civilized, healthy adult from the raw material of dependent infancy. Lizzie Bates employed an apt metaphor to describe the mother/child relationship; she likened it to a sculptor with unformed marble "to be moulded, shaped, polished."[56]

Late-nineteenth-century advice literature on childrearing reflected this revised version of malleable childhood and a new faith in the power of socialization. More striking than these new themes, however, was the growing number of female writers on childrearing. In the early part of the century, the advisors who urged women to change their mothering patterns and who blamed women for infant illness and death were mostly male health professionals. Female writers were not among those who gave detailed instructions on childcare or age of weaning. But in the late nineteenth century, women, with and without professional medical training, replaced male health profesionals as the most popular childrearing advisors.[57] According to this new set of experts, late-nineteenth-century motherhood required knowledge, skills, and a willingness to serve the "best interest" of the child.

The details of proper infant care, including feedings, napping, bathing, and dressing, filled the pages of late-nineteenth-century books written by women for women.[58] Whether the authors devoted a few pages, entire chapters or sections, or whole books to the subject, they assumed that the maternal role required special instruction. Like the earlier male advisors, late-nineteenth-century women praised regularity in eating and sleeping, and they disapproved of handling or feeding a child "on demand." "Now the chief aim of mothers and nurses is to reduce a child's habits to something as nearly akin to clockwork as it is possible to bring a human being," Christine Herrick wrote with approval.[59] Prompted by their new sense of body control, women insisted that infants could also be regulated in an enlightened way; they could be scientifically manipulated toward a healthy life just as the woman could determine her own health and fertility. But in both cases education was necessary. The mother needed guidelines in order to raise a healthy child.

The women who advised other women about the skills of professional motherhood were interested in raising the status of women's work by recognizing the complexities involved. Although their advice was similar to male advisors' ideas, women assumed a different tone in addressing their readers. One male writer warned mothers "with all due emphasis, with all due solemnity" that feeding an infant more than four times in 24 hours "regulated by cryings and not by regular periods" would result in the baby's death: "These words might be rightfully chiseled on the headstone, 'Died from the ignorance of its mother!' "[60] Women also insisted on clockwork feeding and urged mothers to be calm while nursing, but their tone was not accusatory. "If you have the comfort of being able to nurse your children," Maria Dewing wrote, "it must be done with regularity."[61] She specified every two hours for the first two months. Although women provided detailed instructions for professional motherhood, they tended to trust their readers' common sense more than male advisors did. One man felt it necessary to warn his readers that "care must be taken to support the head" when handling an infant.[62] Women were more likely to discuss correct ratios for infant formulas or proper management of sick babies than to offer instructions about holding a child. Advocates of professional motherhood did not intend to arouse feelings of guilt or inadequacy in mothers, but wanted instead to impress mothers with the difficulty and importance of their job.

In addition to instruction on feeding, bathing, and weaning, late-nineteenth-century women advised mothers about the care of older children. Mothers were urged to take socialization seriously and plan the day's activities for their children, much the same way as twentieth-century kindergarten teachers are required to have a lesson plan.[63] Professional motherhood demanded that children be talked to in a respectful way, that children be disciplined without physical force, and that children's play be recognized as essential to healthful development. Lest a woman mistakenly think there was one formula for a mother to master, advisors reminded their readers that each child was different and no rule could apply to all.[64] Amelia Barr enumerated the duties of mothers to their children to include such specific, but vague tasks as: managing children, strengthening them physically, awakening their intellects, engaging their affections, and winning their confidence.[65]

Besides offering detailed instruction for infant and early child care, late-nineteenth-century women also wrote of the "rights of the child" as numerous and complex. The idea of children's rights was a concept new to the late nineteenth century, and it was usually applied to questions of child labor and compulsory education. The child was said to have rights that the state should grant or protect. But late-nineteenth-century women used the term "rights" to apply to a parent/child relationship, with interesting syntactic implications. For instance, many women wrote of the child's right to be "well born." To some, any "wanted" child was considered well born, so the child's right was actually the mother's right to refuse pregnancy.[66] To others, a well-born child was one whose mother was healthy; again, the child's right was the mother's responsibility to take care of herself.[67] Mary Livermore's argument in favor of well-born children was based on the health of mothers, but also could be interpreted eugenically. "We shall by and by come to recognize the right of every child to be well born," she wrote, "sound in body, with inherited tendencies toward mental and moral health."[68] Eutocia Cook's notion of a well-born child included a favorable environment that the parents worked toward actively. She wrote: "Every child which comes into the world has a right to be well born; by this I mean it has a right to the best conditions, physical, mental, and moral, that it is in the power of the parents to secure."[69] Depending on the writer, a child's right to be well born included different things, but in each case the mother (or at least the parents) was responsible to provide for the right.

Other "rights" of children that late-nineteenth-century women advocated specifically involved the mother without naming the mother as responsible. A child's right to a "happy home," to discipline, to truthful answers to questions—which late nineteenth-century women advocated—necessarily obligated the mother.[70] A child's right to "a place of his own, to things of his own, to surroundings which have some relation to his size, his desires, and his capabilities" also assumed maternal duty to provide and keep up.[71] Likewise, a child's right to be happy presupposed a mother's constant vigilance. "A child should be happy; he must, in every way, be made happy; everything ought to be done to conduce to his happiness, to give him joy, gladness and pleasure," Prudence Saur wrote. Addressing mothers, she left no question as to who was responsible for the child's happiness:

Make a child understand that you love him; prove it in your actions. . . . Look after his little pleasures—join in his little sports; let him never hear a morose word. . . . Love! let love be his polar star. . . . Let your face, as well as your tongue, speak love. Let your hands be ever ready to minister to his pleasures and to his play.[72]

The daughters' generation abandoned the idea of pious influence as part of natural motherhood, but they substituted a new array of childhood rights that mothers were duty-bound to provide. The late-century child, deserving of intelligent socialization, had a "right" to professional motherhood.[73]

Although late-century women did not advocate suffering and self-abnegation as essential to good mothering, they championed a new maternal ideal which prescribed behavioral constraints for women similar to those of their mothers' generation. Just as the early-nineteenth-century suffering mother needed to be home to provide pious influence, the late-century mother was warned not to trust her child's early socialization to others. Elizabeth Peabody told her readers not to delegate childcare responsibility during the "nursery period" because "only a mother can respect a child's personality sufficiently."[74] Another woman who advocated professional motherhood advised: "The mother should, so far as possible, have charge of the children."[75] Stella Gilman recognized that late-century women had more extra-domestic activities than earlier generations. "Mothers nowadays have so many outside engagements . . . that they are taken from home a great deal, and our children have less of their companionship than we had of our parents," she wrote; but she urged women to plan their time efficiently so that they could be home during the pre-school years and home when their children came back from school.[76] Whether she was to provide influence or socialization, the home-focused mother was still essential to the daughters' feminine synthesis.

Likewise, the late-century maternal ideal specified that the mother be unselfish, prompted by duty and altruism, with behavioral requirements similar to early-century self-abnegation. "If we are selfish in one single thought we are not true mothers," Andrea Proudfoot wrote. "The children's interests and

happiness must be our first consideration," another woman urged.[77] Echoing
the earlier emphasis on mother-love as selfless devotion to children, late nineteenth-century women also wrote of maternal feeling as "the only unselfish
love." Elizabeth Blackwell asserted that maternal sentiment included "a special
divine gift of unselfishness and profound devotion to the well-being of husband
and children," and Amelia Barr described "mother-love" as "the spirit of self-
sacrifice...the meat and drink of all true and pure affection."[78] Ella Wilcox
included unselfishness, perseverance, patience, cheerfulness, and tact as the
traits essential to successful motherhood, and Mary Blake reminded her readers
that anything conflicting with a "mother's first duty" to her family was neither
"womanly" nor "proper."[79] Women were urged to pass on this high regard for
altruism to their daughters: "Teach them by experience the blessedness that
comes from deeds done for others, the farthest removed from selfish consideration."[80] Even Antoinette Blackwell argued that women were not as naturally
self-centered as men because of women's childcare duties.[81] While freeing
women from the biological necessity of suffering femininity, the late-nineteenth-
century maternal ideal still required selfless devotion to others in the name of
duty.

In spite of the fact that the daughters' synthesis demanded home-focused,
unselfish motherhood, the concept of chosen duty and altruism was a shift in
consciousness from the earlier idea of innately feminine self-sacrifice and suffering. Altruism was a conscious choice from a position of strength and enlightenment about the needs of others and the power of self.[82] More importantly,
altruistic service to others did not require sacrifice of the woman's health and
happiness; to the contrary, service demanded strength and purpose. Finally,
altruism and unselfishness, while linked to women "naturally," required intelligent impetus. Whereas the suffering woman could rest assured that her
very pain was proof of her passive, natural service, the duty-inspired woman
needed plans and causes to express her altruism in the family or community.
Professional motherhood offered a challenging outlet for unselfish, intelligent
service, still based on woman's nature but requiring more than biological femaleness.

The first two themes in the late-nineteenth-century feminine synthesis prepared women, especially the daughters' daughters, to take a more active role
in "the world." By questioning the biological roots of domestic inclination and
motherly instinct and by asserting that suffering was not essential to the mother-
role, late-century women created a sense of womanhood theoretically com-
patible with self-directed, non-domestic pursuits. But a final, crucial element
was needed in order for middle-class women to feel comfortable and righteous
in following duty into the public sphere. The daughters' synthesis needed to
address the constraints of sexual hierarchy and separate spheres.

Late nineteenth-century women inherited the ideology and lifestyle of separate spheres from their mothers who celebrated domesticity as women's domain and woman's power. In the late-century period, however, women began

to claim (as men had done earlier) that women and men were totally different kinds of creatures. The overdeveloped sexuality of men was the most public complaint made by women about men, but along with that women claimed that men just did not understand women. Florence Winterburn wrote of married women as "alone" within their marriages, dealing with "spiritual 'incompatibilities' which are the ruin of so many ideals of happiness." "The feminine mind which aspired to ideals above the sordid matters of every day," she wrote, "usually dreams and hopes alone, knowing that to confide such visions would bring ridicule and impatience from the 'partner of her sorrows and joys.' "[83] Mary Walker wrote of woman's "thousand unwritten trials and sorrows that God has not given to men the power to comprehend."[84] And Eliza Lyman argued that "thousands" of married people were strangers to each other, "the only point of union being the sexual act," which Lyman claimed women did not usually desire because there was "no love to prompt desire."[85] Being daughters of women who accepted separate spheres as the order of nature, and growing up within a female world themselves, late-nineteenth-century women were more vocal than past generations about the problems and disappointments of living with an alien creature. Amelia Barr complained that husbands were not attentive to their wives, Grace Dodge and Mary Sherwood asserted that marriages were very often not happy, and Haryot Cahoon concluded that "marriage is an institution designed, not for happiness, but for discipline."[86] A sense of psychological distance from husbands and from men in general was evident in late-nineteenth-century women's writings.

This feeling of separation from men, coupled with a new ability and public permission to control marital sexuality, led women to assert for the first time that women, not men, should define feminine needs. "How can men know what is best for women?" Emily Gibbes asked her readers. "Only a woman can understand a woman's needs."[87] This attitude was very clear in the debate over Edward Clarke's *Sex in Education*. Women were incensed not only by Clarke's thesis that education would harm a woman's reproductive organs, but also by the fact that he had the arrogance to comment on women's capacities. Julia Howe called Clarke's book "an intrusion into the sacred domain of womanly privacy." She went on to say: "No woman could publish facts and speculations concerning the special physical economy of the other sex, on so free and careless a plane, without incurring the gravest rebuke for insolence and immodesty."[88] Mercy M. Jackson attacked Clarke for "assuming that he is a better judge of what they [women] can bear than they are themselves," and Antoinette Blackwell asserted that men could not say anything useful about the normal powers and functions of women.[89] These women were angry about Clarke's presumptuousness in assuming he could define proper, healthy feminine activity. Because women and men were so different, Clarke's maleness rendered him incompetent to discuss women's capacities.

Similarly, late-nineteenth-century women began to question the validity of male definition and male control of women in general. A few women complained that male physicians "having no corresponding organs, could not possibly understand their [women's] diseases."[90] Eutocia Cook, a female physician, asserted that "male doctors can not, in the nature of things, understand the secrets of a woman's life. She can not, nor would he understand her if she could, delineate all her sensations, her longings, her abuses, and sexual depletions."[91] Other women expressed indignation that husbands assumed they could dictate their wives' opinions or that men in general assumed they could tell women what to do and decide what women needed.[92] Lillie Blake, speaking specifically of ministers but also of men in general, wrote: "It would really be amusing if it were not provoking, this calm way in which men undertake to dictate to women what they shall or shall not do; while it never seems to cross their minds that women have any right to dictate to men what they shall or shall not do." She went on in a mocking and bitter tone: "Class A., orchids, very delicate, must be kept under glass and carefully protected. Class B., turnips, useful domestic article, belongs in the kitchen garden. Class C., weeds, to be trampled under foot."[93] These writers shared a common suspicion of male definition of womanhood, and either implied or asserted that only women could define woman's nature and women's needs.

Feeling separate and different from men, late-nineteenth-century women expressed a new sense of female individualism. Freedom of individual decision, the need for self-knowledge, and the right to education were newly claimed by women to be essential to womanhood.[94] Submission to men, whether physical or psychological, was seen as undesirable. But women did not claim the right to self-definition as an inalienable right so much as a sexual right. It was because of the difference between women and men that female definition needed to be in the hands of women. It was because men knew so little of "woman's nature" that women had to describe it themselves. Separate spheres was both enabling and confining in the evolution of feminine consciousness. The separation of the sexes led to an awareness of separate interests and profound differences, which facilitated women's insistence on self-definition while ensuring that the definition would assume innate sexual differences.

The daughters' new definition of true womanhood stretched the boundaries of woman's sphere even while it celebrated the innate qualities of femaleness. Late-nineteenth-century women rejected their mothers' biologically based definition of femininity partly because the daughters' generation had a different experience of female body, but true womanhood continued to be based on women's interpretation of body experience. In keeping with their new experience of physical control and reflecting their inherited high valuation of motherhood as spiritually ennobling and innately powerful, late-nineteenth-century women secularized and politicized maternal superiority. Because of their experience of body as controllable, of mothering as a learned skill, and of submission to men as physically and psychically undesirable, late-nineteenth-century women were able to imagine a motherhood that claimed the world as its domain. Women's popular writing about mothering the world reflected these physical/psychological changes.

Helen Gardener, in *Facts and Fictions of Life*, wrote of the laws of heredity and how they affected women. She was convinced that control and wise planning were possible on a cultural level, just as they were recognizable on a physical level, and she saw women's professional motherhood as a key to a better future. Since Gardener believed women's maternal function, when educated and rationalized, held tremendous potential, she argued that women should not be subject to male authority. "Self-abnegation, subservience to man—whether he be father, lover, or husband—is the most dangerous that can be taught to, or forced upon her, whose character shall mould the next generation."[95] Similarly, Carol Norton asserted that woman's "selfhood" had been "dormant and underdeveloped" because of her confinement to one sphere and to male authority. Norton hoped the "New Woman" of the late-century period would "lift the race" in the name of "Divine Maternity."[96] Eliza Gamble used Darwin to prove innate female superiority based on women's maternity and argued that the inferiority of women was socialized and maintained by the sexual division of labor. Unfettered motherhood promised world reformation, according to Gamble.[97] These writers linked women's world-mothering to physical and psychological release from male control and to a new sense of personal power rooted in self-directed, yet biological, motherhood.

Other women stressed the idea that educated motherhood should exert a direct influence on politics. Women's mothering was seen as innately female, yet in need of training and direction. After acquiring the skills of mothering, it was argued that women could apply these skills in a focused, controlled way to altruistically influence political and social events. Lillie Blake shared her vision of educated motherhood with her readers:

Educated and admirable women, who are doing women's work in caring for women, and laboring to make the world purer and better, who are devoted to their homes faithfully, and then to that larger home which is the world in which we live and in which we have every one of us a work to do.... women who shall lead lives of usefulness, for children, for friends, and for the state.[98]

Other women wrote of "world mothering" and women's "unfinished work" in the world as altruistic, learned, and self-directable.[99]

The women's club movement and movements for social change such as the WCTU and the social purity crusade shared this same image of women's mothering. Frances Willard believed women could deliver the nation from disaster if only they would accept their mission: "to make the whole world homelike."[100] By this she meant that women needed to apply the same generosity and skillful management to politics that they did to their individual homes.

Echoing Willard, Lillie Blake called for motherhood qualities in government: "The purifying, the ennobling, the moral qualities that make the household happy . . . should have their place in the government also."[101] She went on to say:

The state is but the larger family, and the national housekeeping is all out of order for want of that virtue, love of order, and above all, conscientiousness, which woman especially represents. Just what happens . . . in the home during the absence of the mother, is taking place to-day in the nation for the want of woman's influence.[102]

Blake specifically linked that influence to women's domestic skills. "She who for twenty years has superintended a well-ordered family of children and servants ought to be well qualified to govern in a larger community."[103] Middle-class, professional motherhood prepared women for skillful government service.

Neither Willard nor Blake saw women's influence as natural and moral, as their mothers' generation had seen it; instead, they saw women's influence as related to the educated, professional mother-role. According to late-nineteenth-century women, the maternal function was biologically specific to women; but controlled, self-directed, skillful maternity demanded more than a female body. Blake revealed this apparent contradiction throughout her book, *Woman's Place Today*. She repeatedly called for education and development for women and wrote of mothering skills as needing conscious direction, yet she argued that only women could bring these cultivated virtues into the world: "What intelligent woman would ever think of putting her husband and sons in charge of the house-cleaning?" she asked.[104] The biological female function was still the root of femininity, but the daughters' generation provided a new interpretation based on their own experience of self-control and the power of socialization and education.

Late nineteenth-century women replaced passive suffering and submission as the base of femininity with active, self-directed but altruistic public service. This came to be the new standard for middle-class true womanhood. As other historians have pointed out, the new feminine synthesis was still very limiting for women because it was based on a variation of the "natural woman" theme.[105] However, in evaluating the usefulness and drawbacks of past states of consciousness, it is important to realize women did not "choose" professional, altruistic motherhood from a variety of options; they developed a feminine synthesis out of the raw material of body experience and socialization within a new social setting. They were not free to disregard their mothers' teachings and their own childhoods; instead, they reinterpreted their inherited feminine thesis in light of changes in material conditions, both physical and social. The daughters were, and are, creators of feminine ideology, within the constraints of an internal and external historical dialectic.

NOTES

1. Haryot Holt Cahoon, *What One Woman Thinks*, ed. Cynthia M. Westover (New York: Tait, Sons & Co., 1893), p. 74; Emma Stebbins, ed. *Charlotte Cushman: Her Letters and Memories of Her Life* (Boston: Houghton, Osgood & Co., 1878), p. 172; *Should Woman Obey?* (Chicago: E. Loomis & Co., 1900), p. 83; Laura Langford, *The Mothers of Great Men and Women* (New York: Funk & Wagnalls, 1883), preface; Eliza Lyman, *The Coming Woman; The Royal Road to Perfection, A Series of Medical Lectures* (Lansing, MI: W. S. George, 1880), p. 205.

2. Mary Elizabeth Sherwood, *Amenities of Home* (New York: D. Appleton & Co., 1884), p. 75. See also Mary Ashton Livermore, *What Shall We Do With Our Daughters* (Boston: Lee and Shepard, 1883), pp. 72–73; Amelia Edith Barr, *Maids, Wives, and Bachelors* (New York: Dodd, Mead & Co., 1898), p. 102.

3. Isabel Mallon, *The Business Girl in Every Phase of Her Life* (Philadelphia: Curtis Publishing Co., 1898), preface.

4. Grace Hoadley Dodge, *A Bundle of Letters to Busy Girls on Practical Matters* (New York: Funk & Wagnalls, 1887), p. 11.

5. Eleanor Cecelia Donnelly, ed., *Girlhood's Hand-Book of Woman* (St. Louis: B. Herder, 1898), pp. 111, 112. Men also expressed this idea. See Charles Fletcher Dole, *Noble Womanhood* (Boston: H. M. Caldwell Co., 1900), P. 52; Puchard Haber Newton, *Womanhood; Lectures on Woman's Work in the World* (New York: Putnam's Sons, 1881), pp. 122–123.

6. Laura deForce Gordon, "Woman's Sphere from a Woman's Standpoint," in *Papers of the Congress of Women*, ed. Mary Kavanaugh Oldham (Chicago: International Publishing Co., 1894), p. 75.

7. Mary Wolker, *A Woman's Thoughts about Love and Marriage, Divorce, Etc.* (New York: Miller, 1871), p. 154. This idea was also expressed by male writers. See Newton, *Womanhood*, p. 18: "Every line of vision converges towards the marriage altar."

8. Jane Croly, *For Better or Worse; For Some Men and All Women* (Boston: Lee & Shepard, 1875), pp. 45, 117. See also Edward Hardy, *How to Be Happy Though Married* (New York: C. Scribner's Sons, 1886), p. 19.

9. Dodge, *A Bundle of Letters*, p. 104.

10. Stella Scott Gilman, *Mothers in Council* (New York: Harper & Brothers, 1884), p. 102.

11. Gordon, "Woman's Sphere," p. 74.

12. Caroline H. Dall, in *Sex and Education, A Reply to Dr. Edward H. Clarke's "Sex in Education,"* ed. Julia Ward Howe (Boston: Roberts Brothers, 1874), pp. 107, 108. This same position was expressed in Helen Gilbert Ecob, *The Well-Dressed Woman; A Study in the Practical Application to Dress of the Laws of Health, Art, and Morals* (New York: Fowler & Wells, 1892), p. 168.

13. Jennie Willing, *The Potential Woman, A Book for Young Ladies* (Boston: McDonald, Gill & Co., 1886), p. 160.

14. Barr, *Maids, Wives, and Bachelors*, pp. 1, 11. See also Howe, *Sex and Education*, p. 138.

15. Mary P. Ryan, *Womanhood in America* (New York: New Viewpoints, 1979), p. 176.

16. Charlotte Perkins Gilman, *Women and Economics* (New York: Harper & Row,

1966); Mallon, *The Business Girl*, preface; Dodge, *A Bundle of Letters*, p. 105. Howe, *Sex and Education*, pp. 52–55. Mary Terhune, *Eve's Daughters; or Common Sense for Maid, Wife and Mother* (New York: J. R. Anderson & H. S. Allen, 1882), p. 397.

17. Harriet Eliza Paine, *The Unmarried Woman* (New York: Dodd, Mead & Co., 1892), pp. 68, 69, 113; Harriet Eliza Paine, *Girls and Women* (Boston and New York: Houghton Mifflin & Co., 1890), pp. 17, 24. Gilman, *Mothers in Council*, p. 23; Cahoon, *What One Woman Thinks*, p. 50. See also Mary Studley, *What Our Girls Ought to Know* (New York: M. L. Holbrook & Co., 1878), pp. 199–201.

18. Lizzie Bates, *Woman: Her Dignity and Sphere, By a Lady* (New York: American Tract Society, 1870), pp. 13, 14.

19. Terhune, *Eve's Daughters*, pp. 128, 259.

20. Paine, *Girls and Women*, p. 56, used the term "majority." See also Sherwood, *Amenities of Home*, p. 75; Donnelly, *Girlhood's Hand-Book of Woman*, p. 128; Anna Callender Brackett, ed. *The Education of American Girls* (New York: G. P. Putnam & Sons, 1874), p. 141; Croly, *For Better or Worse*, p. 117; Walker, *A Woman's Thoughts*, p. 150.

21. *Should Woman Obey?*, pp. 9–10.

22. Gilman, *Women and Economics*; Caroline Lefavre, *Mother's Help and Child's Friend* (New York: Brentano's, 1890), p. 85; Livermore, *What Shall We Do With Our Daughters*, p. 84.

23. Etta Taylor, *How; A Practical Business Guide for American Women of All Conditions and Ages, Who Want to Make Money, But Do Not Know How* (Minneapolis: E. M. Taylor, 1893), preface. See also Jane Croly, *Thrown on Her Own Resources; or What Girls Can Do* (New York: Thomas Y. Crowell & Co., 1891), p. 40.

24. Croly, *Thrown on Her Own Resources*, pp. 156, 157, 159.

25. Croly, *Thrown on Her Own Resources*, pp. 38, 40.

26. Adeline Dutton Whitney, *Friendly Letters to Girl Friends* (Boston and New York: Houghton Mifflin & Co., 1896), p. 177.

27. Taylor, *How*, p. 79.

28. Jane Croly, *The History of the Woman's Club Movement in America* (New York: H. G. Allen & Co., 1898), preface.

29. Martha Louise Rayne, *What Can a Woman Do: or, Her Position in the Business and Literary World* (Detroit: F. B. Dickerson & Co., 1884), p. 3. See also Paine, *Girls and Women*, p. 51.

30. Donnelly, *Girlhood's Hand-Book of Woman*, pp. 127–128.

31. Gertrude Aquirre, *Women in the Business World; or, Hints and Helps to Prosperity* (Boston: Arena Publishing Co., 1894), p. 9.

32. Irene Hartt, *How to Make Money, Although a Woman* (New York: J. S. Ogilvie Publishing Co., 1895), pp. 7, 40, 63–66.

33. Sallie Elizabeth White, *Business Openings for Girls* (New York: The Werner Co., 1899), p. 13.

34. Frances Willard, *How to Win; A Book for Girls*, 5th ed. (New York: Funk & Wagnalls, 1888), p. 18.

35. Livermore, *What Shall We Do With Our Daughters*, p. 15.

36. Willard, *How to Win*, p. 18.

37. Whitney, *Friendly Letters to Girl Friends*, p. 175.

38. About domestic architecture during the late nineteenth century and the house-

wife's job, see Gwendolyn Wright, *Moralism and the Model Home* (Chicago: University of Chicago Press, 1980).

39. Ecob, *The Well-Dressed Woman*, p. 167.

40. Wright, *Moralism and the Model Home*, p. 36.

41. Barr, *Maids, Wives, and Bachelors*, p. 128; Jane Grey Swisshelm, *Half a Century* (Chicago: Jansen, McClurg & Co., 1880), 48.

42. Maria Elmore, in Howe, *Sex and Education*, p. 181.

43. Andrea Proudfoot, *A Mother's Ideal; A Kindergarten Conception of Family Life* (Chicago: by the author, 1897), p. 195; James Caleb Jackson, *American Womanhood; Its Peculiarities and Necessities*, 3rd ed. (Dansville, NY: Austin, Jackson, 1870), p. 62. See also Walker, *A Woman's Thoughts*, pp. 31, 62.

44. Although the professionalization idea was put forward first by Catharine Beecher, of the early-century generation, the idea did not find widespread acceptance until the late-century period. On Beecher, see Kathryn Kish Sklar, *Catharine Beecher: A Study in American Domesticity* (New Haven: Yale University Press, 1973).

45. For examples of this attitude see: Bates, *Woman: Her Dignity and Sphere*, p. 264; Helen Nitsch, *Progressive Housekeeping* (Boston and New York: Houghton Mifflin & Co., 1889); Livermore, *What Shall We Do With Our Daughters*, pp. 72–73; Margaret Sangster, *The Art of Being Agreeable* (New York: The Christian Herald, 1897), pp. 106–107; Sarah Bolton, *Every-Day Living* (Boston: L. C. Page & Co., 1900), p. 24; Terhune, *Eve's Daughters*, p. 270; Florence Hull Winterburn, *Nursery Ethics* (New York: The Merriam Co., 1895), p. 159.

46. Ella Wheeler Wilcox, *Men, Women and Emotions* (Chicago: W. B. Conkey Co., 1894), p. 255.

47. Harriet Storer Doutney, *An Autobiography* (Cambridge, MA: by the author, 1871), p. 25. This same idea of "mother love, deep though misdirected" responsible for girls' lack of domestic training was expressed by Christine Herrick, *A Home Book for Mothers and Daughters* (New York: The Christian Herald, 1897), p. 8.

48. LeFavre, *Mother's Help and Child's Friend*, p. 142.

49. Proudfoot, *A Mother's Ideal*.

50. Terhune, *Eve's Daughters*, p. 271.

51. Frances Willard, *A Great Mother; Sketches of Madam Willard, by Her Daughter* (Chicago: Woman's Temperance Publication Association, 1894), pp. 141–143; Helen Ekin Starrett, *Letters to Elder Daughters, Married and Unmarried* (Chicago: A. C. McClurg & Co., 1892), pp. 17–19; Margaret Sangster, *Winsome Womanhood; Familiar Talks on Life and Conduct* (New York and Chicago: F. H. Revell Co., 1900), pp. 125–126; Bates, *Woman: Her Dignity and Sphere*, pp. 264–266.

52. Marie Dewing, *From Attic to Cellar; A Book for Young Housekeepers* (New York: G. P. Putnam's Sons, 1879), pp. 124–125; Rayne, *What Can a Woman Do?*, p. 296.

53. Terhune, *Eve's Daughters*, p. 294.

54. Lefavre, *Mother's Help and Child's Friend*, p. 7.

55. Proudfoot, *A Mother's Ideal*, p. 13.

56. Bates, *Woman: Her Dignity and Sphere*, p. 12. This idea of malleable childhood open to intellegent socialization was also expressed in Donnelly, *Girlhood's Hand-Book of Woman*, pp. 112, 122; Dole, *Noble Womanhood*, p. 53; Sarah Stickney Ellis, *The Mothers of Great Men* (London: Chatto and Windus, 1874); Gilman, *Mothers in Council*, pp. 153, 172–173; Newton, *Womanhood*, pp. 125, 142–143; Mary Lowe Dickenson, "The Next Thing in Education," in *Papers of the Congress of Women*, pp. 641–642.

57. This might have been because women in the late-century period were more frequently living away from female kin than their mothers had, and felt a need to offer advice that in an earlier time would have been part of an oral tradition.

58. For example, see Prudence Saur, *Maternity: A Book for Every Wife and Mother* (Chicago: L. P. Miller, 1891), chapter on infant care; Herrick, *A Home Book for Mothers and Daughters*. p. 18; Lyman, *The Coming Woman*, pp. 235–237; Alice Stockham, *Tokology; A Book for Every Woman* (Chicago: A. B. Stockham & Co., 1889), pp. 204–216; Mary Terhune, *Common Sense in the Nursery* (New York: C. Scribner's Sons, 1885); Dewing, *From Attic to Cellar*, pp. 115–147.

59. Herrick, *A Home Book for Mothers and Daughters*, p. 18. On keeping infants and children on regular schedules, see Winterburn, *Nursery Ethics*, p. 132; Saur, *Maternity*, pp. 254–269; Lyman, *The Coming Woman*, p. 240; Dewing, *From Attic to Cellar*, pp. 113–114; Eutocia Cook, *Easy Favorable Child Bearing; A Book for All Women* (Chicago: Arcade Publishing Co., 1886), p. 387.

60. Edward Dewy, *A New Era for Woman; Health Without Drugs* (Northwich, CT: C. C. Haskell & Co., 1898), p. 334.

61. Dewing, *From Attic to Cellar*, pp. 113–114.

62. William Capp, *The Daughter; Her Health, Education and Wedlock* (Philadelphia: F. A. Davis, 1891), pp. 7–8.

63. Gilman, *Mothers in Council*, pp. 81–83, suggested planning the day in a certain way.

64. Lefavre, *Mother's Help and Child's Friend*, p. 28; Rayne, *What Can a Woman Do?*, pp. 298, 315–316, 398; Sherwood, *Amenities of Home*, p. 13; Elizabeth Peabody, *Lectures in Training School for Kindergartners* (Boston: D. C. Heath, 1893), p. 38; Mary Blake, *Twenty-Six Hours a Day* (Boston: D. Lethrom & Co., 1883), p. 85; Dewing, *From Attic to Cellar*, pp. 119–120.

65. Barr, *Maids, Wives, and Bachelors*, p. 99.

66. Saur, *Maternity*, pp. 168–169; *Should Woman Obey?*, dedication page.

67. Cook, *Easy Favorable Child Bearing*, p. 114; Saur, *Maternity*, p. 165.

68. Livermore, *What Shall We Do With Our Daughters*, p. 21.

69. Cook, *Easy Favorable Child Bearing*, p. 175.

70. Saur, *Maternity*, p. 376; Sangster, *Winsome Womanhood*, p. 135; Cook, *Easy Favorable Child Bearing*, p. 177; Lefavre, *Mother's Help and Child's Friend*, p. 17; Winterburn, *Nursery Ethics*, p. 5.

71. Kate Wiggin, *Children's Rights; A Book of Nursery Logic* (Boston: Houghton Mifflin & Co., 1892), p. 15.

72. Saur, *Maternity*, p. 376.

73. Most of these writers specifically endorsed the kindergarten movement, not only as an institutional pre-school environment but also as a method every mother should learn. About mothers and kindergarten training, see Saur, *Maternity*, p. 389; Rayne, *What Can a Woman Do?*, p. 397; Susan Blow, *Letters to a Mother on the Philosophy of Froebel* (New York: D. Appleton & Co., 1899); Peabody, *Lectures in the Training School for Kindergartners*; Oldham, *Papers of the Congress of Women*, pp. 296, 323–325, 641–642, 747–751; Proudfoot, *A Mother's Ideal*.

74. Peabody, *Lectures in the Training School for Kindergartners*, p. 61.

75. Lafavre, *Mother's Help and Child's Friend*, p. 166.

76. Gilman, *Mothers in Council*, p. 177. Other writers who urged mothers to be home for their children were Adeline Whitney, *The Law of Woman's Life* (n.p. 189?), p.

20; Barr, *Maids, Wives, and Bachelors*, p. 103; Sherwood, *Amenities of Home*, pp. 14, 75; Dole, *Noble Womanhood*, p. 55.

77. Proudfoot, *A Mother's Ideal*, p. 93; Lefavre, *Mother's Help and Child's Friend*, p. 86.

78. *Should Woman Obey?*, p. 83; Elizabeth Blackwell, *The Human Element in Sex* (London: J. A. Churchill, 1894), p. 30; Barr, *Maids, Wives, and Bachelors*, p. 98. See also Paine, *The Unmarried Woman*, p. 165.

79. Wilcox, *Men, Women and Emotions*, p. 8; Blake, *Twenty-Six Hours a Day*, p. 39.

80. Livermore, *What Shall We Do With Our Daughters*, p. 127.

81. Antoinette Brown Blackwell, *The Sexes Throughout Nature* (New York: G. P. Putnam's Sons, 1875), p. 133.

82. For a very interesting discussion of women's altruism from a philosophical point of view, see Larry Blum, Marcia Homiak, Judy Housman, and Naomi Scheman, "Altruism and Women's Oppression," in *Women and Philosophy*, ed. Carol C. Gould and Marx W. Wartofsky (New York: G. P. Putnam's Sons, 1976), pp. 222–247.

83. Winterburn, *Nursery Ethics*, pp. 117–118.

84. Walker, *A Woman's Thoughts*, dedication.

85. Lyman, *The Coming Woman*, p. 207.

86. Barr, *Maids, Wives, and Bachelors*, p. 130; Dodge, *A Bundle of Letters*, p. 43; Sherwood, *Amenities of Home*, p. 64; Cahoon, *What One Woman Thinks*, introduction. See also Richard L. Griswold's excellent study of divorce, "Law, Sex, Cruelty, and Divorce in Victorian America, 1840–1900," *American Quarterly*, 38(1986), 721–745.

87. Emily Gibbs, *Gleanings; A Gift to the Women of the World* (New York: The Caxton Press, 1892), p. vi. See also Cook, *Easy Favorable Child Bearing*, p. 129.

88. Howe, *Sex and Education*, p. 7.

89. Mercy B. Jackson, in *Sex and Education*, p. 154; Blackwell, *The Sexes Throughout Nature*, pp. 6–7. See also Eliza Duffey, *No Sex in Education; or An Equal Chance for Both Boys and Girls* (Philadelphia: J. B. Stoddart & Co., 1874), p. 12.

90. Jackson, in *Sex and Education*, p. 158.

91. Cook, *Easy Favorable Child Bearing*, p. 267.

92. Mrs. Horace Mann, in *Sex and Education*, p. 54; *Historical Account of the Association for the Advancement of Women, 1873–1893*, Twenty-first Women's Congress, World's Columbian Exposition, Chicago, 1893 (Dedham, MA: 1893), p. 43; Abby Diaz, *Only a Flock of Women* (Boston: D. Lothrop Co., 1893), p. 38; Helen Gardener, *Facts and Fictions of Life* (Boston: Arena Publishing Co., 1893), p. 169; Oldham, *Papers of the Congress of Women*, p. 74.

93. Lillie Blake, *Woman's Place Today* (New York: J. W. Lovell Co., 1883), p. 47.

94. Walker, *A Woman's Thoughts*, pp. 27, 33, 108; Jackson, in *Sex and Education*, p. 161; A. C. Garland, in *Sex and Education*, p. 183.

95. Gardener, *Facts and Fictions of Life*, p. 154.

96. Carol Norton, *Woman's Cause* (Boston: Dana Estes & Co., 1895), pp. xiii, xiv.

97. Eliza Gamble, *The Evolution of Woman; An Inquiry into the Dogma of Her Inferiority to Man* (New York: G. P. Putnam's Sons, 1894), pp. 28–52, 62.

98. Blake, *Woman's Place Today*, p. 50.

99. Whitney, *The Law of Woman's Life*, pp. 4, 10; Starrett, *Letters to Elder Daughters*, pp. 164–165; Julia Ward Howe in *Historical Account of the Association for the Advancement of Women, 1873–1893*, pp. 39–40.

100. Willard, *How to Win*, pp. 53–55.

101. Blake, *Woman's Place Today*, p. 74.
102. Blake, *Woman's Place Today*, p. 147.
103. Blake, *Woman's Place Today*, p. 151.
104. Blake, *Woman's Place Today*, p. 149.
105. Rosalind Rosenberg, "In Search of Woman's Nature, 1850–1920," *Feminist Studies*, 3(1975), 141–154; Jill Conway, "Women Reformers and American Culture, 1870–1930," *Journal of Social History*, 5(1971–72), 164–177.

Conclusion

Over the course of the nineteenth century the sexual ideology surrounding reproduction went through dramatic changes. Popular ideas of motherhood shifted from a privatized, moral, home-bound mother devoted to children in a self-sacrificing way to a secular but ethically inspired world-mother in altruistic service to community. My argument has been that the similarities and differences in these two ideals reflect characteristics of the mother/ daughter relationship, on the one hand, and changes in women's physical experience of womanhood, on the other. This is not to say that these two factors are the only determinants of ideology, but rather that *women's* role in shaping ideology and ideology's shaping of women can be understood only through serious consideration of both generational and physical phenomena.

Viewing nineteenth-century feminine sexual ideology and women's physical experience as part of a dialectical process has at least two theoretical consequences important to historians and to present-day feminists. First, it forces us to connect public and private as a unity and to recognize women as agents in history. The sexual ideology defining womanhood upholds, rationalizes, makes palatable, all the "external" conditions of female life. But the social construction of femininity is partially women's creation, built out of a distorted understanding of the physical and material conditions of their lives and a search for meaning and value within the constraints of patriarchal structure. Women also participate in the communication of ideology. "Femininity" is passed on as a generational legacy; the "world" is brought "home" in the intimate bond between mother and daughter. Within this point of view, public and private are not separate, and women are not victims.

However, the nineteenth-century "woman's world" that facilitated the creation and communication of a particular sexual ideology has all but disappeared. In the late twentieth century, mass media and consumer culture, largely controlled by men, have more power in creating sexual ideology than any group of women. Today, more than in the nineteenth-century middle-class women's world, it is possible for women to experience more intense dissonance, conflict between experience and cultural definitions. It is also more likely that women today experience more alienation, a lack of connection between self/world, both "named" by others but not by self. Therefore it is very important that we continue, or re-introduce, consciousness raising as a strategy of twentieth-century feminism. In order for women to envision a new self/world less encumbered by male definitions, it is necessary for us to re-create a female forum for the discovery and expression of women's "naming" experience. If reality and self are socially constructed, and if late-twentieth-century women are separated from each other by the economic and cultural breakdown of the women's community, it is essential that we re-establish woman-to-woman contact in order to facilitate a feminist future.

In addition to seeing public and private as a unity, the second consequence of viewing gender as process is the recognition that female body experience is an essential factor in women's oppression and women's liberation. The body is political in ways we had not imagined before. Funding for girls' sports programs is not a liberal reform, but a radical demand; contraception and sexual freedom are not private, middle-class concerns, but revolutionary necessities; and women's involvement in amateur and professional athletics, woman-centered childbirth, natural therapeutics, and even body-building are not merely passing fads but are also potential sources of powerful new ideals. If body and culture are related dialectically, then changing the structure of women's physical experience can alter feminine consciousness, hasten the re-formation of feminine ideology, and create new behavioral options. However, the recognition that physical experience is a factor in women's historically developing consciousness should also give us pause. In a society in which men control technology and reproductive technology is a rapidly expanding field, men's power over women increases with each scientific "advance," not just materially but ideologically. It becomes more and more imperative that women develop strategies for gaining power in this area.

I began by asserting that both Margaret Fuller and Adrienne Rich were partially correct in their assessment of the relationship between women and sexual ideology. Women shape the meaning of womanhood, and therefore have power in changing that meaning in a conscious way; but women are also burdened by the material and ideological constraints of the socioeconomic structure in which they are born. This can be an empowering point of view for late-twentieth-century feminists to consider. There should be no quarrel between separatism and political activism; feminism demands both. We need a "woman's culture" in order to create a space and expression for women's experience, but we also need a political activism that understands the structural constraints that hamper women's liberation and works toward changing those material conditions. Viewing gender as an internal and external dialectic, with self as the mediating factor, can provide an exciting way to consider historical questions and can give us a new way to see the present dilemma of late-twentieth-century feminism.

Notes on Sources

When I first became interested in the relationship between generational dynamics and ideas about femininity, women's studies and women's history were very new fields. Barbara Welter's "The Cult of True Womanhood" inspired me to read, with generational change in mind, hundreds of woman-authored advice manuals, monographs, autobiographies, and serialized fictional stories from the early nineteenth century to the 1890s. As I went through this material I also read the books and articles on women's lives in the nineteenth century that were beginning to appear at an accelerated rate. Important to my developing sense of middle-class women's life worlds in the nineteenth century was the work of Carroll Smith-Rosenberg (especially "The Female World of Love and Ritual"), Nancy Cott (especially *The Bonds of Womanhood*), Mary Ryan (especially *Cradle of the Middle Class: The Family in Oneida County, New York, 1790–1865*), Barbara Welter (*Dimity Convictions: The American Woman in the Nineteenth Century*), Barbara J. Harris (*Beyond Her Sphere: Women and the Professions in American History*), and Lois W. Banner (*American Beauty*). Also important were studies focused on domesticity and middle-class culture, such as Ryan's *The Empire of The Mother: American Writing About Domesticity, 1830–1860*, Kathryn Kish Sklar's *Catharine Beecher: A Study in American Domesticity*, Karen Halttunen's *Confidence Men and Painted Women: A Study of Middle-Class Culture, 1830–1860*, and Barbara Leslie Epstein's *The Politics of Domesticity: Women, Evangelism, and Temperance in Nineteenth-Century America*.

The books and articles of the past ten years on sexuality, marriage, fertility and contraception, and women's family roles in the nineteenth century are too numerous to list. Some of the more important authors for me were Smith-Rosenberg, Ryan, Cott ("Passionlessness: An Interpretation of Victorian Sexual Ideology, 1795–1850"), Lee Chambers-Schiller (*Liberty a Better Husband: Single Women in America: The Generation of 1780–1840*), Daniel Scott Smith ("Family Limitation, Sexual Control, and Domestic Feminism in Victorian America"), James Mohr (*Abortion in America: The Origins and Evolution of National Policy, 1800–1900*), Linda Gordon (*Woman's Body, Woman's Right*), Robert V. Wells (especially "Demographic Change and the Life Cycles of American Families" and "Women's Lives Transformed: Demography and Family Patterns in America, 1600–1970"), Elaine Tyler May (*Great Expectations: Marriage and Divorce in*

Post-Victorian America), Robert Griswold (*Family and Divorce in California, 1850–1890: Victorian Illusion and Everyday Realities* and "Law, Sex, Cruelty, and Divorce in Victorian America, 1840–1900"), William Leach (*True Love and Perfect Union: The Feminist Reform of Sex and Society*), Ruth H. Block ("American Feminine Ideals in Transition: The Rise of the Moral Mother, 1785–1815"), Bryan Strong ("Toward a History of the Experiential Family: Sex and Incest in the Nineteenth-Century Family"), David G. Pugh (*Sons of Liberty: The Masculine Mind in Nineteenth-Century America*), Charles Rosenberg ("Sexuality, Class and Role in Nineteenth-Century America"), Estelle Freedman ("Sexuality in Nineteenth-Century America: Behavior, Ideas, and Politics"), and Carl Degler (*At Odds: Women and the Family in America from the Revolution to the Present* and "What Ought to Be and What Was: Women's Sexuality in the Nineteenth Century"). Studies focusing on childhood and education in the nineteenth century, some specifically about girls and women, were also significant to me. Philip Greven (*The Protestant Temperament*), Joseph Kett ("Adolescence and Youth in Nineteenth-Century America"), Anne Scott MacLeod (*A Moral Tale: Children's Fiction and American Culture*), Anne L. Kuln (*The Mother's Role in Childhood Education: New England Concepts, 1830–1860*), Thomas Woody (*A History of Women's Education in the United States*), Robert Sunley ("Early Nineteenth-Century American Literature on Child Rearing"), and Barbara Miller Solomon (*In the Company of Educated Women*) were some of the more important studies I read.

Because my reading in the primary sources convinced me that women's sex-specific physical experience was an important ingredient in the formation of feminine sexual ideology, I was drawn very quickly to the growing body of secondary literature about childbirth, medical ideas about women, and changing medical practices. Jane Donegan (*Women and Men Midwives: Medicine, Morality and Misogyny in Early America*), Richard W. Wertz and Dorothy C. Wertz (*Lying-In: A History of Childbirth in America*), Judith Walzer Leavitt (*Brought to Bed: Childbearing in America, 1750–1950*), and articles by Catharine M. Scholten (" 'On the Importance of the Obstetrick Art': Changing Customs of Childbirth in America, 1760–1825") and Jane Bogden ("Care or Cure? Childbirth Practices in Nineteenth-Century America") were especially important to my understanding of nineteenth-century childbirth among middle-class women and how that experience changed over time. The work of Smith-Rosenberg ("Puberty to Menopause: The Cycle of Femininity in Nineteenth-Century America," "The Hysterical Woman: Sex Roles and Role Conflict in Nineteenth-Century America," and with Charles Rosenberg, "The Female Animal: Medical and Biological Views of Woman and Her Role in Nineteenth-Century America"), Regina Morantz (especially "Making Women Modern: Middle-Class Women and Health Reform in Nineteenth-Century America"), and Anita Claire and Michael F. Fellman (*Making Sense of Self: Medical Advice Literature in Late Nineteenth-Century America*), were among the most helpful studies of medical ideas and their significance. More general histories of medicine as a profession and of changing medical practices were also essential to my sense of the context of women's position as patients. The more useful ones include Richard H. Shryock (especially *Medicine and Society in America, 1660–1860*), Erwin Ackerknecht (*A Short History of Medicine*), William G. Rothstein (*American Physicians in the Nineteenth Century: From Sects to Science*), Paul Starr (*The Social Transformation of American Medicine*), Norman Himes (*Medical History of Contraception*), Martin S. Pernick (*A Calculus of Suffering: Pain, Professionalism, and Anesthesia in Nineteenth-Century America*), Regina Morantz and Sue Zschoche ("Professionalism, Feminism, and Gender Roles: A Comparative Study of Nineteenth-Century

Therapeutics"), and James V. Ricci (*The Development of Gynaecological Surgery and Instruments*).

Readers even slightly familiar with the field of women's history or the history of medicine will not be surprised by the works I have mentioned here; however, the final category of reading I want to cover may be less well known to students of history. Theoretical works in sociology, psychology, feminist literary criticism, and political science were essential to my interpretation of historical sources. The feminist theorists who first stimulated my interest in describing women's historical experience in an interactive, process-oriented way were Joan Kelly ("The Doubled Vision of Feminist Theory: A Postscript to the 'Women and Power Conference' "), Gayle Rubin ("The Traffic in Women: Notes on the 'Political Economy' of Sex"), and Ann Foreman (*Femininity as Alienation: Women and the Family in Marxism and Psychoanalysis*). Other theorists writing about women and the family who were important to me were Eli Zaretsky (*Capitalism, The Family and Personal Life*), Zillah Eisenstein (especially "Developing a Theory of Capitalist Patriarchy and Socialist Feminism"), and Mary O'Brien (*The Politics of Reproduction*). Writers who were especially important in illuminating the psychological aspects of the process of gender were Nancy Chodorow (*The Reproduction of Mothering: Psychoanalysis and the Sociology of Gender*), Ethel Spector Person ("Sexuality as the Mainstay of Identity: Psychoanalytic Perspectives"), and Jane Flax ("Political Philosophy and the Patriarchal Unconscious: A Psychoanalytic Perspective on Epistemology and Metaphysics"). The sociological theorists most useful to me were Peter Berger and Thomas Luckmann (*The Social Construction of Reality: A Treatise in the Sociology of Knowledge*), Peter Berger and Stanley Pullberg ("Reification and the Sociological Critique of Consciousness"), George Herbert Mead (*Mind, Self, and Society*), and Karl Mannheim ("The Problem of Generations"). The essays by Eugene T. Gendlin, Joseph J. Kockelman, Maurice Merleau-Ponty, Edward A. Tiryakian, Gerhard Funke, and Donald M. Lowe in *Phenomenology and the Social Sciences* (edited by Maurice Natanson) were extremely helpful in demonstrating a process-oriented approach to various sociological questions. Also important to me was Donald M. Lowe's *A History of Bourgeois Perception*, a beautifully clear application of phenomenological methodology to an historical question, and Carroll Smith-Rosenberg's *Disorderly Conduct: Visions of Gender in Victorian America*, an inspirationally bold application of anthopological theory to the body/culture questions of nineteenth-century women's history. Finally, in my reading of women's popular writing I was influenced greatly by the analyses of women's fiction developed by feminists literary critics. Interpretations of the relationship between writer and text, text and reader, and text and the larger cultural setting found in Mary Kelley's *Private Woman, Public Stage: Literary Domesticity in Nineteenth-Century America*, Nina Baym's *Novels, Readers, and Reviewers: Responses to Fiction in Antebellum America*, and Jane Tompkins's *Sensational Designs: The Cultural Work of American Fiction, 1790–1860*, were important to my reading of women's popular non-fiction writing in the nineteenth century.

This very brief note on sources does not begin to acknowledge the books and articles by historians, sociologists, psychological theorists, and literary critics that have been essential to my work. Readers interested in more complete source information should consult the appropriate endnotes, purposefully long and more exhaustive.

Index

About the Author

NANCY M. THERIOT is Assistant Professor of History at the University of Louisville, Kentucky. She is the editor of *The Child in Contemporary America* and the author of articles published in *International Journal of Women's Studies* and *Frontiers*.